ALSO BY SENATOR JOE LIEBERMAN

The Power Broker:
A Biography of John M. Bailey, Modern Political Boss

The Scorpion and the Tarantula:
The Struggle to Control Atomic Weapons, 1945–1949

The Legacy:
Connecticut Politics, 1930–1980

Child Support in America:
Practical Advice for Negotiating—and Collecting—A Fair Settlement

In Praise of Public Life (with Michael D'Orso)

An Amazing Adventure:
Joe and Hadassah's Personal Notes on the 2000 Campaign
(with coauthor Hadassah Lieberman and Sarah Crichton)

The Gift of Rest:
Rediscovering the Beauty of the Sabbath
(with David Klinghoffer)

With Liberty and Justice:
The Fifty-Day Journey from Egypt to Sinai
(with Rabbi Ari D. Kahn)

★ ★ ★ ★ ★ ★ ★ ★ ★ ★ ★ ★ ★ ★ ★

THE CENTRIST SOLUTION

How We Made Government Work
and Can Make It Work Again

★ ★ ★ ★ ★ ★ ★ ★ ★ ★ ★ ★ ★ ★ ★

SENATOR

JOE LIEBERMAN

DIVERSION
BOOKS

For my family and yours
with faith in the future of America's democracy

For more information, email info@diversionbooks.com

Diversion Books
A division of Diversion Publishing Corp.
www.diversionbooks.com

First Diversion Books edition, October 2021
Hardcover ISBN: 9781635769043
eBook ISBN: 9781635769050

Printed in The United States of America

1   3   5   7   9   10   8   6   4   2

Library of Congress cataloging-in-publication data is available on file

CONTENTS

INTRODUCTION

The Nightmares of John Adams

"There is nothing I dread so much as a division of the republic into two great parties, each arranged under its leader, and concerting measures in opposition to each other.

"This, in my humble apprehension, is to be dreaded as the greatest political evil under our Constitution."

—JOHN ADAMS,
Second President of the United States

For the last few decades, the American people have been living through what John Adams considered "the greatest political evil under our Constitution"—and our country has suffered greatly. In this dreaded nightmare, we have become more divided, our largest problems remain unsolved, and our international leadership has been compromised.

For the future of our country and our children, we must find a way to do better. I have written this book with the goal of helping our leaders and the people who elect them find that better way. Within these pages, I will share stories that illustrate what I learned during forty years in elective office—twenty-four in the US Senate—about how to make America's government work. This book is a call for the restoration of bipartisanship and centrism to Washington. When put into practice, those methods have always enabled our democracy to function best.

Centrism is not an ideology like liberalism, conservatism, socialism, or fascism. It is a strategy for how to govern in a democracy. It is the bringing together of people from different parties and ideologies to genuinely listen to each other so they can negotiate compromises and get things done for their constituents and country. The ideologies and priorities of the Republican and Democratic parties have naturally changed over the course of American history, but the need for bipartisanship and centrism to bring them together has not. It remains the best—often the only—way for democratic governments to produce results.

Centrism is not the same as moderation. However, being a moderate makes it easier to find the way to the center because most moderates are already there on matters of policy. Centrism is anathema to extremists of the Left and Right because getting together in the center requires that they compromise, which they abhor. They don't understand that the compromises required in the problem-solving center are not compromises of principle, morality, or ethics. As I learned in my ten years in the state senate and two dozen in the US Senate, the big choices are not between right and wrong. They are between solving problems or having another futile political fight; between demanding 100 percent of what you want or engaging in some give-and-take with the other party to actually get something done.

Here is a simplistic illustration of my point in the area of economic policy. The Far Right argues for pure, free market capitalism with no governmental involvement. The Far Left argues that the government itself should control most of the economy. Center-left and center-right leaders avoid those extremes and find a common ground that preserves private property ownership and free markets but regulates them to protect the public interest. Centrists understand these words from the Talmud: "Without governments, people would treat each other like fish—the big ones would eat the little ones." But centrists also remember Winston Churchill's wisdom: "Some regard private enterprise as if it were a predatory tiger to be shot. Others look upon it as a cow they can milk . . . A handful see it for what it really is—the strong horse that pulls the whole cart."

It's no coincidence that I chose private enterprise and a quotation from Winston Churchill in my illustration of centrism; one is a hallmark of democratic nations and the other is a man who spent a lifetime in government service under a parliamentary democracy. Both were bulwarks against dictatorships.

Centrism is irrelevant in a dictatorship because the dictator stifles all differences of opinion.

But in a democracy, centrism is essential. Why? Because in democracies, the perpetual challenge is to form a majority from the multitude of parties, factions, and opinions that freedom—freedom of speech, assembly, religion, conscience, and more—makes possible.

It's valuable to look back at American history, which shows how important centrism has been to our national journey— beginning with the critical compromises that allowed our founders to reach agreement at the Constitutional Convention to form our government and protect our independence. I will do that in Chapter One.

As I look back on my two-plus decades in the US Senate, all of the important legislation I helped enact began and ended in the bipartisan center. I will describe the legislative products I am most proud of in the pages ahead. They span a wide spectrum of policy, including the Clean Air Act of 1990; the legislative campaign to support American military action to stop post-Cold War aggression and genocide in the Balkans; the creation of the Department of Homeland Security and the reform of America's intelligence agencies after the terrorist attacks of 9/11/2001; the Balanced Budget Act of 1997 made possible by the odd-couple centrist partnership of President Bill Clinton and Speaker of the House of Representatives Newt Gingrich; and the repeal of the anti-gay "Don't Ask, Don't Tell" policy in our military, which I cosponsored with my Republican colleague, Senator Susan Collins of Maine.

My centrism also helped give me some of the most unexpected political opportunities of my career, such as being asked by Al Gore to be his vice-presidential running mate on the Democratic ticket in 2000, then eight years later being vetted by John McCain to be his running mate on the Republican ticket.

Bipartisanship and centrism also caused a lot of political controversy and upheaval in my career. And that's another part of the story I want to tell. For example, my position on one issue during the George W. Bush administration—my opposition to Democratic demands that the president withdraw American troops from Iraq—led to a Democratic primary against me in 2006. I lost but was re-elected as an independent.

America's freedom, security, and prosperity depend on a healthy political center, a center that avoids chaotic and self-destructive extremes and instead produces progress and stability. On public opinion poll after public opinion poll, the American people show they understand these truths. Large majorities say they prefer elected officials who are willing to compromise with the other party to solve problems, rather than sticking absolutely to policy positions they have endorsed in their campaigns. And yet the representatives who the voters elect to lead them in Congress and the White House seem more frequently to avoid the center like it was a hot zone of infectious disease.

After the presidential election of 2020, Mark Penn, Chairman of the Harris Poll, which is among the oldest and most prestigious trackers of American opinion and social sentiment, wrote: "We are one country divided by two parties." America remains primarily a moderate, centrist country in which, as Penn explains, "Most voters prefer compromise on health care, immigration, and other thorny issues that the extremes of the parties have pushed to the limits."

As the Harris exit polls show, the election of Joe Biden as our 46th president was, in good measure, a victory of centrists over the partisan and ideological extremes. Almost all self-identified liberals (23 percent of all voters) voted for Biden, and almost all conservatives (38 percent of all voters) voted for Trump. It was the moderates—the centrists—(also 38% of all voters) who made the difference. In 2016, Hillary Clinton carried self-identified moderate voters by 12 points, but in 2020 Biden carried them by 30 points, an enormous 18 percent increase that helped decide the election. In some very encouraging ways, the 2020 election can be seen as a centrist uprising against partisan and ideological divisions, harsh personal rhetoric, and the resulting governmental gridlock in Washington.

It is also true, however, that President Trump ran way ahead of the predictions of most pollsters in 2020, receiving more than 74 million votes, and, in 15 battleground states, actually running more than a million votes ahead of Biden. Many Republican candidates for Congress and state offices who are loyal to Trump did even better. They got elected. In fact, the number of Republicans and Democrats who took the Senate or House oath of office to serve in January 2021 was almost even. It also seems clear that President Trump intends to remain the leader of the Republican Party at least until 2024, which will definitely work against it becoming more centrist. In sum, there is compelling evidence from the 2020 election—in spite of the polling and Joe Biden's centrist election—that shows there is still a big partisan divide in our country. As Mark Penn said, "We are one country divided by two parties."

There is a lot of work to do before bipartisan centrism is back conclusively in American politics. President Biden has said he is a proud Democrat, but intends to be the president of all Americans, working across party lines in Washington, and hoping thereby to unify the rest of our country. I know from serving in the US Senate with Joe Biden for twenty-four years that he means what he says; it's what he *regularly did* in the Senate and it helped him build an impressive record of legislative accomplishments. Now, President Biden and members of both parties in Congress have to find their way to the center to listen to each other respectfully, negotiate thoughtfully, and compromise productively. It's the only way we will solve some of our serious national problems and seize some of our great national opportunities. It will require Republican members of Congress to break away from Trump, and it will require Biden and Democratic members of Congress to declare their independence from Far-Left Democrats who won't compromise.

I hope the stories in this book and the lessons I draw from the bipartisan successes in which I was privileged to participate during my Senatorial career will be helpful to Republican and Democratic elected officials who are fed up with the political dysfunction that has crippled our government and diminished our great country. I know the overwhelming majority of them want to make our government work better again. Bipartisan centrism is the way. That's the pivotal lesson I learned.

And so, for all who follow in elective office, I aim to illustrate and emphasize how effective and beneficial our government has been when the voters have received the bipartisan problem-solving they want. I also will offer suggestions about how to close the gap between the dysfunctional and divisive government the American people have endured and the problem-solving, opportunity-creating government they deserve. In the last chapter, I will describe my work with an organization called No Labels, which I have supported since it was founded in 2010. My Senate Chief of Staff, Clarine Nardi Riddle, was one of its five official founders. When I left the Senate in 2013, I became personally active in No Labels and since 2014 have been its national chair.

Today, I believe No Labels has done more than any other political organization to bring America's government back to the bipartisan, problem-solving center. It is one of our best hopes for a brighter American future.

1

THE ROOTS OF AMERICAN CENTRISM

America's founders were educated in the Greek classics, Judeo-Christian theology, and the philosophy of the Enlightenment—all of which guided their creation of a centrist government.

In Greek philosophy, Aristotle held that the middle way between extremes was the best way. Harmony that moderated extremes was the goal. Courage is a favorite example of Aristotle's centrism. Courage is a human virtue, he said, but if taken too far to one side becomes reckless and dangerous. If it slides too far to the other side, it becomes cowardice, which is also dangerous. The center point of courage—between the cowardly and reckless—is the place to be.

Aristotle's lesson is memorably illustrated in Greek mythology. Daedalus builds wax-and-feather wings for himself and his son Icarus so they can escape the control of King Minos by air. Daedalus instructs Icarus to "fly the middle course" between the heat of the sun and the cool of the ocean. But Icarus is infatuated by his ability to fly and goes higher and higher, closer and closer to the sun until the wax on his wings melts, the wings separate from his body, and he falls into the sea and drowns. That was a large price to pay for leaving the centrist course!

America's founders were well-educated in Greek philosophy and mythology, but it was Judeo-Christian theology that influenced them more. There, they also found great value placed on the center path. In the Talmud, Rabbi Judah offers a parable that reads like Daedalus:

> There is a highway that runs between two paths, one of fire, and the other of snow. If a person walks too close to the fire, this person will be scorched by the flames; if too close to the snow, this person will be bitten by the cold. What is the person to do? This person is to walk in the middle, taking care not to be scorched by the heat nor bitten by the cold.

Maimonides, the 12th-century Spanish-Jewish philosopher and scholar, wrote:

> The right way is the mean . . . namely that disposition that is equally distant from the two extremes in its class.

Christian texts are full of appeals for personal and societal moderation as the natural result of living Christian values.

> Evil consists in discordance from their rule or measure . . . This may happen by exceeding the measure or . . . falling short of it.
>
> Therefore, it is evident that moral virtue observes the mean. (St. Thomas Aquinas)
>
> Let your moderation be known unto all men (because) the Lord is at hand. (Philippians 4:5)
>
> All things are lawful unto me, but all things are not expedient: all things are lawful for me but I will not be brought under the power of any. (1 Corinthians 6:12)

Many leaders among the founding American generation brought to our nation's shores a belief in the Hebrew Bible and the New

Testament. The theologian who most influenced them was John Calvin.

"There is no kind of government more salutary," Calvin wrote, "than one in which liberty is properly exercised with becoming moderation and properly constituted on a durable basis."

Calvin's Protestant reform theology can be described as centrist, sitting as it does between the "extremes" of Anabaptist liberalism and Catholic legalism. Although Calvin was a theologian and religious leader, he had strong political views—centrist political views—based on his wonderful phrase: "becoming moderation."

"The purpose of political government and law," Calvin said, "is to cultivate civil restraint and righteousness in people, and to promote general peace and liberty."

Michael Novak, the Roman Catholic theologian, wrote that the American eagle took flight in the eighteenth century with two wings: One was the Calvinist faith of the founders, particularly their knowledge and love of the Bible, and the other was the philosophy of the Enlightenment. Our forefathers were very much aware of the Enlightenment's great European philosophers, including Montesquieu, Voltaire, Rousseau, Hume, Locke, and Bacon.

Those great thinkers believed in the primacy of reason and embraced the scientific method of their time. Tolerance, particularly religious tolerance, was very important to them. They advocated for a government that upheld civic virtue and protected freedom of religion and speech, as well as individual equality and opportunity.

The operative political strategy of the Enlightenment was centrist. In his "Spirit of the Law," Montesquieu writes that the essence of his political philosophy is "the spirit of moderation."

Voltaire's guiding philosophy for government, meanwhile, was one that has been repeated by political centrists since he wrote it in the eighteenth century: "The perfect is the enemy of good."

In other words, the compromises that centrist politics require are the best way to solve society's problems and bring about progress. If you accept only "perfection," you will not solve or build anything. Voltaire's pithy statement is not only a wise comment on the general imperfection of the human race, but also an inescapable fact about the impossibility of achieving perfection in the work of political leaders who must find common ground to produce results.

The great values of Faith and Enlightenment motivated and directed our founders as they drafted America's Declaration of Independence in 1776 and our Constitution in 1787.

In the case of the Constitution, there were large and fundamental differences of opinion about America's future government that needed to be reconciled. Compromises were therefore imperative to achieve the unity America needed to secure its independence from England.

However, there were no disagreements about our founders' purpose in adopting the Declaration of Independence at the Continental Congress at the State House in Philadelphia in the summer of 1776. The resolution for independence from England passed unanimously. Differences of opinion arose around the actual words the delegates chose to explain their Declaration, and those choices have greatly influenced American history since.

The Declaration preceded the Revolutionary War. America's values were therefore declared before its boundaries were secured, meaning the words chosen for the Declaration were important. They emerged from admirable discussion, negotiation, and compromise among the delegates to the convention. The most important phrases of the 1,337-word Declaration constitute some of the most important words ever written in the English language:

> We hold these truths to be self-evident, that all men are
> created equal, that they are endowed by their Creator with
> certain unalienable rights, that among these are life, liberty,
> and the pursuit of happiness.

To make clear how determinative those sentences are, the Declaration immediately goes on to say: "To secure these rights, governments are instituted among men, deriving their just powers from the consent of the government."

In other words, the new nation was being established for the primary purpose of implementing the universal declaration of human rights made in the first paragraph. But there was not unanimous support for the words Thomas Jefferson proposed for that pivotal paragraph from the outset. The original language he sent to the other four members of the Drafting Committee of Five (John Adams of Massachusetts, Benjamin Franklin of Pennsylvania, Robert Livingston of New York, and, may I say with some parochial pride, Roger Sherman of Connecticut) was:

We hold these truths to be sacred and undeniable.

Franklin asked that the words "sacred and undeniable" be replaced by "self-evident." Why? Walter Isaacson, a great Franklin biographer, believes Franklin was reflecting the philosophy of the Enlightenment, particularly as he had learned it from David Hume, the philosopher with whom he had become friendly during the years he was in London. Franklin wanted the new nation to be founded on rationality, not religion. Everyone, including Jefferson, looked up to Franklin—who was much older and more worldly than the other delegates in Philadelphia. Jefferson himself was thirty-seven years younger than Franklin. The Committee accepted Franklin's edit, but John Adams was not satisfied with the result. He wanted to add words that reflected the other wing of Michael Novak's American eagle—Calvinist Christianity. He asked that the Committee add the sentence: "They are endowed by their Creator with certain unalienable rights."

In the spirit of compromise, Jefferson and the Drafting Committee—and ultimately the Continental Congress—accepted the amendments that both Franklin and Adams offered, resulting in the timeless words of the Declaration that have defined our national purpose and shaped our history since then.

That was not the only compromise in the drafting of the Declaration of Independence. Take, for example, the section listing the misdeeds of the British Crown that justified the Americans' claim to independence. Jefferson originally included the charge that Britain had forced slavery on the colonies. The Drafting Committee accepted that wording. When it came before the full Congress, however, some of the delegates argued that this language went too far and would offend people in Britain who might otherwise support the American Revolution. In the interest of moderation, pragmatism, and unity, that charge against Britain was removed from the Declaration.

As significant as these compromises were in leading to unanimous adoption of the Declaration of Independence, they were modest compared to the great differences that had to be bridged to reach agreement at the Constitutional Convention eleven years later.

When the delegates left their home states for Philadelphia in May of 1787, there wasn't even unanimous consent about the purpose of the convention. A majority agreed that the Articles of Confederation were not working well, primarily because the states had too much power and the national government too little. But most of the delegates saw the convention only as an opportunity to modify the Articles to achieve a bit more authority at the center of the US government. A few delegates had larger goals. They wanted to abandon the Articles and write a new Constitution for a new, stronger national government. Alexander Hamilton of New York and James Madison of Virginia united in making this case in the Federalist Papers. With the support of the hero of the American Revolution, General George Washington, they ultimately prevailed.

But it wasn't easy, and it required more than the force of the Federalist Papers' reasoned arguments and Washington's stature. It required hard, practical compromises to protect and strengthen their experiment in independent self-government. The states were, after all, very different from one another. There were large and small population states, and slave and free states. They had different ideas about how much power they should give the citizenry in the republic they were creating, and how much authority should be added to the new national government and taken from the state governments.

Like all compromises, the great ones reached in Philadelphia at the Constitutional Convention were not perfect. Remember Voltaire's warning that the quest for perfection cannot be allowed to block the achievement of good results. In the end, the delegates wrote a Constitution and strengthened America in a way that has sustained and guided our nation since. In fact, it changed the vision of government throughout the world. And it only happened because the delegates in Philadelphia came to the center and made difficult, imperfect compromises.

First, most of the delegates ultimately accepted that it was necessary to write a new Constitution for a new government—but they still had to work out their differences about its form and content or they would not have the votes necessary to adopt a Constitution and send it back to the states for ratification.

When it came to the new national legislative body, there was a consensus that it should have two chambers. That was what the delegates were familiar with from Britain and had adopted in all of the states, except Pennsylvania, which had a unicameral legislature. But how would they apportion representatives from the states to the new Congress, and how would they select the representatives? Those were very divisive questions. Large population states were pitted against small ones; slave states against free ones.

The large population states naturally wanted representation in both chambers of Congress to be based on population. They were led by Virginia which, together with Massachusetts and Pennsylvania, contained almost half of the young country's population. But the small population states at the convention—led by New Jersey—were larger in number, and they wanted each state to have equal representation in both Chambers of Congress. Without their support, no Constitution would be adopted at the convention. This dispute threatened to break up the convention, and effectively end the American experiment. The delegates were gridlocked during the summer of 1787. The breakthrough came when the Connecticut delegation, led by Roger Sherman and Oliver Ellsworth, proposed what became known as the Connecticut Compromise. It was sensible and simple: Representation in the House would reflect the population of the states, but in the Senate each state would have equal representation regardless of its population.

Would enslaved Americans who constituted 40 percent of the population of the Southern states at that time be counted in the apportionment of seats in the House? The Southerners wanted the slaves to be counted, but, of course, not to be freed. Many of the Northerners argued that if Black slaves were to be counted, they should be liberated.

James Wilson of Pennsylvania, appreciating that the larger population states like his, Massachusetts, and Virginia needed the support of some of the Southern states to adopt a system of representation based on population, proposed that seats in the House be based on the "free population" plus 3/5 of the slave population. This dehumanizing compromise not only left slavery in America untouched, but gave the Southern states about a dozen more seats in the Congress, and a dozen more votes in the Electoral College.

Nine states supported the 3/5 compromise; only New Jersey and Delaware voted against it.

The anti-slavery forces were upset by the 3/5 compromise and pressed for a ban in the Constitution on international slave trading into the US. In other words, although the Constitution would not alter the status of the current slave population, they wanted to legislate an end to the importation of more slaves. The Southern states opposed that, and another compromise was reached. International slave trading would be banned in America but not until twenty years later, at the earliest, in 1808.

There were also various proposals for how to elect members of Congress, many of them not really democratic. Hamilton proposed that the House be elected for set terms by the voters, but that the Senate be elected for life by a new group called "Electors" who would be chosen by the state governments. Charles Pinckney of South Carolina recommended that members of the House should be elected by the people, and the Senate should then be elected by the House. Some argued that both chambers should be popularly elected, but that proposal was defeated in a vote.

Then, a compromise was offered to have the House popularly elected and the senators chosen by their state legislatures. That process was adopted and stayed in effect until the 17th Amendment—which required the popular election of US Senators—was ratified in 1913, more than 125 years later. It is important to understand that although the delegates to the Constitutional Convention wanted to create a republic based on classic, liberal principles, they were also landed aristocrats who worried about what the citizenry might do if there were no limits on the new power they had in voting. Thus, they chose the state legislatures, which were generally controlled by establishment figures, to elect the members of the US Senate, one layer removed from the voters.

The delegates to the Constitutional Convention did the same when it came to the election of the president. First, they had to decide the basic question of what form the executive branch of their new government would take. There were some proposals made by great men in Philadelphia that seem very odd today. Hamilton proposed that "Electors" would choose the president who would serve *for life*. Franklin proposed a plural executive of three people. And in his Virginia Plan, Madison provided that the president would be chosen by Congress.

James Wilson of Pennsylvania again listened, negotiated, and offered a compromise. He argued that a president chosen by Congress would be too dependent on the legislature and would not be a check on its power. So, he recommended a unitary executive. Wilson's proposal gained support because many of the delegates had George Washington, who they had chosen to preside at the convention, in mind as their first president. A majority of the delegates still wanted the president to be popularly elected, and that worried a minority that feared who the voters themselves might chose as their president. So again, there was gridlock.

To break it with another centrist compromise, Wilson took Hamilton's idea of Electors chosen by the states (which had been rejected for the selection of the members of the Senate) and proposed instead that the Constitution establish an Electoral College, whose members would be chosen in the states, and actually select the president. The voters in presidential elections would be voting for Electors, presumably supporting a presidential candidate, not for the candidate himself.

As the summer of 1787 was coming to a close, most of the big questions for the Constitution had reached a consensus. Then the convention chose a Committee of Detail, chaired by Benjamin Franklin, to bring it all together—and they did. For example, on the most difficult political question regarding the degree to which population would determine the selection of members of Congress,

Franklin embraced the Connecticut Compromise but sweetened it for the still dissatisfied large population states by proposing that the House, whose membership would be based on population, would have exclusive power to originate revenue bills and propose salaries for government workers.

When Franklin presented his committee's agreed-upon language for the new Constitution to the convention, he reminded the delegates that he had come to the convention favoring a single House and no Senate. Now he was offering a very different compromise proposal, a change of opinion which he justified with a wonderful story from his earlier life:

> When we were young tradesmen in Philadelphia, (and) we had joints of wood that didn't quite fit together, you'd take a little from one side and then shave a little from others until you had a joint that would hold together for centuries. And so too we here at this convention must each part with some of our demands if we're going to have a Constitution that will hold together.

"Compromises may not make great heroes," Franklin said, "but they do make great democracies."

Franklin's statements are eternal truths that have been validated in American history at every point when our elected leaders have come together to protect our security, increase our prosperity, and, in many other ways, make ours a more perfect union. They did it compromise by compromise.

That was certainly what I experienced in my 40 years in American government, an era when bipartisanship and compromise were much more achievable than today. Many times during gridlock, I would appeal to my colleagues in the US Senate to look back at our Constitutional Convention and remember that our founders were capable of compromising as much as they did to establish our government, including in the very make-up of the Congress in which we were privileged to serve. Surely, we could find a way to come together to solve the problem we were facing that day.

2

A PERSONAL CASE STUDY: THE SOURCES OF MY CENTRISM

My first political memory is Election Day in November 1952, when I was just ten years old.

My father, mother, grandmother (my mom's mom, who lived with us), and I were sitting in our house on Strawberry Hill Court in Stamford, Connecticut, watching the returns from the presidential election on our new television which had a cabinet much bigger than the screen. The candidates were Republican Dwight Eisenhower and Democrat Adlai Stevenson. My grandmother and I were quite logically supporting Eisenhower. He was, after all, the great general who had led the American military to victory over Hitler's Nazi armies in Europe.

As the evening went on, it became clear to me that my father and mother were supporting Stevenson which puzzled and irritated me. But I was only ten and besides, in the end, Ike won and that was what counted.

A few years later, I asked my dad how he possibly could have supported Stevenson over Eisenhower. Was it because he always supported the Democratic candidate? "Oh no," he answered. "I admired Eisenhower a lot. But I thought Stevenson was more ready, based on his experience as governor and his intellect, to be president. I don't always support the Democratic candidate if I think the Republican will do a better job. In fact, in 1940, I supported the Republican candidate, Wendell Willkie, instead of President Roosevelt, because I didn't think it was good for any president to serve more than two terms, even during a world war, and I thought Willkie was a very honorable, able, and independent-minded man."

Needless to say, those paternal words—bipartisan, centrist—stuck with me.

The 1952 election night was not the only way my parents influenced me to become a centrist or, for that matter, to go into public service. They raised my sisters and me in a religiously observant home where faith was the foundation of all we did. We believed in God—our Creator, Sustainer, and Redeemer. We saw our lives as the result of an intentional Divine act, not an accident of nature. The same was obviously true of all lives, of every other person, which meant we should treat everyone as we hoped they would treat us.

How do those beliefs connect to politics and centrism?

If you see everyone you meet on the street or serve with in politics as a child of God, just as you are, it should lead you to treat them respectfully, listen to what they are saying, and try to better understand and learn from them. Those are the ingredients of centrism, and the opposite of the reflexes of partisans and extreme ideologues who view people in the other party, or of different ideologies, as enemies to be defeated, not as fellow human beings to engage, debate, and work with.

My study of the Talmud added values and stories from the rabbis of old that also influenced me.

One of the most important values I learned was the process by which the Talmud itself was composed—discussion and disputation leading to a consensus in values and law. In other words, disagreements can be a good thing if they are made with mutual respect and open minds because they usually lead to greater insights and understandings than an individual can reach alone.

Take the following story I was taught from the Talmud, for example. It's about a great rabbi who regularly studied, learned, and argued matters of faith and law with another rabbi, who died suddenly. The surviving rabbi was heartbroken. His students worried about him and decided they should find another rabbi to be his new study partner. After a few days, the older rabbi told his students to never bring that new study partner to him again. "With my friend who has died," he said, "when I would make a point, he would find many reasons to question my position which we would discuss and argue, and the result was a better conclusion between the two of us. I know this Rabbi you brought to me is learned, but every time I propound a position, he finds only reasons to agree with me. That is not the way to help me or lead to the truth."

That Talmudic ethic is an ideal precondition for centrism and problem-solving politics.

So is civility. You are much more likely to be able to meet people of different views in the center if you have treated them civilly and they have treated you that way, as well. Here too, religious tradition and my parents were great teachers and role models. The rabbis of the Talmud instructed the faithful to greet people with a smile and, if you knew them, with a friendly, interested word. This was to be done not with an ulterior motive but because it was the respect each of us owes our fellow human beings.

My mom and dad lived by this rule, and it had an effect on my sisters and me. As I realized later when I became a parent, we teach our children as much or more by how we behave than by how we tell them to behave. In that way, my parents were great educators. My mom was a naturally warm, outgoing, and accepting person with the widest variety of friends. My dad was more cerebral and quieter, and that made it all the more impressive when I saw how warmly and civilly he greeted people in public and in his store.

There is another side of civility—one closer to what used to be called manners—that I also grew up with. Both of my parents were raised in lower-income, one-parent families, and neither had the opportunity to go to college, but they were as refined in behavior and speech as any high-income college graduate I ever met. In our home, foul language, stories about improper subjects, and gossip about other people were not tolerated. Today, those taboos of my youth are publicly broken every day in political discourse. That, too, contributes to the difficulty politicians have finding their way to the problem-solving center. Coming to common ground begins with mutual trust, which is eroded when people in public life attack each other and spread stories (often false) about each other in language that is coarse and insulting.

Just as I was blessed to have excellent personal teachers and role models, I was fortunate to have public heroes who motivated me into public service and helped shape my centrist politics.

In 1954, when I was twelve years old, Abraham Ribicoff was elected governor of Connecticut, the first Jewish person to hold the highest office in our state's history. Ribicoff's election was a source of great pride, excitement, and optimism in the Lieberman household. The governor himself spoke of his election as the realization of the American Dream.

A few years later when I was following current events more closely, I read a lot about Ribicoff and was particularly impressed that he titled his first "State of the State" address as governor "The Integrity of Compromise." Ribicoff was a Democrat. The majority of both houses of the General Assembly were Republicans. Ribicoff said they would have to compromise to get anything done for the people who elected them. That kind of compromise was honorable and necessary, he argued. Coming to the center, Governor Ribicoff extended his hand to the Republicans in the General Assembly and, to their credit, they took his hand and joined him there in a number of bipartisan accomplishments, including reforming the state's judicial system, eliminating outdated county governments, and increasing state government support for local public schools.

Governor Ribicoff was connected to the other great political hero of my youth, John F. Kennedy. He and the longtime Connecticut Democratic Party Chairman John M. Bailey supported then Senator Kennedy from neighboring Massachusetts when he sought and lost the Democratic nomination for vice president in 1956 and stayed with him all the way to the White House in 1960.

For many Americans of my generation, Kennedy was our inspiration and catalyst into public service. To me, his views were attractively balanced: liberal on social policy, moderate on economic policy, and conservative on foreign and defense policy. He was a proud Democrat—and also a centrist because he wanted to get things done. As he said right at the opening of his memorable inaugural address on January 20, 1961, "We observe today not a victory of party, but a celebration of freedom . . . "

The lessons I learned from my parents and my faith together with the role models and heroes I had in Governor Ribicoff and President Kennedy combined to arouse my interest in public service and my understanding of how to be an effective public servant, which was from the bipartisan center.

In the fall of 1960, I left Stamford and, with my dad behind the wheel, traveled up I-95 to New Haven and Yale College. Like most freshmen, I had no idea about what I wanted to do when I graduated. I was just excited to be there—the first in my family to go to college—and anxious that I not flunk out and thereby embarrass my family and "ruin" my life.

Seven years later, on a sunny day in June 1967 when I graduated from Yale Law School, if you'd asked me what I hoped to do in life, I wouldn't have given you the truthful answer because it seemed too presumptuous. I would have said that I was very happy to have a job with a wonderful, old New Haven law firm, Wiggin and Dana. I might have added that one day I could go into public service. The unrevealed part of the answer was that I had a specific goal—really a dream—and that was to become a United States senator.

What happened during my seven years as a Yale student that so dramatically clarified and raised my ambitions and planted that dream?

First, I took some great courses in history, political philosophy, political science, and economics. I also did a lot of reading on my own, mostly history and biography, but also some political novels. Robert Penn Warren's *All the King's Men* was my favorite and is one of the greatest American political novels ever.

From this studying and reading, I came away with a growing appreciation of the large role leaders play, for good or bad, in the lives of the people at local and national levels. I also learned how the best leaders in democracies like America's—leaders like Washington, Lincoln, Theodore Roosevelt, Franklin Delano Roosevelt, and Harry Truman—achieved the most good. It was through important personal qualities like patriotism, principle, and persistence, together with a practical willingness to work with people who disagreed with them. Today I would call that centrism.

In 1962, after my sophomore year at college, I volunteered to work on the US Senate campaign of Abe Ribicoff, who had returned to Connecticut after two years as Kennedy's Secretary of Health Education and Welfare. During that summer, I attended the Connecticut State Democratic Convention, my first ever. Ribicoff was nominated over a liberal, populist challenger, Congressman Frank Kowalski.

Connecticut Party Chairman John Bailey was at the center of that convention, as he had been at every Democratic Convention since the mid-1940s. His control of the nominating process at those conventions was usually conclusive because primaries for nominations were not even legal in Connecticut until the mid-1950s, and the first statewide primary didn't happen until 1970.

Watching Bailey operate at that 1962 Convention fascinated me. He looked as if he had been sent from Hollywood to play the role of an old-time political boss, moving from delegate to delegate, glasses on his forehead, cigar in his hand, whispering to each, or sending an aide to ask a delegate to come for a discussion in the private room he had backstage at the convention hall. The more I asked people about John Bailey, the more their answers intrigued me. In some ways, he was actually like the old American political bosses in the power he exercised. But he did it differently. Bailey was a consensus builder, not a dictator. He had made a transition to a new generation of politics, embracing new groups (that year, he put an African American man on the state ticket, a first for Connecticut), and using new campaign tools like public-opinion polling.

When Ribicoff defeated his challenger Kowalski for the nomination, Bailey offered Kowalski re-nomination as congressman-at-large, but he balked. He was angry that Ribicoff had returned from the Kennedy Cabinet to take the Senate nomination away from him. The convention then went into recess for several hours during which Bailey and others negotiated with Kowalski. The congressman threatened a first-ever statewide primary, made increasing demands, and refused to compromise.

Bailey walked away from the negotiations, which was unusual for him, and directed his aides as follows:

> Get me three Polish American Catholics who have good clean records, and, if possible, can speak Polish. We will interview them right now.

From that process, Bernard Grabowski, a lawyer and former municipal judge from New Britain, emerged. He was nominated that night, elected in November, and served three successful terms in Congress. Frank Kowalski never held office again.

I decided I wanted to do my senior paper at Yale on John Bailey. I applied for and was accepted to a unique program called Scholar of the House, to which a dozen seniors were admitted each year. It freed me from all course requirements to work with a faculty advisor on a project and readings before writing a thesis. I was very fortunate to be assigned to James David Barber, then a young faculty member at Yale, later to become a renowned professor of political science at Duke University. At the end of the year, my paper was submitted to a panel of three faculty members who read it, questioned me, and graded it. One of them, William Lee Miller, was a graduate of the Yale Divinity School, teacher of political ethics at Yale and later at the University of Virginia, and a historian and prolific author. After reading my paper, Bill Miller contacted me to say he thought it was unique and should be published. If it was okay with me, he would send it to his publishers, Houghton Mifflin, in Boston. I was grateful, excited by the possibility, and absolutely thrilled when Houghton Mifflin said they wanted to publish it, which they did in 1966 under the title *The Power Broker*.

I recently looked back at that book and was surprised at how much my college study of John Bailey educated me and contributed to my later political life as a centrist.

I began my senior paper and the book with a quote from Robert Penn Warren's *All the King's Men* in which Willie Stark, the fictional governor of Louisiana, tells a reporter who becomes his chief aide: "One thing I understand and you don't is what makes the mare (government) go, I can make the mare go." That was John Bailey. He knew how to make the mare go. He wanted Democrats to win elections, and then get things done while they were in office so they could be re-elected.

I ended my book with some relevant conclusions about John Bailey:

> Bailey is . . . temperamentally a competent centrist who
> views political issues as a technician, not as an ideologist. He
> is not at ease with zealous partisans of either right or left . . .

This approach was reflected in Bailey's choice of candidates whom the Connecticut Democratic Party would support. As I observed then:

> With the cold and professional detachment of the surgeon
> he once thought he might be (his father was a doctor), Bai-
> ley goes about gauging popular sentiment. He becomes the
> unemotional receiver of feedback from the voting public,
> the computer absorbing data and then turning out the name

of the candidate most likely to receive the vote of a majority
of citizens . . . Bailey's personal attitudes have no place in
these investigations or in his ultimate choice.

The proof of that stoicism is the number of times Bailey supported people with whom he had disagreements. As Abe Ribicoff once told me, "John has never allowed himself the luxury of
revenge."

Here are some other words I wrote at age twenty-two that bring
a smile to my face now:

> Probably Bailey's most caustic critics within the Connecti-
> cut Democratic Party . . . are liberals who charge him with
> bringing too many "mediocre" men to office, mediocre here
> seeming to mean more moderate than they would prefer.

In fact, John Bailey did support many candidates who most
people considered liberal in their time and were also high-quality
public servants, including Governor Chester Bowles, Senator William Benton, Senator Abe Ribicoff, President Kennedy, and later
Governor Ella Grasso. The deciding factor in his candidate-selec-
tion process was never ideology, but who he believed had the best
chance to get elected. As he said to me, "I go with the bird who
can fly; not with the pigeon who can't get off the ground."

Bailey had rules that enabled him to find those birds who could
fly and then to help them soar. And he had what he called "political feel."

In the 1954 gubernatorial campaign, for example, he chose Abe
Ribicoff as the breakthrough Democratic candidate for governor
because he saw Ribicoff as a "Yankee Jew" who could receive support from the still large voting block of white, Protestant, moderate
Republicans, while holding on to the surging number of working,
middle-class Roman Catholic Democratic voters. His "political
feel" in that case worked brilliantly, as it did for John F. Kennedy
for president in 1960, and in 1974 for Ella Grasso, the first Italian
American governor in Connecticut history and the first woman

ever elected governor of any American state, not succeeding her husband.

Another of Bailey's rules was to balance Democratic state tickets ethnically and religiously, and later racially and in gender. Congressman Grabowski was a beneficiary of that balancing. I once asked Bailey whether he still thought all that ticket balancing was necessary, and he answered: "To be honest with you, I really don't know, but we keep winning, don't we?"

John Bailey was more involved in Democratic policy formation in the Connecticut legislature than most state political bosses of his time. He loved the legislative process and was a skilled negotiator and problem solver for Democratic governors. His goal was always to give his Democratic governors and legislators a good record to take into the next election. Those records of accomplishment were almost always centrist because Bailey knew Connecticut was a competitive political state where the plurality of voters was registered as independents.

John Bailey turned out to be invaluable in my education as a centrist.

I graduated from Yale College in 1964 and was lucky to be admitted that fall to Yale Law School—which also contributed to my education as a centrist, but in very different ways. I learned about the compromises at the Constitutional Convention that were necessary to reach agreement to form our new country, and the negotiations in the legislative center that enabled the enactment of the most important laws in our history. I also was taught that laws enacted by legislators, enforced by lawyers, and adjudicated by courts are the embodiment of our aspirations for ourselves and our country. They are the expression of our best values and the enactment of rules for behavior to achieve it. Laws say what we would like to be and should be but are not yet. Without law, there would be chaos, violence, and probably societal self-destruction.

The faculty at Yale Law was superb, spanning a large spectrum of political ideologies and legal philosophies. The student body was impressive and taught me a lot, as well.

Those lessons deepened my desire to be a lawyer and lawmaker, perhaps a law enforcer, and maybe even a judge.

I also benefitted greatly from my extra-curricular activities while at Yale College and Law School. As an undergraduate, I was a reporter on the *Yale Daily News* and eventually became the editor (called "Chairman of the Board" at Yale). As such, I spent a lot of time with a wonderful group of classmates who wrote for the "Yalie Daily"—two of whom became managing editors of great American newspapers: Paul Steiger at the *Wall Street Journal* and Bob Kaiser at the *Washington Post*. As Chairman, so the tradition held, I wrote all the editorials. Although I used "we," it was me who had to learn enough about issues in the world, our country, and on campus to take policy positions. And I would say that during my year as Chairman, our newspaper's editorial policies are best described as center-left.

Thirty-six years later in 2000, as part of Vice President Gore's vetting of me as a possible running mate, a Washington lawyer went back and read all of my *Yale Daily News* editorials to make sure I had not taken any positions that would come back to hurt the Gore ticket if I were selected. I was later told that the three most controversial editorial positions he found were: appeals for civil rights for African Americans, coeducation for the still all-male Yale College, and the opening of diplomatic relations between the United States and a country I called "Red China."

In 2000, the Gore vetting team fortunately concluded that none of those editorial positions would compromise my possible candidacy for vice president. Nor would the fact that during college I got personally involved in the civil rights movement, first in New Haven in protest against low-income housing policies. Then, during the summer of 1963, while I was a summer intern for Senator Ribicoff in Washington, I joined in the March on Washington for Jobs and Freedom behind Dr. Martin Luther King. I was at the Lincoln Memorial on that summer afternoon when Dr. King delivered his "I Have A Dream Speech"—one of the great orations in American history. It was built on the centrist American foundation of religious faith and values. When I returned to New Haven, I wrote about that influential experience in the *Yale Daily*.

Soon thereafter, Yale's Chaplain, William Sloan Coffin, challenged me to use my position as Chairman of the *Yale Daily News* to organize and lead a group of Yale students to Mississippi to join in a mock freedom vote election to protest the disenfranchisement of African Americans there, one hundred years after the Civil War. It was a thrilling, threatening, and ultimately transformational experience, which taught me what it meant to be a leader and gave me the special feeling of satisfaction that comes from serving a cause larger than one's self.

It was quite an education I received inside and outside the classrooms at Yale, and during two "Mr. Lieberman Goes To Washington" summer intern experiences working with Senator Abe Ribicoff in 1963 and Democratic National Chairman John Bailey in 1964. By 1967, when I left law school, I knew that I would practice law, but I also wanted to try public service, and, undoubtedly because of my experiences with Abe Ribicoff, dreamed of being a US senator.

I was blessed in the years that followed "to live the dream." I lived it, as I will describe, in the bipartisan center of American politics—the most fertile ground, I believe, for an effective life in government.

3

THE MAKING OF A CENTRIST ELECTED OFFICIAL

When young people have asked me how to begin a political career, I naturally base my answer on my own experience.

The first part of my response usually surprises people: I urge them to read histories, biographies, and books on current events so they can learn about the lives of political leaders and better understand what their own political aspirations are. You shouldn't become a politician just because you want to have a title, I say. You should have a purpose and policy priorities. You should stand for something.

Next, I tell them to get personally involved so that they understand what political life is like. Experience will teach them whether a career in politics is what they really want. Volunteer in a campaign or in an elected official's office. Get active in the community where you live—perhaps in a public service organization and definitely in the political party of your choice.

Depending on how great the competition is among potential candidates in the party and place you have chosen, it is possible that they will ask you to be their nominee for a particular office. More likely, at some point, you will have to decide to take the risk of just running, regardless of who your party is supporting.

But I add two conditions. First, you have to conclude that you can do a better job than the incumbent or the other candidates. You'll have to convince the voters of that. Second, I caution would-be candidates before they seek office to conclude by some means (public opinion polls or conversations with voters) that it is possible they can win the nomination and election—not that they are *sure* they will win but that it is plausible they *can* win. Some people so deeply hold the beliefs that motivate them to run that they don't care whether they can win. They just want to make a point. I have never felt that way. I have never wanted to live through the demands of a political campaign unless I believed there was a chance I would be elected and could serve.

In recent years as politics has become more partisan and personal, I now add this plea to aspiring politicians: In your campaign, you will want to distinguish your opponent's record and policy positions from yours, but don't treat him or her as evil unless you are the rare political candidate whose opponent actually *is* evil, and, incidentally, others agree with your conclusion. If you become your party's nominee, remember that the other party's candidate is your opponent, not your blood enemy, and his or her party is the other political party, not a country with which you are at war. If you win the election, you will have to come to the center and work with people in that other party if you want to get anything done for the people who were good enough to elect you.

All that counsel is essentially derived from the way I started my political career in New Haven. After I began my law practice, I got active in the community, working, for instance, to stop an interstate highway from going through one of the city's most beautiful parks. I also became co-chair (with a Republican lawyer!) of the New Haven Jewish Community Relations Committee, and I volunteered in the 1967 re-election campaign of New Haven's pioneering, long-time mayor, Richard C. Lee.

In 1968, I got involved for the first time in a Democratic presidential campaign in Connecticut. My choice of candidate showed that I had already found my way to the Center-Left of the Democratic Party, as opposed to the Left-Left.

The war in Vietnam had turned bad and so too had President Lyndon Johnson's political fortunes. He was challenged by the anti-war movement and its candidate, Senator Eugene McCarthy of Minnesota. While I was also against the war and Johnson, I was not comfortable with McCarthy or the movement around him, one that seemed to reject more about America than our policy in Vietnam. I didn't think McCarthy could defeat Johnson for the nomination either—or, that if he did get the Democratic nod, that he could win the election in November. When McCarthy finished a surprising second to President Johnson in the New Hampshire primary, Senator Robert Kennedy entered the race. I was thrilled, and immediately volunteered to work for him in Connecticut. I contacted a friend from Yale who was on Kennedy's staff in Washington as well as John Bailey, assuming he was "in touch" with the nascent Kennedy campaign—even though, as Democratic National Committee Chairman, he had to remain "neutral."

President Johnson announced on March 31 that he would not seek re-election. Because the Connecticut liberals were for McCarthy and the organization Democrats had been for Johnson and were now waiting for Vice President Humphrey, I became one of the two leaders of the Robert Kennedy presidential campaign in Connecticut, despite being only twenty-six years old. The other leader was James Fitzgerald, an East Hartford Democrat who was close to John Bailey. Through "Jimmy Fitz" and me, Chairman Bailey had friends in charge of the Kennedy campaign in Connecticut. Less than three months after Kennedy declared, it all ended tragically. After winning the crucial California primary that day, he was assassinated, and I and so many others were literally heartbroken.

Later in 1968, the leaders of the Connecticut McCarthy campaign joined with a group of us from the Connecticut Kennedy campaign to form a political committee in support of the re-election of Senator Abe Ribicoff, who had emerged from the tumultuous Democratic Convention that summer as a hero because of his criticism of the Chicago police's treatment of the anti-war protesters. Ribicoff was easily re-elected and Vice President Humphrey carried Connecticut by 5 percentage points, but of course, lost nationally to Richard Nixon.

After the election, the leaders of the former McCarthy campaign in Connecticut invited me and others from the Robert Kennedy campaign to join them in creating a new reform Democratic organization called the Caucus of Connecticut Democrats (CCD). The chairman of the McCarthy campaign, Rev. Joe Duffey, became chairman of the CCD and I was vice chairman. In 1969, we lobbied in the Connecticut General Assembly for a policy platform we had adopted at a CCD Convention. It was somewhere between center-left (Kennedy) and left (McCarthy). In 1970, Joe Duffey ran for the Democratic nomination for US senator, which had opened up when the incumbent, Senator Thomas Dodd, said he would run for re-election as an independent. One of the two other candidates for that nomination for the US Senate was the Democratic State Senate Majority Leader, Edward Marcus, who was also the state senator from the district in New Haven where I lived.

I began to think about running for Marcus's state senate seat even though I assumed there would be many other candidates—more senior than I was and already in office—who would also seek the nomination. When none of them declared, I asked why. The answer: They all expected Ed Marcus to lose the primary for the US Senate and return to run for his state senate seat, so they didn't want to waste their time.

Marcus was known as a very tough, vengeful man, and nobody wanted to get on his bad side. I was twenty-seven and held no office. I had nothing to lose. I was also too young and eager to appreciate that being on Ed Marcus's bad side could be perilous for my political future in New Haven. I had watched Marcus operate as the power in the Connecticut legislature during the 1969 session. I didn't like what I saw. He was autocratic, sometimes abusive, and treated John Bailey more harshly than any Connecticut Democratic leader ever had.

From conversations with people in New Haven (a public opinion poll was beyond my financial reach), I learned that Marcus's personality was not wearing well with his constituents and, like so many politicians who attain power in "the Capitol," he had lost touch with a lot of people back home.

I had answered the two questions I would later urge others to ask themselves before seeking office. I believed I could do a better job for the district than Ed Marcus, and I thought it was possible (but surely not probable) that I could win.

The campaign was more personal and generational than ideological, and it was bitter. My slogan was "A Strong, New Leader For A Better New Haven."

I have always been skeptical of the influence of political endorsements in campaigns, but if you are as new and unknown as I was in 1970, endorsements matter. I was blessed to be endorsed in that campaign by Senator Ribicoff and former Mayor Lee. Both had become valued mentors to me, and both had quarreled with Marcus in previous years.

From the beginning, I made it clear that I was in the race to stay, whether or not Ed Marcus came back to run for the state senate. Most people didn't believe me. But, when Marcus lost the state primary for US senator to Joe Duffey and returned and took the nomination away from me at the New Haven convention, I stayed in. The primary campaign was rough and tumble. I won by a couple of hundred votes out of more than seven thousand cast. The State Senate District was overwhelmingly Democratic, so I was easily elected in November and on my way to public service in Hartford in January 1971.

In the three-way US Senate race that year, Joe Duffey and Tom Dodd lost to the Republican congressman from Fairfield County, a fellow named Lowell Weicker. I never could have imagined then that I would myself meet Weicker on the field of political battle eighteen years later.

During my ten years in the state senate, I learned how to make the legislative process work, and even though the two major parties in Connecticut were alive and well, I also learned how important bipartisanship and centrism were in producing legislation. For the first four years, I actually got to work with John Bailey, who remained Democratic State Chairman until his death in 1975. For the last six of my ten years in the state senate, I was the majority leader while Ella Grasso served as governor. She was a great governor, a brilliant politician, and a wonderful mentor to me. Ella was also a practical and effective centrist.

As majority leader, I had the authority to determine what bills would be brought up in the senate. I met each day with my Democratic caucus to decide the bills we might take up and I also met with the Republican leader of the senate each day to discuss the same. He and I divided the bills on the calendar into three categories: those we could pass without partisan controversy, others we could probably negotiate to a compromise and passage, and still others we decided we would be unable to "negotiate" and therefore either I would not bring up or we would "let them fly" in partisan or personal debate on the floor. It was a very productive process in which the two gentlemen who were Republican leaders during those six years, Richard Bozzuto and Lewis Rome, and I developed a warm friendship and trusting working relationship that enabled the process to benefit our state. That successful, bipartisan experience guided me in the years ahead.

In 1980, my congressman, Robert Giaimo, surprised everyone by announcing he would not seek re-election. I had never thought of being in the US House of Representatives. My aspirations were set on governor and then senator, undoubtedly reflecting Abe Ribicoff's history. But I now asked myself and my family and friends whether I was remaining a state senator for too long—ten years—and would regret having missed this opportunity to seek higher office. I decided to run for Congress, and I won the nomination. It was a Democratic district, and I was expected to win easily in November, but I lost because of the surprising Reagan landslide (he carried Connecticut by 10%) and because I ran a bad campaign.

Defeat is not just an orphan, as the old saying goes. Defeat can also be a painfully good teacher. It was that for me in 1980. I ran a status-quo campaign in a year in which people were unhappy and wanted change. It was the first time I had used national media and polling consultants, and it didn't work well for me. My slogan was "Joe Lieberman, a Proven Leader You Can Count On"—not the right message in a year when people wanted new leaders.

Toward the end of the campaign, my Republican opponent began to attack me as a big spending, big taxing liberal (making our race suddenly more ideological and me seem like a Far-Left liberal). I anxiously called my consultants and they told me not to worry about it. We had taken a poll three weeks before the election and I was 19 points ahead. "Let's just stay on message and you will be fine," they said. So I did. On Election Day, I was not fine. I lost by 5½ percentage points.

It stung. I had lost a race that everyone, including me, thought I would win. One of the lessons I learned from that defeat was never to allow your opponent to define you without responding. Another was to poll more frequently because a campaign is always subject to sudden change. Third, I would never again yield control of a campaign to national consultants who didn't really know my district or state as well as I did. In the future, I would employ national experts and consultants but bring my judgment and experience to bear on the big strategic decisions of the campaign.

After about a month in a daze and a steady stream of condolences, I snapped out of it and said to myself, "You haven't died. You just lost an election and you have learned some things about why. You are only thirty-eight years old. You believe in public service. Go make your future."

In 1982, there would be a state election. Ella Grasso had died too young of cancer and was succeeded by Lieutenant Governor Bill O'Neill. He would run for election on his own in 1982, but there were rumors that the incumbent attorney general, Carl Ajello, was not going to seek re-election. I got excited about seeking that office. It would give me an opportunity to enforce public interest laws, particularly environmental, consumer, and human rights laws.

Before the incumbent decided whether he was going to run again, I jumped in and declared my candidacy. It was a risk, just as it was when I ran for state senate twelve years earlier. In fact, I knew that if I lost in 1982, it probably would be the end of my political career; but I had learned in 1980 that I could lose an election and life would go on. I also learned that in politics, as in so many other areas of life, the biggest rewards often come when you take the biggest risks, not when you play it safe.

So, I had again asked and answered my traditional two-threshold campaign questions. Attorney General Ajello was well-liked but not active. It was still legal for the attorney general in Connecticut to work part-time, which enabled the incumbent to maintain a private law practice. When I announced my candidacy, I promised that if elected I would end my law practice and work full-time as attorney general for the people of Connecticut.

How did I conclude this was a race I could win? Frankly, it was mostly by intuition this time, influenced by a desire to get back on the field after my defeat in 1980. I believed in my reason for running, and that I could convince others I could do a better job as the people's lawyer.

I had one other big asset which may not count as much anymore in the age of big money politics and social media campaigning as it did in 1982. I had the support of my hometown New Haven Democratic organization led by two wonderful friends and loyal supporters, Mayor Biagio "Ben" DiLieto and Town Chairman Vincent Mauro. They stood with me and my family on a cold day in the winter of 1982 in front of the Connecticut Supreme Court building in Hartford as I declared my candidacy for attorney general. Their presence and support were less an act of political logic than personal friendship for a candidate who, after all, had just lost an election he should have won. I shall forever be grateful to them.

A few months later, Attorney General Ajello announced he would not run again. Three other Democrats declared for the nomination. It was a good, tough campaign that ended with me receiving the nomination at the convention. My opponents decided not to carry their campaigns into a primary.

The convention was also memorable for me (and maybe for Connecticut, too) because, according to Connecticut tradition, it was held on a Saturday, the day which, according to Jewish law and tradition, I observe as Sabbath and therefore could not attend. In an inspired decision, my campaign manager, Sherry Brown, chose as my theme song at that convention the title song from *Chariots of Fire*, a popular movie about a Christian Sabbath observer who would not compete in the Olympics on Sunday.

Only in America!

On Election Day, the Democratic ticket led by Governor Bill O'Neill swept to victory, and with it, I became Connecticut's new attorney general.

During the campaign that year, former Vice President Walter Mondale came to Connecticut to speak at a big Democratic dinner. When we met and he learned that I was the candidate for attorney general, he told me that before he became a US senator and vice president, he had been attorney general of Minnesota. "Of the three offices, my favorite was attorney general of Minnesota," Mondale said. "Because when you are a state attorney general, all you do is sue the bastards."

That was a funny one-liner, but Mondale had made a great point. The job of attorney general is a public interest advocacy position. It is not ideological. I always thought of being attorney general as inherently centrist—as I wrote earlier, the law is inherently centrist in that it exists to balance freedom and order in society, keeping us on the middle path, far from the extremes of tyranny on one side and chaos on the other. The law provides our society with a non-violent, non-chaotic way to change and reform. That, too, is the work of a state attorney general.

After I was sworn in, I reorganized the Connecticut attorney general's office, bringing in new leadership from outside state government and promoting others from inside the office. Together we made it into a pro-active, innovative, public interest law firm, and we gave good counsel to all the agencies of state government, which was also my responsibility. Like Mondale, I loved the job, and I sued a lot of "the bastards." It made me grateful in new ways that I had gone to law school. And it opened an unexpected path to the US Senate.

4

MY UNEXPECTED CENTRIST PATH TO THE US SENATE

In 1986, I ran for re-election as attorney general and again, along with the Democratic ticket led by Governor O'Neill, won a big victory. Afterward, I started to think about the future and 1990, when it was widely believed Governor O'Neill would not seek re-election. Senator Weicker was up for re-election in 1988, but he looked unbeatable to most everyone, including me. So, I was focused on the '90 gubernatorial race.

There was some money left in my campaign fund after the 1986 run, and in early 1987 we used it to ask our new pollster, Stan Greenberg, to assess my chances in a campaign for governor in three years. Stan was a local consultant, an assistant professor of political science at Yale, and after my unhappy experience with national consultants in my 1980 congressional campaign, that made me feel better. A few years later in 1992, Stan would become very national—as Bill Clinton's presidential pollster.

The results of Stan's poll in March 1987 were both discouraging and provocative. In a projected Democratic primary for governor against two Democratic congressmen who were also thinking of running for the office in 1990, I came in third. Stan said I had a positive statewide public image and pretty good recognition, but they each had a very positive image and very high recognition in their respective congressional districts.

My wife Hadassah and my campaign manager Sherry Brown were there with me. I very clearly remember the next moment—in hindsight, the beginning of a major turning point in my life. We were in Stan's small, second-floor office above a popular Greek restaurant on State Street in New Haven. He had just given us the bad news about how difficult a gubernatorial campaign in 1990 would be for me. Then, with a devilish half smile, he said:

> Even though I know you are thinking about a gubernatorial campaign, I decided to put in a few questions about Senator Weicker and you. The results were interesting. In a head-to-head contest, he runs well ahead of you, but his personal "re-elect" numbers are not good. He is more vulnerable than most people think, and you are exactly the kind of centrist Democrat who could defeat him. All I'm saying now is that you should *think* about running against Weicker. You could possibly win, but, even if you don't, you will raise your visibility around the state and make yourself a much stronger candidate for governor in 1990. Please think about it and if you are at all interested, we should do a broader "benchmark" poll on you and Weicker in the next few months.

Hadassah, Sherry, and I were surprised, unsettled, and a little excited by what Stan told us. We were all doubtful that Senator Weicker could be beaten. So were most of the other possible Democratic opponents, which is why a concerted effort began to convince me to run for the Senate. It came from the leadership of the Connecticut and national Democratic Parties, led respectively by my longtime friend, supporter, and advisor, John Droney, who was then Chairman of the Connecticut Democratic Party, and another longtime friend from Yale College, John Kerry, who was a senator from Massachusetts and chairman of the Democratic Senate Campaign Committee (DSCC) during that two-year cycle. The arguments Droney and Kerry made were the same:

> We know Weicker will be difficult to beat, but we believe he can be beaten and that you are the best positioned of any Democrat to do it because you are a centrist, a moderate. Politically, you will be in the middle of your second term as attorney general and no one will ask you to give that up. So, as demanding as this would be, we think it is without risk. If you lose, you will still be attorney general.

Interestingly, the heart of Weicker's political strength in Connecticut was his reputation as a moderate Republican. He had opposed Nixon during Watergate and was pro-choice. He was disliked by many Republicans, but in elections he received a lot of support from independents, a respectable share of Democrats, and convinced a majority of Republicans—including those who didn't like him—that he was better than the Democrat running against him.

I described the Weicker profile to Kerry and Droney and said I needed to formulate a good case to make *against* Weicker and *for* me—in other words, why I would be a better senator. Based on what I knew about Weicker's record, I told them it would be a challenge.

John Kerry promised that he would have the DSCC do a top to bottom report on Weicker's career. At the same time, I was now interested enough to ask Stan Greenberg to do that benchmark poll he had talked about.

Kerry came back with a report of several hundred pages on Weicker's seventeen years as a senator. I learned that Weicker had a surprisingly negative record on environmental and consumer issues, law enforcement, and social service programs that was largely unknown by people in Connecticut, and by me. He was also close to the special interests in Washington, and on many occasions had

given speeches to their associations and received a personal hono-
rarium. That was legal at the time, but, I thought, unethical, and
surely looked bad. Again, no one in Connecticut knew about that.
He also had been critical of President Reagan's strong foreign policy, for example, opposing an airstrike Reagan had ordered against
Libya after Gaddafi's intelligence agency was implicated in a terrorist
attack on a nightclub in Germany that killed American soldiers. I
was also surprised to learn that Weicker was cozy with Fidel Castro and had vacationed and gone scuba diving with him in Cuba.

Then, during Labor Day weekend in 1987, Stan Greenberg
came over to our house in New Haven to present the results of
his benchmark poll to Hadassah, Sherry Brown, and me. We sat
around the kitchen table and listened.

Here is my reconstruction of the narrative Stan gave us on that
September morning:

> Weicker is vulnerable and you are exactly the kind of
> Democrat who can defeat him because you are indepen-
> dent-minded. After your years as attorney general, you are
> seen as a non-ideological advocate for the public interest.
> You can run as a centrist Democrat. To be more explicit,
> you can run to the left and right of Weicker at the same time
> because those are the positions you have taken and he has
> taken—to the left of him on environmental, consumer, and
> social service issues, to the right of him on law and order,
> foreign and defense policies, and family values. And you can
> also run directly at him on ethics issues.
>
> You are more than 20 points behind Weicker in a head-
> to-head matchup, but his re-elect numbers are very low for
> an incumbent. You can beat him, but even if he wins, as
> long as you don't make big mistakes, which I assume you
> will not, you will be a much stronger candidate for governor
> in 1990.

Although those urging me to run against Senator Weicker argued
that it was riskless, I knew it was anything but and that it would

be a very demanding campaign at a very demanding time for our family. Hadassah was pregnant and due in March 1988. She and I believed that I could do a better job than Weicker and that I had a chance to win a campaign against him, although it was not likely I would. In other words, big risk, big reward. Hadassah (God bless her) and I decided we would take our chances; we could handle the disruption.

On another cold winter day late in February of 1988, we all returned to the steps of the Connecticut Supreme Court Building in Hartford, where I had declared for attorney general five years before. I announced that I was a candidate for the Democratic nomination for US senator.

I could write a separate book about my 1988 Senate campaign because there were so many ups and downs, and so many stories to tell. But here I want to abbreviate the telling and focus on the campaign through the prism of centrist politics. From the moment I declared until Election Day in 1988, we executed the plan Stan Greenberg had laid out at my kitchen table in New Haven on Labor Day weekend in 1987. It was centrist and independent. I staked out positions to the left and right of Weicker because, as Stan said, that is who I was, what I believed in, and what I had supported in office. I campaigned through personal appearances, press releases, and local radio and television whenever I could get on. In 1988, of course, there were no social media opportunities.

Raising money against an incumbent is usually difficult, and it was particularly so in Weicker's case because of his reputation as a man with a long memory. Many potential contributors were reluctant to support me and oppose him. I worked very hard to find donors in Connecticut and around the country. It was not natural for me, but I knew I had to do it, so I got busy. When I raised enough, we began to invest in paid television ads, highlighting my public interest record as attorney general on environmental and consumer policies, and contrasting it with Weicker's record of supporting special interests.

We had four debates, beginning in the spring and ending in October. The general opinion was that I did well in taking the fight to Weicker. He stayed above the battle in the first three debates and generally ignored me in the campaign until the middle of October, when the race suddenly got close. The last debate was a scorcher.

During the third week in September, I was frustrated by my lack of progress and called my media consultant in Washington, Carter Eskew, who had become a trusted friend during that campaign.

"Carter, I am really disappointed," I began. "We are hitting Weicker hard on his record and contrasting it effectively with mine and my promises of what I would do differently in the Senate, but I am still more than 15 points behind him in the polls, and there is only a little more than a month left until Election Day."

Carter's answer was wiser than his years, and turned out to be prescient:

> I am at least as disappointed as you are, Joe. We should be doing much better in the polls by now, and, believe me, I have been thinking about why we are not. I think there are two possibilities. The first is that a lot of Connecticut voters have put their arms around Weicker over the years because of his opposition to Nixon or his independent positions on issues like choice, and no matter what we tell them about him, they will not let him go. The second possibility is that every time we tell them something about his voting record or closeness to the Washington special interests that they had not known, they loosen their embrace of him and then something will happen that will convince enough of them to let him go that you will win. That's my hope.

That's exactly what happened during October 1988. There is still enough mystery to America's campaign process, notwithstanding public opinion polls, that I cannot say for certain why a *Hartford Courant* poll released during the last month of the campaign suddenly showed me in a "dead-heat" with Weicker, but I think it was Carter Eskew's "Sleeping Bear" television advertisement. It was not ideological. But it made the case for change.

It was about Weicker's style of public service and about his ethics in government. The main message was that Weicker was more focused on his own needs than on his Connecticut constituents' needs. We illustrated that with a listing on the screen of the number of times he had spoken to special interest groups for a fee that went into his own pocket and missed Senate votes to give those speeches. It was not done in a harsh attack mode but in a colorful, animated cartoon that showed a bear named Weicker coming out of a cave growling and then going back into the cave. The voice-over said that Weicker was like a sleeping bear, spending most of his time in a cave (missing votes to meet with special interest groups whose names and dates scrolled along the side of the screen). He only came out when he had something he wanted to growl about, whether or not it mattered to the people of Connecticut, and then he went back in the cave. Like most political ads that work, this one expressed what a lot of people had come to think of Lowell Weicker. In other words, it did not attempt to make a sow's ear out of a silk purse. It built on feelings that a lot of people already had about the man being more self-involved and entangled in Washington politics. To keep with the light cover to the powerful message, the tag line at the end of the ad was: "Does a bear sleep in the woods?"

Soon after this ad ran for several days, the *Hartford Courant* poll showed me surging to a dead heat with Weicker. Senator Weicker's response was to buy a lot of television time for commercials that attacked me and my record. We slugged it out for the last few weeks of the campaign and during a final, tough debate at the Old State House in Hartford, which the media said I won. That debate had some memorable moments, such as his criticizing me for taking contributions "from the right-wing Cuban community in Florida." My response: I would rather stand with those patriotic Cuban Americans than vacation with the Communist dictator of Cuba and accept a gift box of Cuban cigars from Castro, as Weicker had reported in his Senate Ethics filing.

For Republicans who didn't like Weicker already and independents who had supported him before but had doubts about him, my record as a centrist made me an acceptable alternative. In previous campaigns, those Republicans and independents had stayed with Weicker despite their doubts or distrust because he portrayed his Democratic opponent as way too far left for them to support. He could not do that with me.

In fact, there was an unexpected series of endorsements of my candidacy by prominent Republicans who happened to be friends of mine but who also really did not like Lowell Weicker. The most well-known of those surprising Republican supporters was William F. Buckley, Jr., the renowned conservative intellectual and writer. Bill had been Chairman of the *Yale Daily News* in 1950, fourteen years before I had assumed the role. He loved the *Yale Daily* and had reached out to me during my year as Chairman. We became friends. Bill and his wonderful wife, Pat, lived in Stamford, Connecticut, which made it easy for us to see each other once or twice a year. Those evenings at the Buckleys' were always stimulating, elegant, and enjoyable. One day, in 1988, Bill called me and said, "Joe, I am thinking of endorsing you against Lowell Weicker, but will only do so if you are sure it will not hurt your campaign. If I do endorse you, please understand it will be the only time I ever do. Of course, you are my friend and I admire you, but I will only get involved in this because I so despise Lowell Weicker."

That was classic Buckley. I thought about it and told him I would be honored to have his support and believed that on balance it would help me. I am convinced it did.

Buckley "despised" Weicker because of the regular criticism Weicker had leveled against President Reagan, and also because Weicker had blocked his brother, James Buckley, from appointment by President Reagan to the Second Federal Circuit Court in New York. I knew an endorsement from him would upset some Democrats, but I also believed that a Buckley endorsement would sway the many Republicans who were unhappy with Weicker but hesitant to vote for a Democrat. For many independents, it could also make me a certifiable independent, centrist candidate.

Buckley's support came in a couple of his syndicated columns, which became national and state news stories. It also came in his own collegiate, prankster way—through the formation of a political organization Bill called "BuckPac," which he said was open automatically for membership to anyone in Connecticut named Buckley.

Another Republican endorsement I was thrilled to receive was from Dick Bozzuto, with whom I had a very good working relationship and a strong personal friendship when he was the Republican minority leader in the state senate and I was the majority leader. Dick thought Weicker was an arrogant, unkind person, who was also not a Republican team player. He saw me as a bipartisan centrist, and a friend. Dick's endorsement was made in a public statement during the last month of our campaign, and in a letter which my campaign sent to tens of thousands of registered Republicans in Connecticut. Both were very important to me on Election Day.

The third prominent Connecticut Republican who endorsed me publicly was Pat Sullivan, who had led the Reagan campaign in Connecticut in 1980 and had also clashed with Weicker. Pat had become a personal friend of mine, and in 1988 he was both a valued strategic adviser and a very credible contact to many Republicans throughout the state.

There was another surprising factor at work among Connecticut voters that year, one never considered by analysts because it was hard to measure. It was Stan Greenberg's insight that family values—in this case faith—would be a point in my favor over Weicker.

I can support this contention not with polling data but with a wonderful "Only in America" story. About a week before the election, I received a call from a good friend, Democratic State Senator Cornelius O'Leary from Windsor Locks, Connecticut. "Con" told me that he was confident I was going to win. "I'm thrilled to hear that Con," I responded, "but you and I are in a small minority who hold that opinion. Why do you think I am going to win?"

Here was Con's answer:

> I visited my mom yesterday afternoon, and she was having tea with three lady friends, all seniors and all Roman Catholics. I asked who they were going to support on Election Day for president between Governor Dukakis and Vice President

Bush. They all said Bush, and I couldn't talk them out of it.
Then I asked about your race with Weicker, and they all said
that was easy, they were going to vote for you.

"Why is that so easy?" I asked.

And they all said, "We like the fact that he is a religious man
and that he cares so much about his faith that he doesn't do politics
on his Sabbath."

Joe, that is why I think you are going to win.

On Election Day, I did win, by less than 1 percent of the 1.3
million votes cast. Who can say whether Mrs. O'Leary's friends
and people like them all over Connecticut gave me my margin
of victory? When you win by as little as I did that day, a lot of
people can rightfully claim they elected you. I put Mrs. O'Leary
and her friends in that group—fellow citizens to whom I will
always be grateful.

On election night, it was so close that I was not comfortable
declaring victory until 11:30 p.m. Nor was Senator Weicker willing to concede. And he was right not to do so. But by the next
afternoon, both campaigns had rechecked the votes and agreed I
had been elected. Senator Weicker conceded, and I began a thank-
you tour of the state.

The vote totals were fascinating. In most of the traditional
Republican towns and suburbs, Weicker won, but by less than
Bush defeated Dukakis on that same Election Day. In a few of
the Republican towns, I won surprising victories. I carried the
Democratic cities, but by less than Dukakis was defeating Bush.
In the inner blue-collar Democratic suburbs and the pivotal Nau-
gatuck Valley, which were full of "Reagan Democrats," I won big.
In sum, I was supported by a majority of Democrats, a majority
of independents, and a surprisingly large minority of Republicans.

Years before, my Yale College friend, Bob Kaiser, had introduced me to his uncle Jerry, a businessman who lived in Westport,
Connecticut, and was involved in local politics. Uncle Jerry gave
me sage counsel: "In politics, you cannot do it all yourself. There
is just too much to do, particularly in campaigns. You have to have

help. You have to be dependent on others. But here is my advice to you, Joe, as you think about going into politics: spread your dependency. Never allow yourself to become overly dependent on *one* individual, *one* group, or *one* special interest. That is the road to losing your independence once you are in office."

As Hadassah and I prepared to move to Washington, I was empowered by the knowledge that because I was a centrist Democrat, my election was the result of support from Democrats, Republicans, and independents, and I owed them all my best non–partisan effort as their new US senator. In 1988, I had been lucky to have been able to spread my "dependency."

LESSONS FOR CENTRISTS

1. It is natural and good to dream and plan for the future, as I did in 1987, about running for governor of Connecticut in 1990, but sometimes an unexpected opportunity comes along first that may be worth changing your plans for. That was what the US Senate race in 1988 turned out to be for me.

2. But first, I had to be convinced that it really was worth trying. That meant concluding that I could make the case that I would be a better senator for Connecticut than Lowell Weicker, and that I had a real chance to win. Senator Kerry and the Democratic Senate Campaign Committee he then chaired gave me the answers to my first question, and my pollster, Stan Greenberg, convinced me of the second, with some caveats and a lot of faith.

3. Although my two questions about running were answered to my satisfaction, going against Senator Weicker was still a high-risk decision, but, in politics, business, science, technology, and most of the rest of life, including love, the higher the risk,

the higher the reward. In other words, playing it safe rarely produces progress.

4. As a political pro told me early in my career, "politics is about addition, not subtraction." To win elections, you have to add supporters rather than lose them. That seems obvious, but, particularly in recent years when core constituencies in the Republican and Democratic parties have played such an outsized role in our politics, many elected officials have not tried to add supporters to their base. In some states or districts, where one party dominates, it may be possible to be elected with only (or mostly) the support of members of your own party. But, in national elections and in most state elections, including Connecticut's, you need to add independent voters, who are the fastest growing segment of our electorate. If you can, you should also try to add the support of members of the other political party. In 1988, I was running against an unusual Republican incumbent who in previous campaigns received a fair share of Democratic support, a slim majority of independent votes, and a majority of Republicans. Many of the latter were reluctant supporters who chose Weicker as the lesser of the evils over his Democratic opponent, whom Weicker usually portrayed as Far Left.

In 1988, I knew I had to secure my Democratic base but also win among independents—and try to convince enough Republicans that I was a centrist alternative to Weicker. When my friend, Bill Buckley, offered to endorse me because he "despised" Weicker, I knew it would make some Democrats uneasy; but I also bet that it would help me add more Republican voters to my totals, so I gratefully accepted Bill's offer. Support from two Connecticut Republican leaders, Richard Bozzuto and Pat Sullivan, helped a lot. In other words, bipartisanship and centrism can help win elections as much as they help to enact laws.

5. The 1988 Senate campaign was the second time I had used national campaign consultants. The first was my losing 1980

congressional campaign. My conclusion after the 1988 campaign was that I could not have won without national consultants, but I would not have won if I had done everything they recommended. Sometimes, the candidate has a better sense of his constituents than the consultants because he has had political experiences in his own state or district that consultants don't usually have. This lesson is a good one for anyone using consultants in any business or profession.

The bottom line is not to be intimidated by expert consultants, not to blindly believe they always know better than you do. They don't. But always be willing to listen to them, because they have had a different kind of experience than you have—and they might just be right.

5

FINDING THE BIPARTISAN CENTER IN PARTISAN WASHINGTON

For most of American history, we have had only two major political parties—Democrats and Republicans. The former goes back to an original Democratic-Republican Party led by Thomas Jefferson and James Madison. A schism caused by the controversial presidential election of 1824 created a new political organization that backed Andrew Jackson's victory in the presidential election of 1828, cementing its status as a major party—now called the Democratic Party. The Republicans were organized in 1854 by anti-slavery Whigs and came into their own in 1860 when their candidate, Abraham Lincoln, was elected president.

America is the exception among democracies in having only two political parties. Most have multiparty parliamentary systems. Nowhere in our Constitution or laws is it ordained that our country must have only two political parties. In fact, one of the sternest warnings President George Washington gave future generations of

Americans in his Farewell Address was not to allow the political factions or parties to become so strong that they would divide our country.

While the Democratic and Republican parties grew into their historic reality, they protected their duopoly through laws, rules, and customs. For instance, state laws were adopted that gave Republicans and Democrats unique power in the selection of candidates for state and federal office. The nomination of the Republican and Democratic Party candidates for president happens in a process that is established by state laws and by the rules of each party. Participation in the all-important presidential debates is determined according to rules adopted by a non-profit corporation, which is composed of representatives of the two major political parties. Not surprisingly, they make it hard for third-party candidates to qualify for the debates.

There are many more examples of the cementation of the two-party system, the self-legitimization and self-strengthening of the Democratic and Republican parties since their birth.

Some of the best examples are to be found in the rules and customs of the US Congress which divide both houses into Republican and Democratic caucuses, making clear to members that the two major political parties control the ladders up to greater influence in Congress through committee assignments and leadership.

Even though I was elected to the US Senate in 1988 because I received support from a broad coalition of Democrats, independents, and Republicans, when I arrived in the Senate in January 1989, I entered a very partisan world.

There was no choice but to live within the system as I found it. If I'd done otherwise, I would not have been an effective senator for the people of Connecticut. Democrats were in the majority after the 1988 elections, and I had supported the winning Democratic candidate for majority leader, Senator George Mitchell of Maine. He gave me my first two committee choices. My first was the Environment and Public Works Committee, because the policies it determined were important to me. I had said during the 1988 campaign that I would focus on environmental protection.

I was also appointed to the Governmental Affairs Committee, the Senate's investigative and oversight committee, which I asked for because its chairman, Senator John Glenn of Ohio, had urged me to seek membership. He described it as the "sleeper among Senate Committees because we can investigate anything related to the federal government we want and that means anything." Glenn added that he wanted to return a favor that Senator Abraham Ribicoff had done him. "When I came into the Senate, Abe urged me to ask for the Governmental Affairs Committee, which I had never heard of. I did and now I am the chairman." That's how I became a member of the Committee on Governmental Affairs and, as Glenn prophesied and fate would have it, I became its chairman in 2001, presiding over its post-9/11 transformation into the Senate Committee on Homeland Security and Governmental Affairs.

George Mitchell also gave me some very good additional advice as I began my Senate service:

> The Senate has seniority rules, and they are important, but even as a freshman you can have a lot of influence if you choose two or three policy areas that are priorities for you and learn them well so your colleagues in the Democratic caucus come to trust you and rely on your judgment and recommendations in those areas.
>
> Remember, Joe, there are fifty-five Democratic senators this session but there are hundreds of issues that will come before the Senate. Each senator, including you and me, cannot be an expert on every issue, so each of us has to rely on colleagues, usually in our own party, whose honesty and judgment we trust.

When the votes began in the Senate, I saw how accurate George Mitchell's counsel was and how partisan customs enabled delegation of decision-making. There are two tables in the well of the Senate in front of the podium. One of the tables is for Democrats, the other for Republicans. Partisan caucus staff members sit at each table. When a roll-call vote is called, each caucus staff puts sheets of paper on the table describing the matter being voted on, how the respective party leaders are voting, and, if relevant, how leading senators in one's own party are voting. That is a custom. It is not in statute or in the Senate rules, but it certainly strengthens the party caucuses and encourages senators to pay some attention to those sheets of paper.

At the same time, it was clear to me that it almost always takes more than members of your own party to get something done in Congress. Another rule of the Senate that is not in the Constitution or any law is the filibuster rule, which provides that before you can try to get fifty-one votes to adopt legislation, you have to get sixty votes to stop debate. It is very rare that one of the two major parties elects sixty or more senators. So, you have to get some support from the other party to get sixty and allow a vote on your legislation. In this way, the filibuster rule can be an inducement to bipartisan compromise.

It is also true that in each party's caucus, there are a variety of ideologies and opinions, so a senator has to be ready to negotiate and compromise with members of his own party, as well as members of the other party, to get to sixty votes to break a filibuster. Those negotiations necessarily occur in the center, not the margins, of both political parties.

In 1990, my second year in the Senate, I had the privilege of participating in one of the greatest bipartisan accomplishments of my twenty-four years in Congress—passage and enactment of the Clean Air Act. It should be studied by senators and students of government alike.

It began with a principled policy agreement between Republican President George H.W. Bush and Democratic Senate Majority Leader George Mitchell that air pollution was compromising the American people's health and damaging some of our most cherished natural resources. Both the president and the majority leader wanted to reduce air pollution, but each knew they did not have the votes alone to pass a bill. Even though there were fifty-five Democrats in the Senate that year, Mitchell knew he would lose some Democrats whose states would be adversely affected by changes in law that were necessary.

Bush and Mitchell agreed to cooperate and convene a bipartisan negotiating process. It met regularly for weeks in Mitchell's elegant, book-lined conference room in the Capitol, adjacent to his office. President Bush was represented at every meeting by either his White House Counsel, Boyden Gray, or the Director of the Environmental Protection Agency, Bill Reilly. Senator Mitchell came and went from the meetings, which were presided over by Pat Moynihan, the Democratic senator from New York, who was second in seniority on the committee and acting in the place of the ailing committee chairman, Quentin Burdick of North Dakota; and John Chaffee, the senator from Rhode Island, who was the ranking Republican on the committee.

Moynihan and Chaffee were great people and great senators who were always willing to come to the bipartisan center to solve problems. I was eighth in seniority of the nine Democrats on the Environment Committee, but that was enough to get me into the room and give me a seat at the table for one of the best legislative learning experiences I could have had early in my Senate career. It taught me how good laws about difficult and controversial matters could be enacted in Washington.

The negotiations over the bill began among the people in the room, but we soon invited in senators and private sector leaders representing different regions and interest groups—some from businesses, others from environmental groups; some from Midwestern states whose power plants were emitting dirty air, and some from downwind states that were being hurt by that dirty air; some from high sulfur coal states, and others from low sulfur coal states.

These were not easy issues, but with the united leadership of Bush and Mitchell and a bipartisan consensus for clean air on our Environment Committee, we worked together, pushing and cajoling other senators and interest groups to negotiate and cooperate with us to reach a consensus. An important incentive was, as we said often, "This train is going to leave the station," because President

Bush and Leader Mitchell were demanding it, so "it would be best for you to figure out a way to get on the train before it leaves."

One of our most difficult challenges was how to reduce acid rain from coal-burning power plants in the Midwestern states that was being carried by wind currents to the Northeastern states where it was killing forests and poisoning lakes and ponds.

George Mitchell was not only the Senate majority leader; he was the senator from Maine where a lot of acid rain had fallen and hurt the local environment. Mitchell was a strong environmentalist who needed to protect his state.

In previous years, there had been proposals to curb acid rain by authorizing the EPA to issue traditional command and control regulations on the Midwestern power plants. But the Bush administration didn't like that big-government approach. They were convinced by the Environmental Defense Fund (EDF) that there was a better way—a market-based approach in which declining acid rain limits would be set by law and regulation and credits bought and sold on markets to achieve the required reductions.

President Bush made it clear to Senator Mitchell that it was very important to him that this innovative approach to environmental protection was in the bill. It was not an easy ask of Mitchell because the market-based approach was untried. Environmental organizations and some Democrats were skeptical about it, even though it had originated with the EDF. Eventually, Mitchell concluded it would probably work—and he also knew he had to at least try it in order to get the Republican votes he needed to pass the bill. His willingness to include the market-based response to acid rain genuinely solidified the relationship between the Republican president and the Democratic Senate majority leader.

A political bonus that came with cutting acid rain was that the requirement to reduce emissions from coal-burning Midwestern power plants would inevitably favor states like Wyoming, which produces low-sulfur, less-polluting coal. The two Republican senators from Wyoming, Alan Simpson and Malcolm Wallop, both conservative Republicans who were not known as environmentalists, voted for the bill.

Another important compromise was reached on how to reduce emissions from cars and trucks—a big part of the national air pollution problem that was making people sick and causing many premature deaths. The automobile industry and senators from states where cars were manufactured nonetheless pleaded for time and less strict requirements. In the original Clean Air legislation, emissions standards were phased in. The second, stricter phase automatically went into effect by a certain date. The final bill took out the mandatory toughening of standards in the second phase and replaced it with a requirement for findings by the government before the demands on the car manufacturers would be increased. The two Democratic senators from Michigan voted for the bill.

One of the other big battles on the Clean Air legislations was, in its way, a personal contest between Senator Robert C. Byrd of West Virginia, the former majority leader, and George Mitchell, the current majority leader. The coal industry had long been at the heart of West Virginia's economy, and the coal it produced was high-sulfur, and therefore highly polluting. It was the cause of the most harmful emissions from power plants. Senator Byrd offered an amendment to provide very large amounts of economic aid to states that would be adversely affected by reforms in the Clean Air Act. Senator Mitchell thought the amendment would cost more than many Republicans would support and wondered whether that was part of why Senator Byrd was offering it. In other words, it could kill the bill. In fact, President Bush told Mitchell that if the Byrd Amendment passed, he could no longer support the Clean Air Act reforms. What followed was not just a debate about different environmental policies and costs in the bill, but a generational struggle between the previous and current Democratic leaders of the Senate. It was intense and close, but Mitchell won. Senator Byrd and his West Virginia colleague, Jay Rockefeller, who was a strong environmentalist, voted against the bill.

In the end, the compromise bill passed both houses of Congress and was signed into law by President Bush on November 15, 1990. It has extended lives and protected the natural environment since then. The law reduced four significant environmental pollution problems: acid rain, urban air pollution, toxic air emissions, and stratospheric ozone depletion. It established a national permit program to guarantee implementation of the law and strengthened the tools available to the EPA and prosecutors to enforce the law. And it improved performance standards for new vehicles, which have made cars and trucks much cleaner since then. Carbon monoxide pollution, mercury pollution, ozone pollution, and pollution from power plants have all been greatly reduced as a result of the law enacted in 1990. The EPA has estimated that in 2020, the Clean Air Act of 1990 prevented 230,000 premature deaths.

The Clean Air Act Amendments of 1990 were not the last environmental protection success I was able to be part of during my four terms in the Senate. But they became harder to achieve as the parties grew more divided, and too many members became risk averse because they feared being primaried by someone further to the left (Democrats) or right (Republicans) in their own party.

But the Clean Air Act of 1990 shows that it can be done, and it shows how. With strong bipartisan leadership, bipartisan member support, and a willingness to talk, listen, and negotiate, Congress can solve real problems.

In an earlier generation, Arthur Vandenberg and Harry Truman showed that could also be done in foreign policy.

Vandenberg was a conservative Republican newspaper editor from Grand Rapids, Michigan, before he became a US senator in 1928. During the 1930s, Vandenberg consistently opposed President Roosevelt's New Deal domestic programs. On foreign policy, his record was decidedly isolationist. He was a well-read, thoughtful man and had developed his political philosophy during his years as an editorial writer. Convinced that America's entry into World War I had been a tragic mistake, Vandenberg spoke out during the 1930s against American involvement in World War II, even urging

Roosevelt to seek an accommodation and peace with Japan. Then came Pearl Harbor and Vandenberg reversed his course. As he wrote later, "at Pearl Harbor, isolationism died for any realist."

Vandenberg was a realist and supported the US and Allied forces throughout World War II. On January 10, 1945, he went to the Senate floor and gave an important and much-honored speech in which he described how he had changed from an isolationist to an internationalist, and why he intended to remain so after the war was over. Only three months later, President Roosevelt died and Vice President Harry Truman, Vandenberg's longtime colleague from the Senate, became president.

In the years that followed, the former haberdasher from Missouri and the former newspaper editor from Michigan built a partnership that has become the gold standard for bipartisanship in American foreign policy. Truman and Vandenberg agreed on the need to create the United Nations, adopt and fund the Marshall Plan, establish NATO, and oppose the spread of Soviet Communism in Turkey and Greece through military and economic aid in what became known as the Truman Doctrine.

The value of Vandenberg's support of Truman rose significantly after the 1946 midterm congressional elections when Republicans won a landslide victory and Vandenberg became chairman of the Senate Foreign Relations Committee.

When his fellow Republicans complained to Vandenberg that he was giving too much support to the foreign policy of the Democratic president who they confidently hoped to defeat in the presidential election in 1948, the senator from Michigan famously responded, "politics stops at the water's edge." There would naturally be disagreements over foreign policy, he said, but they must not be allowed to be determined by partisan politics. That would reduce our strength in the world, and embolden our enemies, particularly the Soviet Communists.

Together, President Truman and Senator Vandenberg, more than any other two Americans, secured the post-war world, strengthened our relationships with our allies in Europe, built the stability that was necessary for great post-war American and global economic growth, and embraced policies in the Cold War that eventually led us to victory.

There has been nothing quite like the Truman-Vandenberg bipartisan partnership on foreign policy since then.

When I arrived in the Senate in January 1989, I aspired to be guided by the Truman-Vandenberg model. I knew I wanted to make foreign and defense policy one of my personal priorities because I saw those as unique and indispensable responsibilities of the national government that I was now a part of. I came to the Senate with strong opinions about national security and foreign policy. As I look back, I understand that those opinions were formed by a combination of my reading about events that had happened throughout history and my response to events during my lifetime.

The historic sources of my foreign policy beliefs probably go as far back as the Bible and the story of the Amalekites, who attacked the defenseless Children of Israel as they fled from Egypt. Afterward, God warns us all to remember the Amalekites throughout human history, and to stop them before they attack. Unfortunately, my reading of history since then justifies that Divine warning and directive. Forces of evil triumph when good people and good nations don't act forcefully to eliminate or contain them.

In modern times, that was painfully clear in Europe during the 1930s as Hitler armed Germany, implemented his hateful and murderous policies, and invaded and conquered neighboring countries, while leaders in Europe and America found excuses for inaction and sought, with tragic naiveté, to appease the Nazis. The great exception, of course, was Winston Churchill, a hero for millions, including me. But until Churchill finally became prime minister and was able to awaken and rally the British people, bring Roosevelt and the American military into World War II, and defeat the Nazis, too many people were killed. The foreign policy lessons that I took from this dreadful history were deepened when I married Hadassah Freilich, whose parents both were taken by the Nazis but survived and moved to Prague where they met and married and where Hadassah was born.

In my lifetime, as I have written, President Kennedy was a catalyst for public service and also a model for my foreign policy beliefs. So many of the extraordinary words he spoke in his Inaugural Address strengthened the views I was forming. For example, he pledged that the United States would "pay any price, bear any burden, meet any hardship, support any friend, oppose any foe, to assure the survival and success of liberty."

That seemed powerfully consistent with the purpose of America as expressed in the Declaration of Independence, and also consistent with the reality of history as I had read and learned it. Allies mattered and steadfastness to principles was an expression of national strength.

In November 2007, nearly twenty years after I came to Washington, I looked back and offered these reflections on Kennedy's Inaugural in remarks I delivered at Johns Hopkins' School of Advanced International Studies:

> This was the Democratic Party I grew up in, a party that was unafraid to make moral judgments about the world beyond our borders, or to draw a clear line between "the free world" of the West, and the "slave society" behind the Iron Curtain. It was a party that grasped the inextricable link between the survival of freedom abroad and the survival of freedom at home . . . that recognized . . . that the idea of freedom is the most contagious idea in the world. And it was also a party that understood that a progressive society must be ready and willing to use its military power in defense of its progressive ideals, in order to ensure that those ideals survive.

As fate would have it, during my first year in the Senate, the world changed gloriously in the direction of those progressive ideals. In November of 1989, the Berlin Wall began to be torn down, and the mighty Soviet Union began to collapse. That victory brought pride and confidence to the US but also new responsibilities to assure the freedom and safety of the emancipated people of Eastern and Central Europe.

I became active with a bipartisan group of Senate colleagues in moving to secure our victory in the Cold War by protecting the independence of the liberated citizens of what we had called the "Captive Nations of Europe." We pushed for early admission of those countries to NATO and extended financial support to their economies as they transitioned from state-controlled to market-based economic systems.

But history rarely goes on vacation. Even before the Cold War ended, a new, unconventional war had begun, this one with Islamist terrorists—although most people were reluctant to acknowledge it then for what it was.

On December 21, 1988, a few weeks before I entered the Senate, a terrorist bomb exploded on a Pan Am plane to New York, over Lockerbie, Scotland, killing all 259 people aboard, several of whom were Connecticut residents. Investigators later concluded that the attack was sponsored by the Libyan government. It was the first foreign terrorist mass attack on American civilians and should have taught us that we were entering a new chapter in our national security history, one where direct threats to America would come from terrorist groups and anti-American extremist enemies in the Muslim world.

Thanks to John Glenn's generous delegation of authority to me as a freshman senator, I chaired a series of hearings of the Governmental Affairs Committee beginning in 1989. The topic: the threat of Islamist terrorism. I asked Glenn for the opportunity so I could educate myself (and the other committee members who were interested) and the public to this new threat to our security. My personal focus on terrorism continued through the decade of the 1990s, as the number and boldness of terrorist attacks against American targets expanded to our troops, our ships, our embassies, and the World Trade Center in New York with a truck bomb in the garage in 1993. All this work on the Governmental Affairs Committee, then on the Senate Armed Services Committee after I became a member in 1993, and after 2001, when I became chairman of the Governmental Affairs Committee, was done from the bipartisan center. For the growing number of members of the

Senate who were concerned about the threat of terrorism before the attacks of 9/11/2001, and all who were activated against Islamist terrorism after 9/11, it was evident that we faced a common and rising threat as Americans. There were no partisans in that congressional foxhole.

But there was a deep partisan divide on the most serious military challenge America faced during my first years in the Senate, and that came from the totalitarian, belligerent government of Iraq.

On August 2, 1990, the Iraqi dictator Saddam Hussein ordered his military to invade neighboring Kuwait, our close ally. Within two days, Iraq controlled the country. The Kuwaiti emir fled, and Saddam installed a puppet government. There was great concern that Saddam's forces would continue their march south into Saudi Arabia, and thereby control an enormous percentage of the world's oil supply, on which the US and our allies depended. The Iraqi invasion also disrupted the territorial stability of the Middle East and the security of other American allies in the region.

President George H.W. Bush made clear that the US would not allow the Iraqi invasion to stand. His administration worked with our allies in Europe to secure condemnation of Iraq in the United Nations and the imposition of economic sanctions on Saddam's government, while at the same time methodically deploying American troops, eventually 700,000 of them, to the region around Iraq. I agreed totally with President Bush's goals in this conflict and his policy reasons for them. We were confronting Saddam with a clear choice: withdraw from Kuwait in response to the economic sanctions or be pushed out by a massive, US-led military force.

In the months after the August invasion, there was a slow-motion quality to our military deployment, but the pace of diplomatic activity was frenzied. In the meantime, throughout the fall and early winter of 1990, I was struck by how few Democrats and how many Republicans in Congress gave public support to the possible use of our military to liberate Kuwait.

Early in December, I was invited to a luncheon of Democratic senators with our leader George Mitchell, in the same conference room where we had just negotiated the Clean Air Act improvements.

There were about fifteen of us there, so I assumed George was dividing the fifty-five Senate Democrats into three or four luncheons to discuss Iraq and Kuwait.

He began by describing the large troop deployment and saying it was putting us on the path to a war we might well not need to fight if we were willing to give the economic sanctions more time to convince Saddam to withdraw from Kuwait. The question George posed, however, was procedural—that is, whether each of us shared his belief that under these circumstances President Bush needed to ask for and receive congressional authorization before he could direct our military into action against Iraq.

I was seated at the rectangular table in a chair that meant I would be one of the last to speak. All of the senators who spoke before me said we should demand that Bush ask for congressional authorization. Many volunteered to vote against it if he did, while others remained silent on how they would vote. Not one Democratic colleague said they would vote to authorize a war in the Gulf to liberate Kuwait.

As I listened, I thought that some of the statements I was hearing were based on a much more benign and naïve view of Saddam Hussein than I held. Others seemed motivated by a personal, ideological distaste for war. And, sadly, some seemed mostly influenced by partisanship. President Bush was a Republican. We were Democrats. If he wants to go to war, let him take the risks without bipartisan support.

When it was my turn to speak, I was feeling separated from my Democratic colleagues on a big issue for the first time. It was my first "moment of truth" in Washington. Would I speak up right away for what I believed or remain silent? I decided it was best to make clear where I stood from the beginning. I began by saying why I felt strongly that the peace and prosperity of America and a lot of the world required that Saddam be pushed out of Kuwait. I then said that my reading of the Constitution led me to conclude that President Bush should come to Congress for authorization before initiating military action against Iraq—the deployment of troops had been slow, and not an immediate response to an urgent challenge that would allow no time for prior congressional approval. Then I added:

> But I do want to make clear now in this room that if President Bush does seek authorization, I will definitely support him because Saddam has had plenty of time to respond to the economic sanctions and hasn't, and because bipartisan congressional support of military action will strengthen the hand of our commander in chief and reassure our troops that the American people are with them.

The room was silent. It was awkward. I stood and said that I had to return to my office to meet with some constituents, which I really did. As I left, Mitchell said, "Joe, I want to continue this conversation with you personally as soon as possible." And I responded, "Of course, leader."

We soon had a good, thoughtful discussion, but I remained convinced of my position in support of military action against Saddam, and soon announced it publicly. I was the first Senate Democrat to say that I would support the war in the Gulf. The leading Senate Democratic authority on national security, Senator Sam Nunn of Georgia, held back at first and then made clear he intended to vote against the authorization for war. He wanted to give the sanctions more time. I had great respect for Sam, so I was very surprised and disappointed that he took that position.

As we approached the vote on authorization during January 1991, I received a call from Larry Eagleburger, the deputy secretary of state, asking me if I would become the lead Democratic co-sponsor of the resolution. The lead Republican co-sponsor would be Senator John Warner of Virginia, another senatorial national security titan who was then the ranking Republican on the Armed Services Committee. I told Eagleburger that I was surprised to be asked, but I was honored and would be proud to lead this effort with Senator Warner. Eagleburger thanked me and added that President Bush would be very happy I had said yes, because "the president wanted a Democratic sponsor who really supports his policy toward Iraq." At the time, I was one of the few who did.

Soon I was meeting with John Warner, Senate Republican Leader Bob Dole, and the White House liaison to Congress to try to line up votes for the resolution. It was going to be close, closer than it should have been. One of the most important Democrats who remained undecided until the day before the Senate vote on January 12, 1991, was Senator Al Gore of Tennessee. He and I had long conversations about his decision, during which our friendship deepened. In the end, Gore and I were two of only ten Democrats who voted "aye," but that was enough to pass the resolution by five votes, 52–47.

Right after the roll call, one of Senator Dole's aides came over to me on the Senate floor to tell me the Republican leader wanted me to immediately come to his office, which was a short walk up the hall. I went right over. Dole was waiting for the president to come to the phone and wanted me to be there. He then formally informed President Bush that the Senate had just authorized him to order the US military to go to war in Kuwait. "I asked Senator Lieberman to be here because his help was so important to us. Please hold on, Mr. President," and Bob handed me the phone. The president graciously thanked me, and I told him what I believed: "I support your policies on this, Mr. President, and I also have great confidence in you personally. I know that you will use the enormous power Congress has now given you wisely and in our national interest."

It was quite a moment for me. I was way above my "pay grade" as a freshman senator. I was lucky to be there, but I also knew it was because I was willing to stand up for what I believed was right and to work across party lines to get it done.

I also made some friendships in that experience that were important to me throughout my time in the Senate. Senators Dole and Warner and I worked together on many different projects, domestic and foreign, over the years ahead. It was the first time John McCain and I had taken note of each other, and it began the unique, close friendship we had that took us around the world together in support of America's values, security, and troops. And Al Gore and I continued to work together on foreign policy (and environmental policy) right through his 2000 presidential campaign when he took me way beyond my political dreams to a national candidacy.

On the battlefield in Kuwait, the American military, under the command of General Norman Schwarzkopf, scored a spectacular victory over Iraqi forces, liberating Kuwait in 100 hours. The Middle East was stabilized and our allies there were very grateful. Our economy was protected from becoming a hostage to Saddam Hussein's control of oil, and America's credibility in the world rose at a critical time of global change when terrorism from the Middle East was rising, and the Soviet Union was collapsing.

It was those enormous changes in Europe that brought me into the second big foreign policy debate of my early years in the Senate. This one took a different turn on the road to foreign policy bipartisanship with a small group of us trying to convince our congressional colleagues and a reluctant Republican president, George Bush (and then a reluctant Democratic president, Bill Clinton), to act to stop Serbian aggression and genocide in Bosnia, after the Communist dictatorship of Yugoslavia had collapsed.

I felt strongly that this was a test of whether we and our NATO allies would allow conflict to break out again in Europe after the Cold War ended and whether we would allow genocide—in this case by Bosnian Serbs against Bosnian Muslims—to begin again in Europe less than fifty years after the Holocaust of World War II had ended. "Never again" meant never again, regardless of the nationality or religion of the people being murdered.

During 1992, Bob Dole, John McCain, Joe Biden, and I began to work together and speak out about the aggression and brutality that had broken out in Bosnia. We believed that it was a turning point in Europe. The US and NATO needed to take action against the war in the Balkans or it would spread. We called on President Bush to act through NATO to lift the existing UN embargo on sending arms to the Balkans (and therefore the Bosnian Muslims) and to deploy NATO air power to strike Serbian forces. Our policy became known as "Lift and Strike." President Bush ultimately chose not to get involved. During the 1992 presidential campaign, at the urging of Joe Biden and me and others, Arkansas Governor Bill Clinton criticized President Bush for his passivity in the Balkans and explicitly endorsed the policy of "Lift and Strike."

When George Bush was president, Bob Dole and John McCain did not hesitate to push the leader of their party to act to stop the slaughter in Bosnia, or to criticize him when he did not. They put America's values and interests, as they saw them, ahead of partisan loyalties. When Bill Clinton became president, Joe Biden and I and others were challenged to do the same—and we did, alongside Dole and McCain.

President Clinton assured us he would keep the campaign promise he made to implement the "Lift and Strike" policy. Then he dispatched his secretary of state, Warren Christopher, to Europe to discuss the proposed new policy with our allies in England, France, and Germany. They told Christopher they would not join such an initiative because it would jeopardize the lives of European volunteers who were doing humanitarian work in Bosnia. To us, it sounded like the Europeans wanted to celebrate the end of the Cold War in peace, not in another hot war in Europe, no matter how much it threatened the tranquility they had just won. They wanted a holiday from history.

European opposition was enough for President Clinton to pull back from "Lift and Strike," leaving our bipartisan group deeply disappointed but resolved that we would keep pushing until the US and NATO entered and ended the Bosnian War. We continued to introduce the "Lift and Strike" resolution we had first offered in 1992, fighting uphill because the public mood about international action had soured after the tragic "Black Hawk Down" events in Somalia where American servicemen died. Public support for our cause slowly rose as the media focused on the horrors of what was then called "ethnic cleansing" of Muslims in Bosnia.

In 1994, our bipartisan group added an amendment to the Defense Authorization Act, imposing new sanctions on the Serbs. In the fall of 1994, Senator Dole and I negotiated and offered a compromise resolution requiring President Clinton to attempt to reach an agreement in the UN Security Council to lift the arms embargo on the former Yugoslavia, and authorizing unilateral US lifting of the embargo if that failed. We received the most support yet in the Senate from members of both parties, but still not enough to pass.

Then in July 1995, because the atrocities in Bosnia were more horrific and visible on television to millions of Americans, our bipartisan resolution to lift the embargo on arms sales to the Bosnian Muslims passed both houses of Congress. We had been introducing it in various forms for four years. Unfortunately, President Clinton was still unconvinced and vetoed the resolution.

Then, history intervened in the darkest way. Later, in July 1995, it became clear that a massacre of more than 7,000 Bosnian Muslims, mostly men and boys, had occurred in Srebrenica, Bosnia, earlier in July. At the order of Serbian Commander Ratko Mladic, the Bosnian Muslims were taken from refugee camps, shot and killed, and pushed into mass graves. It was the largest single-day loss of life in Europe since the end of World War II, and it reminded me of the Nazis' forced march of thousands of Ukrainian Jews in Kiev in 1941 to a massive ravine at a place called Babi Yar, where the Jews were shot, killed, and pushed into the ravine.

The pressure on President Clinton was now irresistible. The US and NATO began air strikes against Serbian forces in Bosnia, which brought the leadership of the Serbs, Bosnians, and Croats to Dayton, Ohio, where Clinton's gifted representative, Ambassador Richard Holbrooke, pushed, cajoled, and negotiated the Balkan leaders into a peace agreement which ended the slaughter in Bosnia and created stability in post-Cold War Europe.

Too many lives were lost before the Bosnian War was ended, but it was finally stopped. Part of the reason was that a bipartisan band in Congress pressured two presidents and our colleagues of both parties in Congress to end it. I was privileged to be a member of that group.

A final word of tribute to Bob Dole, who kept Vandenberg's bipartisan spirit alive. In early 1996, after the Dayton Peace Conference, President Clinton asked Congress for funding to send 60,000

American troops to the Balkans to enforce the peace agreements. Most Republicans fought against it, saying he was asking for too many troops and there needed to be a time limit on how long they would stay. Bob Dole, the Republican leader of the US Senate and the presumptive Republican candidate for president against Clinton that year, supported the president's request, and it passed. That was Dole putting country over politics in circumstances that would have compromised the principles of lesser people.

For Bill Clinton, the Bosnian experience was also transformational. He emerged more confident in foreign policy and the clear leader of NATO in support of building and protecting the European continent so it could be "whole and free."

It seemed to me that the principled, strong, internationalist, centrist Democratic foreign policy of the Kennedy era was back under Bill Clinton.

LESSONS FOR CENTRISTS

FROM THE 1990 CLEAN AIR ACT

1. Leadership always matters. In Congress, nothing matters more than bipartisan leaders who share the same legislative goal, as President George H. W. Bush and Senate Majority Leader George Mitchell did about the Clean Air Act in 1990. They both accepted the science that said that many Americans were dying earlier than they would have if the air was cleaner and that death was also near for some of our most beautiful forests and lakes. Bush and Mitchell agreed that the best way to fix those life-and-death problems was to amend the existing Clean Air Act of 1970.

2. The bipartisan agreement at the top pushed members of Congress with personal interests in favor or against the clean air reforms to come to the center to negotiate the best result they could for their states' people and businesses.

It wasn't easy. It required compromises by everybody. But the everyday presence in George Mitchell's conference room of the president's most important environmental assistants, the Senate Democratic majority leader or his most important aides, and the bipartisan membership of the Senate Environment Committee was a message to every senator, energy industry leader, or environmental group that came in to negotiate that the conferees were committed to getting something done. The overriding message was that the human and natural consequences of dirty air were too serious for us to fail. So, they better be ready and willing to negotiate.

President Bush, Senator Mitchell, and our committee made clear to all that we, too, were ready to compromise to achieve our goals. In other words, we would try as best we could to smooth the way to the changes in behavior we were asking them to make. In announcing his support for the bill, Senator Mitch McConnell, who was finishing his first term in 1990 and running for re-election from Kentucky, a coal state, said, "I had to choose between clean air and the status quo. I chose clean air." The process of negotiation had enabled McConnell to make that tough decision.

3. Some of the best allies we had in achieving bipartisan agreement and enactment of a new Clean Air Act were not politicians. They were new technologies and new ideas.

For example, at the heart of the agreements between President Bush and Senator Mitchell, and the bipartisan membership of the Environment Committee, was the new, centrist idea that we could achieve cleaner air with market-based systems such as emissions banking and trading and performance-based standards, not with traditional regulatory requirements.

And the 1990 law encouraged the use of cleaner energy in cars and trucks through alternative fuels and new technologies, promoted cleaner/low-sulfur coal and natural gas, and subsidized new technologies to clean high-sulfur coal.

4. Sometimes a higher purpose can motivate great legislative accomplishments. That was the case with the Clean Air Act of 1990. Most members of Congress rose to the challenge because they could see that the result of not doing so would be thousands of premature deaths in America and the destruction of some beautiful natural resources. It is the dream of such accomplishments that motivates most members of Congress to run for office. In this case, they knew they had to transcend partisan parochialism and political fear to do what was right for our country and our people. The Clean Air Act of 1990 passed the Senate 89–11, and the House 401–21.

FROM FOREIGN POLICY DEBATES

1. Partisanship should have no place in the conduct of American foreign policy, but increasingly it has. As a result, our country has suffered in the world. Politics should stop at the water's edge, as Senator Vandenberg said. He didn't say that differences of opinion about American foreign policy should stop, but that those differences should not be based on the desire to achieve political and partisan advantage at home.

In the debate over whether to authorize President George H. W. Bush to go to war in the Gulf in 1991, there were sensible policy reasons to be for or against. But I also heard and saw too many Democrats who were opposed and too many Republicans who were in favor primarily for partisan reasons. As the day of the vote approached, it was clear that almost all of the Republicans would vote to authorize the president to go to war, and almost all Democrats would vote against. The outcome was unclear. That was unnatural. It was too partisan, and it risked an enormous defeat for our president, as commander in chief, that would send an embarrassing message to the rest of the world that the United States was politically divided and irresolute in the face of a major challenge to us and to allies of ours in the Arab world.

2. The Gulf War vote in 1991 was not only my first major confrontation with partisanship and politics in foreign policy—it was the first time I had to decide whether to vote with the majority of the Senate Democrats out of loyalty to my party or keep the promise I made to the voters in Connecticut in 1988 that I would be a bipartisan centrist senator. I did what I thought was right and voted for the war, and kept my promise to the centrist coalition that had elected me as their senator.

There was risk in doing so but the reward turned out to be great. I was able to help encourage nine other Democrats to join me. Without us, the resolution would not have passed.

In the Gulf War that followed, America's military won a quick and important victory.

FROM THE BOSNIAN WAR AND SUPPORTING NATO EXPANSION

1. The other two big foreign policy decisions that America made in the 1990s were not partisan. Both were consequences of the end of the Cold War, which itself had for more than four decades received bipartisan support in the spirit begun by President Truman and Senator Vandenberg. Perhaps that is why debate and decision-making about what to do after our victory in the Cold War was also not partisan.

    The first big question was whether the US should give support to the newly independent nations of the former Soviet Union (FSU) and what form that support should take. Under President Bush 41, and then under President Clinton, there turned out to be broad bipartisan support for giving economic assistance to those countries and moving quickly to bring them into NATO as the best way to guarantee their independence and freedom.

    In the Senate, these efforts were spearheaded by a bipartisan group of us, led by the Republican leader Bob Dole and the Democratic Chairman of the Foreign Relations Committee Joe Biden. Looking back over the years since then at the long, repressive, and aggressive reign of Vladimir Putin, it is clear that we acted even more wisely than we believed in bringing liberated nations of the FSU into NATO.

The American congressional and presidential reaction to the outbreak of invasion and genocide in the Balkans after the fall of the Communist government of Yugoslavia was not partisan but it was badly divided for years. There were Republicans and Democrats united in advocating US and NATO military action to stop the bloodshed in the Balkans and there was a larger group of Republicans and Democrats who were opposed.

In the end, President Clinton, Congress, and NATO acted militarily to make clear that such inhumane and destabilizing behavior would not be tolerated in post-Cold War Europe.

It took too long, but finally happened because of the persistence of our bipartisan group of congressional advocates, and, more important, the increasing public awareness in America and Europe of the World War II-like horrors that were being carried out in the Balkans.

The lesson to learn is that when you are in a battle in which you are confident that you are fighting for what is right, you must heed Churchill's famous dictum:

"Never, never, never quit."

6

A CENTRIST IN THE WHITE HOUSE

When I came to Washington as a centrist Democrat in January 1989, my party was moving left, and our national politics were becoming more partisan. I was a stranger in a new land, but I soon found a philosophical and political home in the Democratic Leadership Council (DLC), an organization that had been founded only four years before in 1985 after the second Reagan landslide election.

The DLC had three stated purposes: to move the Democratic Party back to the center; to reconnect the Party to middle-class America; and to elect a Democratic president as soon as possible. In policy, the DLC said it wanted to move on from both the New Deal of the 1930s and the New Politics of the 1960s to create a Third Way to a New Democratic Party of "progressive ideas, mainstream values, and innovative market-based solutions." In foreign policy, the DLC was internationalist and strong on defense. If the DLC had its way, never again would anyone be able to use the phrase made famous by Jeanne Kirkpatrick to describe the Democratic Party she left in 1984 to join President Reagan's Republican Party: "Blame America First Democrats."

The DLC was the brainchild of Al From and Will Marshall, staff members of Louisiana Congressman Gillis Long. Among its founders were Senators Sam Nunn, Al Gore, and Chuck Robb; Congressman Dick Gephardt; and Governor Bruce Babbitt of New Mexico.

When I joined the DLC in 1989, Sam Nunn was its chairman. A year later, in March 1990, at its annual convention in New Orleans, the DLC chose the governor of Arkansas, Bill Clinton, to be its new chairman. For me, it was a reunion.

In 1970, Bill Clinton was at Yale Law School and responded to my appeal for help in my primary campaign against the incumbent state senator. Do I remember Clinton from among all the students who were good enough to support me in that campaign? I do, because he was memorable—a tall, engaging law student with a great smile and a Southern drawl, campaigning on the streets of New Haven.

I remember meeting him again during the Carter administration when I was state senate majority leader attending a fundraiser for the Democratic National Committee in Washington. I was excited to see Clinton in the receiving line, standing next to Bob Strauss, the powerful chairman of the DNC. He gave me a big, warm greeting, which made that moment also feel like a reunion, and then he turned to introduce me to Strauss: "Bob, this is Joe Lieberman, the state senate majority leader in Connecticut. He gave me my start in politics and my first campaign experience while I was at law school in New Haven." I laughed and thanked him.

It is possible my 1970 campaign was the first he had ever worked in, but I know that I did not give him his start in politics, because that happened on the day he was born. Bill Clinton was a natural politician with the best skill set that I have ever seen. As we learned later, he also had personal weaknesses—but there was no one smarter, harder working, and more effective at campaigning and getting the government to produce what he wanted when in office than Bill Clinton. Like John Bailey and Robert Penn Warren's fictional Willie Stark, Clinton knew how to make the "mare" go.

In his speech at the DLC Convention in New Orleans in 1990, Governor Clinton said it was time to go beyond the stale either/or partisan debate in Washington and create "a dynamic but centrist progressive movement of new ideas rooted in traditional American values."

This was political music to my ears. It was a centrist vision like the one I had articulated in my Senate campaign in 1988 and begun to work on in the Senate. From the first meeting I had with Al From and Will Marshall at the DLC, it seemed to me that they had the right set of ideas for a new, centrist Democratic Party. After that New Orleans convention, I began to think we might also have a candidate for president who could carry those new ideas into the White House.

Clinton was already beginning to think along those same lines. During the rest of 1990 and into 1991, he regularly left Arkansas to carry his message and that of the DLC around the country. In May of 1991, the DLC convened for its annual meeting in Cleveland and Clinton gave what he later called "the speech of my life."

In it, he described America's biggest problems, and criticized Republicans for neglecting them. But then he turned to his own party and bemoaned its inability to win elections "because too many of the people that used to vote for us . . . have not trusted us in national elections to defend our national interests abroad, to put their values into our social policy at home, or to take their tax money and spend it with discipline." He put forth a policy agenda that would create opportunity for people but also demand responsibility.

That speech to the DLC in Cleveland became the blueprint for his 1992 presidential campaign. He added three more speeches later in 1991 at his alma mater, Georgetown University, in which he set out what he called a "New Covenant" for the American people. The first speech was about opportunity and responsibility, the second specifically about economic opportunity, and the third about national security. I was impressed that Clinton was not just running for president because the office was there. He had a *reason* for running and a vision of how he could change our party and country. It was new and centrist and full of hope. In my opinion, it was also just what the Democratic Party and America needed.

On October 3, 1991, at the Old State House in Little Rock, Arkansas, Bill Clinton announced that he was a candidate for the Democratic nomination for president. A few weeks later, he called me. The conversation went something like this:

> "Joe, do you remember how in 1970, in New Haven, I supported you for state senator and you were elected?"
>
> "I sure do, Governor."
>
> "Now, as you know, I am running for president and I think you owe me one, so I am calling to ask for your support for president and I believe it will help me get elected like mine helped you in 1970."

I laughed heartily and said of course I would support him. The campaign scheduled my endorsement announcement for January 1992, right before the New Hampshire primary. I was the first senator from the Northeast to support him. A few days after my endorsement, the allegations that Clinton had a long-term extramarital relationship in Arkansas with a woman named Gennifer Flowers went public. My Democratic colleagues in the Senate teased me about the timing of my endorsement: "You are a real political genius, Joe. Now, who is your second choice for president?"

Of course, as has often been the case with the "comeback kid," Clinton had the last laugh, and so did I. He finished a strong second to Paul Tsongas in New Hampshire and then won a bunch of primaries. Governor Jerry Brown entered the contest and ran against Clinton from the left, but Clinton prevailed and was nominated.

The Clinton campaign sent me out to campaign for him during the months that followed, and he asked me to serve on the drafting committee for the Democratic platform "to make sure it is a DLC platform." I also went to work raising money for the campaign with my Senate colleague, fellow DLC member, and great friend, John Breaux of Louisiana. We brought together a varied group of contributors reflecting our different backgrounds. At our first successful dinner in Washington, one of the contributors said he was so impressed by the range of people in the room that we should give our group a special name. Based on the dominant groups there, John and I called our group the Kosher Cajun Caucus for Clinton. At our next event, we distributed a memento which one of John Breaux's staff had found—a Kosher Cajun cookbook written by two Jewish ladies from Metairie, Louisiana. We had discovered a centrist cuisine to go along with Bill Clinton's centrist politics.

When Clinton chose Senator Al Gore to be his vice-presidential running mate, happy days were there again for centrists like me. There was some criticism at the time that Clinton had chosen someone too much like himself—another Southern, centrist Democrat—instead of balancing this ticket with a nominee who was left of him and from another region of the country. But Clinton believed that a centrist Democratic message was the only way he could defeat President Bush, so he wisely doubled down on it. He also believed that Gore balanced him in other ways. Unlike Governor Clinton, Gore was a senator who came with Washington and international experience—and one of the few Democrats who had supported the Gulf War of 1991, the most popular thing President Bush had done.

In the general election, Clinton was not the only centrist candidate. Bush was a relatively moderate Republican who had moved right under Reagan. The unusual new force in the center was a third-party candidate—Texas businessman and philanthropist Ross Perot, who highlighted two issues. The first was his call for a balanced budget amendment to stop the growing annual federal deficits. The second was his strong opposition to trade laws which were "sucking" jobs from America, especially to Mexico. On Election Day, Perot received 19 percent of the total, which was the highest percentage received by a third-party candidate since Teddy Roosevelt won 27 percent in 1912. The 1992 exit polls said that Perot took about the same percentage of votes from Bush and Clinton.

During the campaign, Clinton and Gore focused on the economy which was weak at the time, and they were influenced by Perot, joining him in support of a balanced budget amendment. On the other hand, they endorsed NAFTA, the trade agreement with Mexico and Canada that Bush had negotiated and Perot strongly opposed.

On Election Day, Clinton and Gore won with 43 percent of the popular vote and 370 electoral votes, to President Bush's 37.4 percent and 168 electoral votes. The centrist Democratic ticket carried states in every section of the country, including parts of the South.

The DLC founders' vision of how to elect a Democratic president again had worked earlier than they expected. It happened because their centrist platform was what voters wanted and it was carried in 1992 by two extraordinary candidates.

In the White House, as in his campaign, Bill Clinton showed he was capable of focusing on policy and politics at the same time, usually doing well at both. When he didn't succeed, he figured out why and tried again. During his first two years as president, Clinton had some wins and some bigger losses. The biggest defeat was on health-care reform. He had set its adoption as a goal during the campaign and then put his wife, Hillary, in charge of it. That made it personal.

In 1993, I introduced a separate, bipartisan health-care reform bill drafted with the DLC, called the Managed Competition Act, with Senators Nunn, John Chafee, and David Durenberger, two Democrats and two Republicans. It would have resulted in comprehensive health-care reform but with less bureaucracy and government regulation than the eventual Clinton plan.

Nobody knew yet exactly what the Clintons were going to propose. We hoped our legislation would influence them so they could receive enough bipartisan support to enact a health-care reform bill. We were trying to keep the administration in the center.

When we met with Hillary to talk about our plan, she agreed we had the same goals and some good ideas that she would consider. But our ideas didn't make it into her proposal. The First Lady was criticized for developing the administration's plan through a closed process that did not engage people from the health care or health insurance industries. When she and the president finally issued their proposal, the industry began a devastating television advertising campaign against it. In the end, the polls persuaded the president to withdraw the proposal before it even got to a vote in Congress.

A second Clinton setback was about gay rights.

The president put an early-administration focus on repealing the prohibition of gay and lesbian Americans serving in our all-volunteer military; he had promised he would do exactly that during the campaign. When some of the leaders of the military publicly opposed the change—with most Republicans and some Democrats joining them—Clinton accepted a compromise which came to be called "Don't Ask, Don't Tell." I thought it was unfair because it made the sexual orientation of a soldier, not his or her quality of service, the determining factor in whether they could continue to serve in the US military. As a member of the Senate Armed Services Committee, I voted against it. To me, "Don't Ask, Don't Tell" was a reminder that not every compromise to get something done is better than doing nothing.

However, four significant laws were enacted in Clinton's first two years as president, each of which was the result of good compromises in the center, including a domestic peace corps called AmeriCorps (Clinton was also inspired by President Kennedy) and a Family Medical Leave Act, creating a new right for American workers and their families.

The other two successes of Clinton's first two years were doubly significant because they also showed he was a "New Democrat" and a centrist. The first was a massive anti-crime bill which responded in a balanced way to the high public anxiety about crime at that time. It transcended the either/or, left/right debates about law and order that had generally put Democrats like Michael Dukakis on the losing side. Clinton negotiated hard with both Republicans and liberal Democrats and produced a bill that expanded the federal death penalty, mandated that convicted criminals serve 85 percent of their sentence, and adopted the tough three-strikes-and-you're-out law which imposed a mandatory life sentence on people previously convicted twice of violent crimes.

But it also provided $6.1 billion for crime prevention programs, adopted the Federal Assault Weapons Ban and Violence Against Women Acts, and provided funding for 100,000 community police around the country.

In other words, the anti-crime bill went right and left. I strongly supported the bill. And in the end almost all members of Congress did, as well. It passed the Senate 95–4. It was a big breakthrough for the country and the Democratic Party's brand because it responded to a real domestic problem that had unsettled the American people.

An equally big but less popular turning point accomplishment of Clinton's first two years, and the hardest to pass, was the Budget Act of 1993. It was his follow-through on his promise to reduce and eliminate the national debt, and another opportunity to prove that the Democratic Party was no longer the party of "tax-and-spend liberals." Clinton's first budget proposal raised taxes some, cut spending some, and promised to bring the federal government back to fiscal balance.

Early in the budget process, the Republicans in Congress announced in a classic partisan move that none of them would vote for Clinton's proposal. The budget battle would be fought out totally within the Democratic Party, which seemed right because it was a battle for the heart and head of the Democratic Party.

For me, it was not an easy vote. Clinton's proposal included an increase in the gas tax, which I had campaigned against in 1988, and some of his spending cuts would hurt Connecticut defense industries. I made my concerns known and was lobbied aggressively by the administration, most effectively of course by the president himself in meetings with other Democratic senators at the White House, personal calls at home in the evening (which he would not end until he felt he had made some progress), and an invitation to go jogging with him on the Mall early one hot, summer morning—with news photographers stationed to take a great picture of us. The president assured me that he would restore some of the reductions in defense spending and reminded me that he too had opposed a gas tax increase in his 1992 campaign because he believed it was regressive. He was trying to change the gas tax increase to a broader energy tax.

As the climactic budget vote neared, seven Senate Democrats had said they would vote no, which meant the administration would need the support of every other Democrat to get to fifty votes. Vice President Gore would break the tie. The filibuster rule did not apply to budget process votes.

There would be two votes on the budget, one on passage of the Senate bill, and then another, after the Senate and House reconciled their differences, on the Conference Report. I ultimately voted "aye" on both votes. Both were 50–50 ties which Vice President Gore broke to enact the bill.

Before the Senate vote, I had lengthy negotiations with the president and the majority leader, George Mitchell. I urged them to put in more job-creating incentives along the lines of legislation I and others had sponsored, and to eliminate the gas tax. They promised me they would try their best to do both in the Conference Committee with the House and, based on that, I told them I would vote for the Senate bill.

When the Conference Report came back, I saw they had kept their promise as best they could. It included several of the changes I asked for, including the Enterprise Capital Formation Act, which I had introduced with a bipartisan group of sponsors, to provide targeted capital gains tax reductions for investments in new businesses that would create new jobs; a research and development tax credit; a deduction for small businesses that bought new equipment; and three enterprise zone incentives to bring more jobs to our poorest urban and rural areas. The gas tax increase was still in, but it was smaller than it had been, and some of the big cuts to the Pentagon budget had been eliminated.

Overall, it was a very good bill, one I believed I had helped make better. Remembering Voltaire, I was not going to let the perfect be the enemy of the good. I also voted for that 1993 budget act because it was so important to Clinton's new presidency, which I strongly supported, and to the reputation of the Democratic Party, which I wanted to help change. In the years that followed, most economists concluded, and I certainly agreed, that the Clinton budget of 1993—a centrist Democratic budget—built a foundation for the extraordinary economic growth and job creation that occurred during his presidency.

However, raising taxes and cutting spending is never popular. And, as the mid-term elections of 1994 approached, the polls showed that Clinton and the Democrats were decidedly unpopular. The failed attempt at health-care reform had hurt the administration. The Republican campaign was led by Congressman Newt Gingrich and put forward a detailed alternative agenda. They called it a Contract with America, and it helped sweep them to an historic victory. Republicans gained eight seats for a majority of fifty-four in the Senate, and fifty-four seats and the first Republican majority in the House in forty-two years.

It was a serious personal defeat for President Clinton. As I wrote earlier regarding my loss in my 1980 congressional campaign, defeat can teach painful but important lessons. It certainly did for Clinton in 1994. Probably too much is made of Clinton hiring political consultant Dick Morris after the 1994 election, because Clinton himself is a political genius who has usually figured out how to right himself after a fall. But Dick Morris definitely made a difference. I knew Morris because he lived in Connecticut, and I had been impressed by him. In the increasingly partisan politics of America, it was very unusual for a Democrat—let alone the president—to retain a consultant who had mostly worked for Republicans. Together they developed a strategy called "triangulation"—rejecting leftist Democratic ideas and rightist Republican ideas and building a center-out coalition from both parties which adopted some of Clinton's centrist Democratic agenda and some of Gingrich's conservative Republican "Contract with America." To me, "triangulation" was just another word for centrism. America needed it, and it worked.

The new strategy was brilliantly implemented by Clinton. He used political sticks and carrots and produced some significant bipartisan results. In the process, the president developed a surprisingly good, working relationship with Newt Gingrich. Clinton understood that Gingrich was as much of a "policy wonk" as he and engaged him on that level. But he also knew that Gingrich needed to deliver on some of the "Contract with America" promises he had made, just as he needed to do more to show he was a "different kind of Democrat" who could solve problems.

The progress that the odd couple of Clinton and Gingrich achieved did not happen in a smooth, straight line. They often fought and blocked each other, but they also learned when to compromise. The testing and jousting began early in 1995. Gingrich had promised a "Republican revolution" of tax cuts, welfare reform, and big cuts in federal spending, but because it is easier to stop action in Congress than to pass it, nothing was getting done. The first big confrontation occurred in the fall of 1995 when the Republicans sent the president a budget that cut Medicare and taxes on the wealthy. They gave Clinton a deadline of November 15 to sign it or the government would shut down. Clinton knew he could not yield to that threat, so he sent another budget back to Congress which did not contain Medicare spending reductions or tax cuts for the wealthy, but did have a program for balancing the budget in ten years. Neither side blinked, so the government shut down. I remember the public anger in Connecticut and the negative national media about the shutdown. After twenty-one days, polling showed the Republicans in Congress that the American people were turning against them. They yielded and accepted most of Clinton's budget.

In November 1995, the Democratic Leadership Council held its annual conference at the Washington Conference Center. President Clinton gave the keynote address. After expressing his gratitude to the DLC for being his ideological home, he described significant progress implementing his and our New Democratic platform. And then he set out his goals for the last year of his first term and, hopefully, his second term. It was a big, joyous event. The DLC's time had clearly come.

At that meeting, I was honored to be chosen as the new chairman of the DLC, where I served until 2001. It brought me into a closer working relationship with the president.

As 1996 began, the president and Speaker Gingrich had tested each other and were both hoping for a better year because it was an election year. They focused first on welfare reform. For years, Democrats had been criticized by Republicans for reflexively supporting a welfare program that was giving taxpayers' money to "welfare moms who were able to work but did not want to." As governor of Arkansas, Clinton had tried to reform the welfare system. In his 1992 campaign, he famously promised to "end welfare as we know it." During 1994, he had made his first substantial move in that direction, sending a reform bill to Congress that he said would make welfare "a second chance, not a way of life." It would limit people without disabilities to two years on welfare and provide them with training and education during that time to get them ready to go to work. The proposal was attacked as too little by Republicans and too much by liberal Democrats. It went nowhere.

In the 1994 congressional campaign, reforming welfare was a major promise of the Republicans' "Contract with America." By 1996, both Clinton and the Republicans had promised to reform welfare—so that is what they did. First, the Republicans passed two bills that Clinton vetoed, saying they were punitive. Then John Kasich, a Republican congressman from Ohio, put forward a compromise proposal which he had been discussing with both Gingrich and the White House. The president had also been speaking for months with the Senate majority leader, Trent Lott, who was a seasoned and effective deal maker. Trent and I had become friends. He briefed me regularly about his talks with Clinton and asked me about how many Democrats I thought would stick with various welfare reform ideas. Trent was always counting votes, usually accurately.

Clinton invited Gingrich to a series of private meetings to negotiate around Kasich's welfare reform bill. He faced opposition from the Left in the Democratic Party because the bill ended the federal guarantee of a fixed monthly benefit to welfare recipients, contained a five-year lifetime limit on welfare benefits, and cut some spending out of the food stamp program. Gingrich faced opposition from members on the Right in his party who thought

Clinton wanted too much money for education and training, and the compromise bill was not really "ending welfare as we knew it."

When the negotiations went as far as they could, Clinton and Gingrich had to decide between the perfect and the good. And they both chose the good. Part of the reason was political; it was already summertime in a national election year, and both had promised that they would reform welfare. Now was their opportunity.

Clinton later wrote that he agreed with some of the objections to the bill from liberal Democrats and advocates for the poor, but he concluded,

> I had spent most of my career trying to move people from welfare to work . . . I decided to sign the legislation because I thought it was the best chance America would have for a long time to change the incentives in the welfare system from dependence to empowerment through work.

The final bill kept the guarantees Clinton had wanted for medical care. It also increased federal aid to children by 40 percent to $14 billion, enabled stronger enforcement of child support orders, and gave states the power to make welfare payments into wage subsidies as a way of encouraging businesses to employ welfare recipients. The bill passed both houses with strong bipartisan support on August 21, 1996.

President Clinton signed it in a White House ceremony on August 22. The Democratic National Convention convened in Chicago a few days later on August 26. Clinton and Gore were nominated without opposition. In his acceptance speech, the president continued stressing DLC themes, but this time he had a record of accomplishment, including the anti-crime bill, welfare reform, deficit reduction, and the smallest federal work force since the Kennedy administration. And he had an economy that was surging. He could boast about 10 million new jobs created in the US since he took office in 1993; 4.4 million more people in first homes; 1.8 million fewer people on welfare; 12 million people who had used their new right to family medical leave; and a federal deficit that had been cut four years in a row.

The thematic foundation for his speech was from the DLC textbook, "Opportunity and Responsibility" for every American, but he added a new goal: "Build a Bridge to the Twenty-First Century." Earlier in August, the Republicans nominated Senator Bob Dole as their presidential candidate. There was a twenty-three-year difference in age between Dole, seventy-three, and Clinton, fifty. In his convention speech, Clinton declared, "Respectfully, America doesn't need to build a bridge to the past." Notwithstanding the great legislative accomplishments Clinton had negotiated with Gingrich, he also found a smart, centrist (triangulating) way to campaign against Dole by saying the Republican senator would not block the Far-Right ideas of Gingrich and many Republicans in Congress as he had done.

On Election Day, Clinton and Gore won 49.2 percent of the popular vote and 379 electoral votes. Bob Dole and Jack Kemp got 40.7 percent of the vote and 159 electoral votes. Ross Perot ran again as a third-party candidate, but this time got only 8 percent. The voters were more satisfied with the two major party candidates than in 1992. For Clinton and his centrist Democratic platform, the 1996 election was a great victory and validation. It was the first time a Democrat had been re-elected president since Franklin Roosevelt. Again, the victory was nationwide with four Southern states going Democratic.

Bill Clinton was on top of the political world as his second term began, and so was the DLC. He went right to work on one big item of unfinished business—balancing the federal budget. Clinton's 1993 budget of higher taxes and lower spending was a turnaround, but only a beginning. In June of 1995, the year before the election, in a televised speech from the Oval Office, he had offered a plan that he said would balance the federal budget in ten years. He tried to sell it to Republicans and Democrats, but he did not get far.

In his State of the Union speech in January of 1996, Clinton spoke again about the importance of balancing the budget, and how government itself had to change in the information age. In that speech he made one of the signature declarations of his presidency: "The era of big government is over." In a classic centrist (and Clintonist) way, he followed immediately with these words: "But we cannot go back to the time when our citizens were left to fend for themselves." Together, those two sentences made his point (and the New Democratic Party's point) that the government had to change, but it should never change its commitment to help people unable to provide for themselves.

Notwithstanding the big victory for Clinton and Gore in 1996, the Republicans maintained control of both houses of Congress, 55–45 in the Senate, 226–207 in the House. That meant that if Clinton was to achieve his goal of passing legislation that balanced the federal budget, he would have to go to the center, where he was most comfortable anyway, and negotiate with Republicans as well as Democrats. He spent a lot of time with Speaker Gingrich and Senator Lott, and with a wide variety of members of both parties. The White House asked me to help with moderate Democrats and moderate Republicans, which I was glad to do. The bill that took shape became like that proverbial train leaving the station and a lot of members wanted their ideas as part of that locomotive's cargo. That was acceptable to the president so long as those ideas did not compromise his main goals of balancing the budget and growing the economy. It was the legislative process at its best and it worked to produce a great result.

Two bills I co-sponsored with Republican colleagues ended up in the final legislation. Both of them carried through on a policy I had supported since I came to the Senate—lowering capital gains taxes as an incentive to job-growing investments, particularly in poorer areas where they were most needed. The first was the Community Empowerment Act, which I had introduced with Republican Spencer Abraham and Democrat Carol Mosely Braun, to create additional empowerment zones in lower-income urban and rural areas, and to encourage the cleanup of polluted areas called "brownfield sites" for economic development. The second, which

I had co-sponsored with Republican Senator Orrin Hatch, was a broad-based capital gains bill that reduced the top marginal tax rate from 28 percent to 20 percent and the 15 percent bracket to 10 percent. Both of those bills were included in the final budget bill. On May 2, President Clinton, Senator Lott, and Speaker Gingrich announced they had reached agreement on the Balanced Budget Act of 1997. It was a big and transformational package.

On the spending side, the final bill cut Medicare payments to providers but increased appropriations for children's health care. It also created the State Children's Health Insurance Program (SCHIP), and a new program called Medicare Plus Choice, now known as Medicare Advantage. Both of those represented significant health-care reforms for President and Mrs. Clinton, less comprehensive than they wanted, but real reforms nonetheless. The fiscal estimators said the new law would save $116 billion in five years, and $394 billion in ten years. On the revenue side, the companion Taxpayer Relief Act of 1997 reduced several taxes, including capital gains, estate, and gift taxes, and created a tax credit for each child under seventeen years of age.

When the budget and tax bills were brought to a vote, they passed with broad bipartisan support. In the House, 64 percent of Democrats and 88 percent of Republicans supported them (more than a third of House Democrats—primarily liberal Democrats— voted against it), and in the Senate, 82 percent of Democrats and 74 percent of Republicans voted for the bill. It was a big centrist victory. And it worked sooner than expected to balance the budget, thanks in part to a booming economy which the tax relief provisions of the 1997 package helped expand. For the last three years of the Clinton administration (1998, 1999, and 2000), the federal government budget didn't just balance. It ran a surplus.

Bill Clinton was building one of the best records of accomplishment in the modern history of the American presidency.

Then came the Monica Lewinsky scandal.

In January 1998, the media reported that Kenneth Starr, the independent counsel who had been appointed to investigate Clinton's conduct regarding the "Whitewater" real-estate and savings-and-loan controversy in Arkansas, was now reviewing evidence that President Clinton had engaged in a sexual relationship with a White House intern, Monica Lewinsky. After several days of media demands for a response, the president held a press conference at the White House with his wife at his side, and said, "I want you to listen to me . . . I did not have sexual relations with that woman, Miss Lewinsky."

For the next several months, while the media debated whether Clinton was telling the truth, I was agitated but remained quiet. There had long been rumors and accusations about Clinton being involved in extra-marital affairs, so I feared there was truth to the Lewinsky story. But at that point, it was an allegation which the president had explicitly denied. He was my friend, and I was proud of the changes he had brought to our country and to the Democratic Party. I owed him the benefit of the doubt. So, I remained silent.

Then, on August 17, in a televised evening statement from the White House, President Clinton told the country what he had told the Starr grand jury earlier that day. He had "an improper physical relationship" with Monica Lewinsky. In other words, he had been lying. Lewinsky had testified to the grand jury a few weeks earlier that, yes, she'd had a sexual relationship with Clinton. The president was now forced to tell the truth. I was heartsick and angry at him but still uncertain what to do.

The Senate was on summer recess, and Hadassah and I had rented a house in Madison, Connecticut, a beautiful town on Long Island Sound east of New Haven, for our family—our four children, my mother, and us. Wherever we went—to the beach, the movies, the supermarket—people wanted to talk about Clinton and Lewinsky. They appealed to me to speak out against him. They said it was my responsibility to criticize the president because they knew I had been outspoken during the preceding years about the destructive impact of the entertainment culture on our children. It was affecting our kids' attitudes toward sex and violence. Around the dinner table in our beach house, I asked the family what they thought I should do. The four children, ranging in age from ten to thirty-one, said it was my responsibility to speak out against the president's behavior. Hadassah was ambivalent. Only my mother, who loved President Clinton, urged me to remain silent: "He made a mistake, but he is your friend. Let someone else criticize him if they want to."

It was one of the few occasions when I did not take my mother's advice. By the time the Senate came back into session at the end of August, I had been working for days on a speech criticizing the president for his outrageous personal behavior and arguing against his contention that his relationship with Lewinsky was a private matter, not related to his public office. I said that nothing a president does is private because everything he does can become public and affect the behavior and values of our country, as people in Connecticut had told me his behavior was already doing to their children.

I also spent time reviewing the Constitution's impeachment provisions and decided that, however repulsive President Clinton's behavior was, it was not an impeachable offense. However, the president needed to accept more responsibility for what he had done than he expressed in his defensive and indirect confession to the American people. I argued that Congress, on behalf of the American people, should adopt a resolution censuring him for his behavior. That was what I said in the Senate later on Thursday afternoon, September 3, 1998. The chamber was empty when I arrived except for Senator Dan Coats, who was in the chair presiding. I spoke for about twenty-five minutes in what I called "the most difficult and distasteful statement I have made on this floor in the ten years I have been a member of the US Senate."

When I finished, I sat down in my chair, relieved that it was done. It was quiet for a while and then Democratic Senators Bob Kerry and Pat Moynihan, who I did not realize had come over to hear my speech in person, rose to thank me for what I had just said. I felt very grateful. The Senate recessed a short while later and we all went home for Labor Day weekend. The attention the media gave that speech was greater than I expected. I was the first Democrat to speak out against the president, and I was his friend, his supporter, and fellow DLC Democrat.

When we returned to Washington on Tuesday, September 8, I received a call from the president's chief of staff, Erskine Bowles:

> I want to express an opinion to you that is not universally
> held in this White House. Your speech last week helped
> the president because it came from a friend and supporter
> and Democrat. You lanced the boil, Joe, and now this can
> get better.

On Friday morning, September 11, the president invited a group of clergy of all faiths to the White House for a meeting that was carried live on television. He offered a deeply personal confession, apology, and commitment to do better. On Sunday morning, September 13, the president called me at my home in Washington. It was the first time we had spoken in over a month. He told me he agreed with everything I said in my speech and felt terrible about what he had done. He wanted me to know that he was meeting regularly with two ministers who were also family counselors. We spoke for more than a half hour as two old friends. There is nothing that can erase the fact of Bill Clinton's immoral behavior with Monica Lewinsky, but he was now doing everything anyone, including me, could ask to accept responsibility and do better.

On the evening of September 3, after I spoke on the Senate floor, a White House spokesman said, "It's always hardest to hear criticism from a friend. But I am sure the president will consider Senator Lieberman's words with the same care with which they were delivered."

Later, Al From of the DLC said that speech "saved the Clinton presidency . . . by saying what he did was wrong without calling on him to resign." I don't know whether those generous words are accurate. But I would be grateful if my speech helped the country and the president get back on track. I will always be upset by Bill Clinton's behavior with Monica Lewinsky, but I will also always be proud that I supported him in 1992 and worked with him closely during the eight years of his presidency. His record of accomplishment as president and leader of the Democratic Party was extraordinary, and most of it happened exactly where I hoped it would—in the bipartisan center.

LESSONS FOR CENTRISTS

1. Twists of fate play a large part in politics. Let's say that you are working with a group of like-minded people to transform your political party into a winning, centrist organization. Well, it helps to have the sudden appearance of a presidential candidate who is the best natural politician of your time. In the case of the Democratic Party in 1992, that was Governor Bill Clinton of Arkansas.

    From the first speech I heard him give at the DLC Convention in New Orleans in 1990, it was crystal clear that Bill Clinton understood what was needed. It was time, he said, to move beyond the tired, reflex partisanship in Washington to build a new Democratic Party, "a dynamic but centrist progressive movement of new ideas rooted in traditional American values."

    Watching him interact with the delegates at the DLC Convention, I could see that he had winning personal ways. He knew how to "work a room."

    During the next two years he developed those centrist new ideas and carried them via his personal skills to election in November 1992 as the 42nd president of the United States.

    As a centrist Democrat, I was thrilled to support Bill Clinton early in 1992, and proud to have helped him in the campaign.

    As a Senate colleague once said to me, "Sometimes in politics you have to think of yourself as a surfer. Surfers don't create waves to ride to shore. They wait for a good wave and let it take them in." That was a little like the relationship between the Democratic Party and Bill Clinton in 1992.

2. President Clinton was very good, but he was certainly not perfect. He made personal and political mistakes which sometimes knocked him down, but he usually figured out

how to get up and learn from those mistakes. When he was at his best, he was a role model for the kind of problem-solving government we have not seen much of in Washington in recent times. Clinton was very smart and spent a lot of time learning about legislation. He was a "policy wonk" and had the patience to listen to members of Congress in both parties and engage them in negotiations, horse trading, and compromise. Those are skills that we always need in a democracy to get things done.

I was one of the targets of President Clinton's advocacy when he worked to pass a budget in 1993, his first year in the White House. He needed my vote to get to fifty so that Vice President Gore could break the tie. First, he convinced me that his budget was a New Democratic budget which would show people we were no longer a party of "tax and spend" liberals. He then asked me what I needed in the bill and gave me as much of it as he could. As a bonus, he threw in that early morning run on the Mall in front of the cameras that I described earlier.

In 1997, he did a lot of the same to secure one of his great achievements, the Balanced Budget Act, arguing convincingly that it would end annual deficits, stimulate the economy, and help poor people. For me, and many others, he was also happy to include personal projects which secured our votes, so long as they did not work against his larger goals. All of that was done in a remarkable leadership alliance with Republican Speaker Newt Gingrich.

He also supported and signed a Criminal Justice Reform bill that was a classic left–right centrist balance. On this, he received significant support from the chairman of the Judiciary Committee, Joe Biden. The bill was tough on criminals but also provided more than $6 billion for crime prevention, funding for 100,000 community police, and two important legislative goals of liberal Democrats: the Violence Against Women Act and a Ban on Assault Weapons. Not surprisingly, the crime bill of 1994 passed with large bipartisan majorities in both houses.

President Clinton taught us all how to make America's government work.

3. He also taught me in the Lewinsky crisis that there is another aspect of centrism besides breaking away from partisan loyalties to work with the other party to solve a problem. It is standing up and criticizing the leader of your own party if you believe he has acted in a way that is immoral or bad for our country.

For me that was more difficult than building bipartisan centrist coalitions because it meant publicly criticizing a friend whose leadership I otherwise supported. But, looking back, it was the right thing for me to do as a centrist Democrat.

7

AL GORE
BREAKS A BARRIER

After a presidential candidate has clinched a party's nomination for president, the choice of a running mate is one of the most unilateral exercises of power in American politics. The presidential candidate will naturally consult others, but it is his or her call. That is why I will always be grateful to Al Gore personally for asking me to be his running mate in 2000. The fact that he had the courage and confidence in the American people to make me the first Jewish American candidate on a major party ticket deepens my gratitude.

It was a long, unpredictable path that led to my selection in 2000. Many coincidental twists of fate played a role. Besides Gore's evaluation of me, events of the moment and the political climate of the time must have influenced his decision. It may seem strange, but I never asked Al in private why he chose me, and he never volunteered an answer in private. The media speculated on his reasons, and some of his campaign staff anonymously leaked their opinions.

Most believed that Gore's selection of me was his response to the "ups" and "downs" of being Bill Clinton's vice president. The "ups" were the great accomplishments of the Clinton-Gore years, including the booming economy, twenty-two million jobs created, and a surplus in the federal budget, as well as adoption of New Democratic programs like the crime bill, welfare reform, and pro-trade laws that rebranded the Democratic Party. The "down" was the Clinton-Lewinsky scandal. I was a strong supporter of Clinton's presidency and program and a devoted New Democrat, so I could highlight the "ups" of the Clinton record, but I also had publicly chastised Clinton for his immoral behavior with Monica Lewinsky, so I could help overcome the "downs."

That explanation of Gore's decision makes sense to me. But I also learned there were other reasons. One was that by 2000 I had served twenty-eight years in state and federal government. I had experience, which could enable him to say I was ready to do the job. Second, Al and I had become friends during my twelve years in the Senate. We trusted each other and were comfortable with each other. The first question for a presidential candidate is, "Which candidate for vice president will help me most to get elected?" But there is a relevant secondary question: "Do I have confidence that this person will help me be a successful president, and that I will enjoy working with him or her?"

Public opinion polling throughout 1999 illustrated Gore's challenge. In February 1999, in a poll taken days after President Clinton was acquitted in the Senate's impeachment trial, a very high 68 percent of the American people told the Gallup organization that they had a favorable opinion of the job Clinton was doing as president. A few months later in June of 1999, when Gore returned to his hometown of Carthage, Tennessee, to declare his candidacy for president, the Gallup poll found the leading Republican candidate, Governor George W. Bush of Texas, was ahead of him. In fact, Bush led every Gallup poll taken in 1999.

I was aware of Gore's dilemma, and concerned about it, but I was focused on my work on behalf of Connecticut in the Senate. I was very busy in the Senate and traveling around the country raising funds for my 2000 Senate re-election campaign. I supported Al Gore for president right after he declared in June 1999. Senator Bill Bradley was challenging Gore for the Democratic nomination, and I admired and liked him, but Gore was an easy choice for me as the logical continuity of the Clinton-Gore presidency, someone who was ready to be president, and someone I was close to.

Bradley kept saying, "One of the reasons I'm running for president is to restore trust in public service."

By late September 1999, those repeated references to the Lewinsky scandal helped produce polls that showed Bradley close to Gore in New Hampshire and in New York. Al moved his national headquarters from Washington, DC, to Nashville, Tennessee, in an attempt to get as far from Clinton and the Washington status quo as he could. At the same time, Gore "challenged" Bradley to a series of debates, which he accepted. Gore did very well in the debates and then went on to win every primary and caucus until March of 2000 when Bill Bradley withdrew.

But Gore's political dilemma continued. In that same month, March 2000, Gallup showed that 55 percent of the American people were satisfied with the direction of the country, the highest number since 1984. Yet in Bush-Gore polling, Bush remained ahead. In June 2000, Gallup issued a mid-year summary of polling. They had taken thirteen polls in 2000, and Bush had won them all. In the Gallup survey that month, Bush led by four points. Democrats and Republicans overwhelmingly favored their party's candidates, but Bush was leading Gore by ten points among independents. In 1996, Clinton had won by eleven points among independents.

For me, all these numbers were background music to my Senate responsibilities and re-election campaign—until former Secretary of State Warren Christopher called in late March and asked if he could come talk with me about Vice President Gore's campaign. I had gotten to know "Chris" when he was secretary during Clinton's first term, and also on Aspen Institute Seminars on foreign policy because he chaired the Institute. He was an honorable, thoughtful, wise gentleman. His leadership of the Gore vetting process was a good twist of fate for me.

I met with Chris in my Senate office alone. He told me that he was overseeing Vice President Gore's search for a running mate, meeting with a number of people to ask what qualities they thought Gore's choice should have and who they thought he should consider. I had not thought about either of those questions. To the first, I gave a conventional but truthful answer: the running mate should be someone who the American people could see serving as president if necessary, and someone who Vice President Gore trusted and could work with. I told Chris I would think about his second question, but two names that came quickly to mind were former Majority Leader George Mitchell and former Treasurer Secretary Bob Rubin.

Then, Christopher asked, "If the vice president should want to consider you, Joe, would you allow that consideration?" That genuinely surprised me, and I answered reflexively that I would be honored to be considered, but I had no expectation that the vice president would choose me. That answer was not insincere. I had never thought of the possibility and, if I had, I would have concluded it was not possible. That evening, I told Hadassah about the conversation, which she said "freaked" her out.

A month later on Sunday, April 30, Hadassah, our daughter Hani, and I, along with about twenty of Hani's classmates from Washington, returned there from Connecticut where we all had gone to celebrate Hani's Bat Mitzvah. Later that afternoon, Warren Christopher called me at our home in Georgetown to tell me that Vice President Gore had narrowed the so-called "short list" of possible running mates to six, and I was on it unless I did not want to be considered. He said he hoped I would allow myself to be on that list. Then he added, "I feel obligated to tell you that the vetting process will be very intrusive and can be painful and there is nothing I can do to reduce the pain." I knew "Chris" well enough to respond, "You mean being vetted for vice president is kind of like having a colonoscopy without anesthesia?" Chris, who once described himself to me as a "self-contained Norwegian American," burst out with laughter and said, "Exactly."

Then he asked if I had talked to Hadassah, who he knew from our Aspen trips, about this possibility. I told him I had, and that we both agreed that the odds were very low I would be selected, but it would be an honor just to be considered. We had a responsibility to allow the process to go forward if that is what Vice President Gore wanted. Chris said he was happy to hear that. I had one more question: "If asked about this by the media, what should I say?" His answer was: "Say nothing." I took that not just as a request but as a test of my trustworthiness. So, I never responded to media questions about whether I was being vetted.

Soon thereafter I asked Jonathan Sallet, a Washington lawyer I had known since 1992 when we were both on the Democratic Platform Drafting Committee, to represent me in the vetting process. I knew it was going to be demanding and I wanted to get it out of my Senate office to help keep it private. Another good twist of fate: Sallet was a friend and former colleague of Jamie Gorelick, a Washington attorney who had been deputy attorney general in the Clinton administration and was leading a team of eight to ten people who would vet me.

Besides my family, my Senate chief of staff, Bill Andresen, and my executive assistant, Melissa Winter, the only people I told and sought advice from were Al From of the DLC and Carter Eskew, my friend and political adviser since the 1988 Senate campaign. Another positive twist of fate: Carter had been a friend of Al Gore since they were young reporters together on a Tennessee newspaper. Carter was senior adviser on the 2000 Gore presidential campaign. Al, Carter, and I agreed that the vice-presidential nomination was not something you campaigned for, but, if there were discrete ways to advance my name with Vice President Gore, it would be foolish not to do so. Eskew and From both said they would think about carrying out such covert action on my behalf.

Jon Sallet's primary responsibility would be to assist the vetting team in obtaining all the personal, financial, political, and legislative information they wanted about me. And they wanted everything. They interviewed my ex-wife, who told me they had asked her whether she had reason to suspect I had ever had extra-marital relations or used illegal drugs. Fortunately, the answer to both was "no."

Sallet and I decided that in addition to reassuring the Gore team that there was nothing embarrassing in my closet, he would find ways to present positive reasons for the vice president to choose me. Jon began by describing the similar senatorial records Al Gore and I had. We had both served on the Senate Armed Services Committee and were outspoken in support of a strong defense. We both advocated for human rights around the world. We had both made environmental protection, "new economy" job growth, and governmental management reform our personal priorities. We were both certifiable DLC New Democrats in the Clinton tradition.

But, on the other hand, I had spoken out against Clinton's relationship with Lewinsky. Finally, Sallet would say that it appeared to him that Gore and I had become friends, and he knew I would be loyal to President Gore as his vice president. Tipper and Hadassah also had become friends. We really enjoyed each other's company, including one memorable Passover Seder we celebrated together at our home in Washington.

As the vetting process went on through May, June, and July, the media reported that Senators John Edwards and John Kerry were in the lead with the Gore team. Apparently, I was falling behind because I was a centrist and had worked across party lines, which meant that I was not the first choice of some important Democratic interest groups like trial lawyers, teachers' unions, and some African American groups who were suspicious of the DLC, even though I had been a civil rights activist all my life. I told Sallet that he couldn't try to turn me into someone I was not. I was a center-left Democrat just like Clinton, and I had a good voting record on the issues that mattered to most core Democratic interest groups. Our goal should be for the leaders of these groups to say, "If Gore wants Lieberman, we can live with that."

Jon and I decided we needed a trusted covert "ambassador" to advocate on my behalf to some of those skeptical groups. My choice was my friend and Senate colleague from Connecticut, Chris Dodd. During the first week in July, Chris and I were in Branford, Connecticut, to announce we had secured federal aid for the local lobster industry which had been suffering from a disease that had struck their lobster pools. It was a beautifully clear and sunny day on the water. When the announcement was over, I asked Chris if he had a moment to talk in private and we walked down a dirt road along the Sound. I told him I was on the short list for Gore's vice president and Warren Christopher had instructed me not to tell anyone, but, "You are my friend, Chris, and I need your help." He responded with generosity and good advice:

> Joe, this is a moment of great opportunity in your life. You have no way of knowing whether anything like this will ever happen again. You should do everything you can so you never look back and say, "If I had done just one more thing, I might have been chosen." Of course, I understand that you can't go out and campaign for this, but others, like me, can help.

He offered to make calls quietly to some of the core Democratic groups that were raising questions about me.

Later in July, I was invited to the vice president's residence on DC's Wisconsin Avenue for a private discussion and interview. I was picked up by one of the vice president's top aides and driven the mile from my home in a van with darkened windows so that the media could not see me. Al and I sat in his sunlit dining room over breakfast. We were both dressed informally. He said this was awkward because we were friends, but he had to interview me. I told him I totally understood. I knew how important this was and he should feel comfortable asking me anything he wanted to know.

He started by asking the big question: "Why should I pick you?" I answered that, based on my years of public service experience in the federal and state governments, he could make the case that I was qualified to be his partner in national leadership and qualified to step into the presidency if that ever became necessary. I also said that because our policy priorities were so similar, we would send a strong, unified message to the voters during the campaign and work together comfortably in office. We were friends, he knew me well, and I hoped he felt that he could absolutely trust me.

Then, Al said, "Let's talk about some of the interest groups in the Democratic Party and how they might feel if you are selected to run with me." He specifically asked about labor unions and the African American community. I told him I had many friends in both of those groups, but I knew there were also people in both groups for whom I was not the first choice. To those with whom I had disagreed on particular issues, he could say—and I would say—that if I were his vice president, I would always express my opinions to him as president, but in the end his position would be my position.

I also told him that Chris Dodd had spoken on my behalf to some of the leaders of the Democratic constituency groups he had asked me about, and they had told him, "If Al Gore chooses Joe Lieberman, it's okay with us." Al said, "So, Joe, is Chris Dodd your John the Baptist?" I laughed out loud and said, "I haven't thought of him that way, but I like the reference."

The interview ended with an outrageous twist. Al said, "Joe, I am compelled to ask you, even after the thorough vetting you have been through, if there is anything about you that I don't know that I should know before I make my decision?" Perhaps because we were friends and I knew he had a good sense of humor, and perhaps because the whole experience was surreal, I hesitated a few seconds, looked down, then looked up at him, and said: "I once was involved in an act of bestiality." Al looked at me quizzically for a second and then roared with laughter, as did I. "That," he said, "concludes this interview."

The Democratic National Convention was scheduled to begin in Los Angeles on Monday, August 14. The time for Vice President Gore's decision was approaching. On Friday, August 5, his campaign let it be known that Al would make his choice over the weekend, and the "finalists" were Senators Edwards, Kerry, and me.

The scene outside our house in New Haven that weekend became like a circus. About a dozen satellite television trucks had mustered when the networks reported it was down to the three of us. We were followed and photographed when we walked to and from Synagogue on Saturday morning, and Hadassah made it onto national television when she took out the garbage. It was a taste of what might be coming.

By Sunday, there was still no decision, but we were told it was likely to happen by the end of the day. My family and I waited. On Sunday evening, we received a call from a friend at one of the television networks who said they heard from a person in the room with the vice president that Gore had selected John Edwards. I told the family, opened a bottle of wine, and offered a toast of gratitude to America and Al Gore that we had come that close to being nominated for vice president of the US.

It was hard to fall asleep that night because Hadassah and I were downloading everything that had happened and the television trucks were still outside, making a lot of noise. Apparently, they had not been told Senator Edwards had been chosen. So, I woke up later than normal the next morning at about 6:55 a.m. and reached for the remote to turn on the television. The local anchor was saying:

> Now let me repeat that very exciting news. The Associated Press is reporting that Vice President Gore has chosen our own Senator Joe Lieberman to be his running mate.

The phone began ringing and didn't stop. I went downstairs to make some coffee, still in my underwear, and found television cameras in both kitchen windows. Life was changing.

Vice President Gore's team called Sherry Brown to say that the staff they'd selected for my vice-presidential campaign was on a plane to New Haven to pick up my family and me and bring us to Nashville where the announcement would be made the next morning. My new staff had gone to sleep Sunday night, not knowing whether on Monday morning they would be flying to Boston to pick up Kerry, North Carolina to get Edwards, or New Haven to meet me. Before they arrived in the early afternoon on that Monday, I kept a scheduled commitment to speak at the Connecticut State Labor Council annual meeting in Hartford, and then returned to our home in New Haven where I received two memorable calls in my basement office, which we called "The Bunker."

The first was from the Rev. Jesse Jackson, who I had come to know during my time in the Senate. In recent years, he had protested the rising influence of the Democratic Leadership Council I chaired, and he'd even taken to calling us the "Democratic Leisure Class." I was pleasantly surprised by the warmth of his call. "Senator, I am very excited by your selection because I believe you will be an excellent running mate for Al Gore, and a great vice president. But I am also excited because I know that in America when a barrier is broken for one group, the doors of opportunity open wider for every other American." I agreed with Rev. Jackson and was moved by his words. I had felt the same way when John F. Kennedy was the first Roman Catholic to be elected president forty years before. I would repeat Jesse Jackson's words across America throughout the campaign.

The second call was from President Clinton.

He could not have been more gracious or more enthusiastic. He even had some advice about how to handle the speech I had given about him: "Now Joe, you know the press may bring up your speech." I agreed that was likely. He said,

> Well, you just tell them, "I stand by what I said in that speech. And President Clinton himself has said he agreed with me." Tell them we've known each other thirty years, and of course you were disappointed in my behavior. But you can also remind them that you fought against impeachment because you knew that whatever people felt about me personally, two-thirds of them thought I was doing a good job as president and that I didn't deserve to be impeached. And I know you agreed with them Joe, and I remember you argued that the framers of the Constitution could not have intended for impeachment to be used in a case like this. In

fact, the impeachment was an abuse of power that should make voters reluctant to give control of the presidency and Congress to the Republicans this fall. Then, if they ask you about it again during the campaign, you can tell them you already answered those questions.

Interestingly, I wouldn't be asked much about it at all during the campaign.

President Clinton then brought up another speech I had given at the National Prayer Breakfast earlier that year on the appropriate role for faith in our public life. He urged me to circulate it widely. "Stand strong against those who might question your religious beliefs and behavior," he told me. "There will be some people in the campaign who will try to keep you quiet on this, but don't you hesitate to talk about your religion." And when it came to my refusal to campaign on the Sabbath, he said, "Some people are going to start saying to you, 'Gee, how can you give up one of the optimum campaign days on Saturday by not campaigning?' If they say that, just tell them to go straight to hell!" I laughed heartily at that.

Most fascinating and important, Clinton had a clear recommendation about how his own vice president should handle the record of the preceding eight years. "Al should get credit for what the administration did right but not get blamed for my mistakes, which were personal. The American people are too fair and too smart to vote against him for that. By choosing you as his running mate, Al has freed himself from being defensive about my personal mistakes. He can now go out and talk about all that we've done for the country over the last eight years. Nobody understands what I've tried to do as president better than you do, Joe. I know you're proud of our record, so it will be easy for you to talk about how Al and you will build on the prosperity and progress that he and I started."

Finally, he offered me wise counsel on how I should describe the Republican ticket: "Our opponents are not bad people. They love their families and their country. But we have honest disagreements with them. Ideas have consequences. And they have some bad ideas."

"You know all that, Joe," he said. "Just be who you are."

It was pure Bill Clinton—pride in his accomplishments, a willingness to accept responsibility for his mistakes, an understanding that because Al had selected me, he could now unabashedly run on their record and promise to keep the strong economic growth and centrist government going. Unfortunately, the Gore campaign was never able to fully operationalize that insight. I was surprised that President Clinton remembered the speech I had given at the National Prayer Breakfast and appreciated his encouragement to talk about the positive place faith has had—and should continue to have—in American life. I would follow this recommendation during the campaign, sometimes evoking positive responses and other times quite negative.

By early afternoon, the staff from the Gore campaign arrived at our house in New Haven. The only one of them I had known before was Kiki McLean, who had worked for the DLC and was now to be my vice-presidential campaign communications director. They were a skillful, hardworking, likeable group. We bonded with each other during the following intense months of campaigning.

As we prepared to leave our home to go to Tweed New Haven Airport, we had two new experiences. Dave O'Brien, our new trip director, told us the order in which we would leave the house, and that none of us should leave until he told us to. Kiki McLean said to me, "Sir, (she always called me 'Sir' and still does), the first reactions to your selection are well beyond anything any of us had hoped for. Don't stop to talk to the press or anyone else on the way out. Just get into the car." In other words, don't step on a good story.

That is usually good advice, but when Hadassah and I exited the side door of our house, I saw two Connecticut television reporters I had known forever, calling my name. Of course, I went over and talked to them on camera. Kiki came over and gently ended the conversation, giving me a look that said, "So this is how it is going to be. You are an independent spirit in more than your policy positions."

That evening, Al and Tipper Gore and their family graciously hosted Hadassah and me and our family for dinner at the Loews

Vanderbilt Hotel in Nashville. My then-86-year-old mother was with us. When she walked into the room, Mom looked up at Al and said, "Mr. Vice President, you certainly made a great choice for vice president." He and Tipper burst into laughter.

When we sat down to dinner, Al asked me to say grace. There was a lot to thank God for that day, in addition to the meal. During dinner, Al said he wanted me to know that when I made it to his "short-short list" of possible running mates, he thought it was important to talk confidentially with a group of friends and advisors about whether the American people were ready to have a Jewish person as vice president, or whether lingering anti-Semitism would make it unlikely he could win with me on his ticket. Al's conclusions from those conversations were both insightful and courageous:

> I came to understand that there was a difference between the reality of anti-Semitism and the fear of anti-Semitism. Several people told me they thought your religion would be a problem, but I concluded their fear of anti-Semitism exceeded anti-Semitism itself. None of these people were anti-Semitic. In fact, most were Jewish. Most of the Christians did not think having a Jewish running mate would be a problem. That showed me that fear of anti-Semitism was greater than the reality of anti-Semitism: I was free to choose you as my vice-presidential candidate.

Those words say a lot that is great about Al Gore. Many other people in his position would have taken the anxieties about a Jewish candidate as posing too big a risk and never would have distinguished between the fear of anti-Semitism and the reality of it. But Al had more courage than that and more confidence in the American people. In making his decision, he created a new reality. His insight was correct, as was clear from the very positive media and public response to his choice of me.

The front-page headlines in newspapers around the country on Tuesday morning were all about the barrier that Al had broken. The *Washington Post* said, GORE PICKS LIEBERMAN . . . TO BE

FIRST JEW ON MAJOR TICKET; The *Chicago Sun-Times* said, GORE SELECTS ORTHODOX JEW AS RUNNING MATE; and the *New York Times* headline was LIEBERMAN WILL RUN WITH GORE: FIRST JEW ON A MAJOR U.S. TICKET.

Although Al certainly did not choose me because I was Jewish, the media heralded that fact as an act of courage and independence, which helped him start a new chapter on his own, separate from Bill Clinton, in a way that was not hostile to Clinton. Some of the media coverage of my selection also mentioned that Al and I were New Democrats and that I had spoken out about the Clinton-Lewinsky relationship, but that usually appeared lower in the stories.

Two people who were in the room with Al on Sunday night before he made his decision told me that at one point the discussion was moving toward John Edwards as the best choice until Warren Christopher spoke:

> Mr. Vice President, this decision is important, and it will say more about you than it does about the person you choose. Senator Edwards is an impressive young man, but if you ask him to be your running mate, you will have to explain why you asked a person who was a lawyer in North Carolina two years ago to be one heartbeat away from becoming president of the US.

The conversation then turned away from Edwards and ended up with me.

Someone told me during that first day in Nashville that there are three times vice-presidential candidates matter in a national campaign: the day of the announcement, the day of the acceptance speech at the convention, and day of the vice-presidential debate. The first of those would happen the very next day, Tuesday, August 8. Paul Orzulak was the speechwriter the Gore campaign gave me. I liked him from the beginning, and not just because he was a University of Connecticut graduate. I was aware that I had less than twenty-four hours to prepare the most watched speech of my life, so we had a lot of work to do. He told me he had a frame of a speech that he had worked on in advance based on reading many of my previous speeches, supplemented by material from the leaders of the Gore campaign in Nashville.

On the plane from New Haven to Nashville, Paul Orzulak interviewed me about my life and wove some great stories into the excellent speech he produced and I edited for delivery at the War Memorial Plaza on Tuesday morning.

It was a very hot day in the Music City, so Al and I quickly took our jackets off. The crowd was huge and exuberant, and everything worked beautifully. People said there was good "chemistry" between the Gores and Hadassah and me. It was real. Tipper began the program with a wonderful introduction in which she told some of Hadassah's life story. The night before at dinner, Hadassah had talked about being the child of Holocaust survivors and how much Al's choosing me meant to her and her family. Later Al asked Hadassah if she was comfortable speaking about that the next morning when she introduced me. She was, and did:

> Here I am at this place that commemorates veterans of World War II . . . the American heroes, the soldiers who actually liberated my mother from Dachau . . . so I stand before you, very deeply, sincerely thankful that I am an American, grateful that we have such a wonderful family in the Gores, and they made this bold, wonderful choice to make us part of the ticket that's going to win.

The crowd roared. Hadassah was compelling and radiant.

> Let me end now with just this one statement: Whether you and your family emigrated from Europe, as mine did, or from Africa, or Latin America or Asia, I am standing here for you. This country is our country. This land is our land, and anything is possible for us.

These words came from Hadassah's heart. They could not have been more genuine or sincere, and they opened up a broader understanding of what Al and I meant when we talked about protecting and expanding opportunity in America. Tipper came back to the podium and introduced Al as "a man whose faith and family are the cornerstone of his life." Al formally announced me as his running mate, and then he explained the "three simple tests" he applied in making his decision. He wanted someone who could become president on a moment's notice; shared his values and could work with him as a partner; and be "someone who would fight right alongside me for the people, not the powerful."

The third reason was a surprise to me. At times in the next few months, I worried that populist appeals were used too much and risked blurring the winning centrist vision and record of the Clinton-Gore administration. On that announcement day in Nashville, Al made a good case for why I passed his third test. He pointed to my record as attorney general of Connecticut, fighting the "big polluters" and the "big oil companies" who were "price gauging at the gas pumps," and he cited my record in the civil rights movement.

Al also talked about our shared support of the New Democratic record of the administration including welfare reform, fiscal discipline, the crime bill, and health care for children. And then he listed a number of initiatives on social programs he and I would take, and how the two of us had "always stood for a strong national defense . . . (and) broke with our own party to cast two lonely Democratic votes in support of the Persian Gulf War." Then, for the first time, I was introduced as "the next vice president of the United States." It was a thrilling moment. I was full of gratitude and thanked Al for his courage and confidence. Then, as I said that morning, "the spirit moved me" to thank God. In words of prayer from Chronicles, I thanked "the Maker of miracles . . . for making this miracle possible for me and breaking this barrier for the rest of America."

I went on to speak of Al as "a man of family and faith . . . He has never, never wavered in his responsibilities as a father, a husband."

That was right on message and exactly what I thought of Al. Then, for the first of many times, I bragged about the record of the Clinton-Gore administration.

"Are we going to elect the old guard that created the problems? Or the new guard that will continue to work to solve the problems?"

Paul Orzulak answered this question with a great one-liner that I had never heard before but used throughout the campaign, all the better because it was a quote from Vice President Bush in the 1988 campaign:

"If you have to change horses in midstream, doesn't it make sense to get on the one that's going in the right direction?"

The Gore campaign was thrilled with how the announcement had gone. "It was quite astonishing, raw jubilation," was the exuberant reaction of my normally restrained, new campaign manager, Tom Nides.

Modesty prevents me from describing the media reaction the day after the announcement, but I found some words Hadassah wrote about it that I can quote:

> When we read the morning papers and saw how favorable they were to Joe, I thought about that scene in *Huckleberry Finn* when Huck is presumed "drowned" and gets to listen to the eulogies at his funeral. The *Washington Post* editorial was headlined INTEGRITY ON THE TICKET. The *New York Times* praised Joe's "gravity and rectitude." I liked what George Will wrote. He called Joe, "a practicing grown-up—the thinking person's choice." And Richard Cohen of the *Washington Post* wrote: "Some call him sanctimonious and some call him moralistic, but everyone realizes that, in the end, this is a politician with a very demanding constituency: his conscience."

Thank you, Hadassah.

The Gore-Lieberman campaign chairman was Bill Daley, whose brother was mayor of Chicago at the time and whose father had held the same position years earlier. He called the enthusiasm behind my candidacy "Liebermania" and was good enough to add, "The reaction to Lieberman has been about as good as you could hope for leading up to the convention. In a lot of ways, it has really changed the dynamic of the convention." In fact, the polling showed that our ticket was now within two points of the Republicans, even after their successful convention.

The Republicans' first response to my candidacy interestingly validated my bipartisan centrism, but it was aimed at Al Gore. They said Governor Bush and I agreed on more issues than Vice President Gore and I. Paul Orzulak had another great one-line reaction to that one (which I would describe as "Reaganesque"): "With all due respect, saying that George Bush and I think alike is like saying that the veterinarian and the taxidermist are in the same business because either way you get your dog back."

LESSONS FOR CENTRISTS

How do you get to be your party's nominee for vice president of the United States?

Be lucky. Be the right person in the right place at the right time. In other words, you can't really run for vice president. You can't take actions or policy positions years before with the intention of being selected on one distant day as the vice-presidential nominee. You have no idea who the presidential nominee will be, or what the political context will be at that future time.

In 2000, a lot of things I had done or said over the years put me on Al Gore's short list. I was a centrist Democrat, a friend of Al's since I had come to the Senate in 1989, a religious person, as he was, and I had given that speech in the Senate chastising President Clinton for his immoral behavior with Monica Lewinsky. None of those beliefs or behaviors were motivated by dreams of becoming vice president. They resulted from separate decisions I made over the years. In other words, unlike so much else in politics, running for vice president is not a goal you can plan to achieve.

Then, to add to the political uniqueness of the experience once you are on the "short list," you can't campaign to be chosen—which is what you have naturally done during the rest of your political life. You can't talk to anyone in the media about it, and you shouldn't tell one more person than you have to that you are being seriously considered. But very discretely, you can ask a friend, as I did Chris Dodd, to provide some advocacy for me among Democratic core constituencies, without confirming that I was actually on the short list.

That's how I became the Democratic nominee for vice president in 2000. I was in the right place at the right time. I was lucky. I was blessed.

8

THE 2000
NATIONAL CAMPAIGN

After completing the vetting process and being selected and announced as Al Gore's running mate, my next "big moment" as vice-presidential candidate was the acceptance speech I would deliver to the Democratic National Convention on the evening of August 16. But first, after I arrived in Los Angeles, I was asked to visit with representatives from the many subgroups that make up the Democratic Party: African Americans, Hispanic Americans, Jewish Americans, Native Americans, Asian Americans, Pacific Island Americans, and other American constituencies. I had done my basic training in politics in Connecticut, which was a very ethnic state, so I comfortably enjoyed these caucus meetings.

The campaign also asked me to meet with Democratic interest groups that were not enthused that Al Gore had chosen me, including teachers unions, trial attorneys, and some African American leaders. At each of these meetings, I would ask for their support, remind them of the times I had agreed with them, and tell them that as vice president, my door would always be open to them. In each of the meetings, the campaign had prepped one of the members of the group to speak up for me, and that support definitely helped. The tort lawyers arrived with a surprise guest—a prominent trial lawyer from Connecticut who happened to be a good friend of mine since we had met at summer camp when we were six years old. I admired that move and told the trial lawyers so.

In the end, I also told them all that if we were elected, Al Gore would be the president and I the vice president. I would give him my opinion on policy in private, but once he decided, I would support his position. That was my fallback reassurance to all the groups that were uneasy. It probably eliminated the worst fears they had, but did not remove all their concerns. I was about to be the vice-presidential nominee of a political party, some of whose core constituencies were supportive but not enthusiastic about me. That was the result of Al Gore's independent-minded choice and his best judgment about what would help him win the election. As the words on a handwritten sign held high by a woman at the Hispanic American Caucus meeting declared: "Gore-Lieberman/ Viva Chutzpah!"

For Hadassah and me and our family, that convention in Los Angeles was truly a trip to "La La Land." We had suddenly become "celebrities." More exciting to us, we hobnobbed with real Hollywood celebrities. We visited the set of *The West Wing* and were greeted by the iconic show's cast. Our kids went to a house party at the home of Arnold Schwarzenegger and Maria Shriver, and on his thirty-third birthday, our older son Matt went to an event where Sheryl Crow was performing. She serenaded him with a breathy Marilyn Monroe impersonation of "Happy birthday, Matt . . . son of the vice president."

Some people call Washington, DC, "Hollywood East." But now we were in the real Hollywood, the capital of another potential Joe Lieberman problem for Al Gore. For the past decade I had been pressuring the American entertainment industry—including the film, television, and video game industries—to protect our children from the endless violence and sex they were producing. In an article headlined "Moguls Rattled by Gore's Choice," the *New York Times* wrote that Al's selection of me had "chilled wealthy Hollywood Democrats who are upset that Lieberman is one of the most vocal critics of Hollywood." In my conflict with this Democratic interest group, I had a very well-placed ally—Tipper Gore. She had been a pioneer fighter for kids in our coarsening culture, and she'd written a popular book called *Raising PG Kids in an X-Rated Society*. She and I had worked together on this cause.

On a flight the day after the announcement, Al said to me, "I chose you because of who you are, so don't let anyone change you." I appreciated that and remembered it. The Sunday before the convention, I made the rounds of the television talk shows and, when asked, continued to spell out my concerns about the impact of the entertainment industry on America's children. I later found out that in the days before the convention Al called some Hollywood executives and there wasn't any real concern about me. As Rob Reiner told a *Washington Post* reporter, "I'm not really concerned about Hollywood's parochial interests," adding that the industry issues were "miniscule" compared to problems like education, health care, and the environment—concerns he and most people in Hollywood shared with me.

Our big night was Wednesday, August 16. Hadassah and I waited near a long ramp backstage. Soon we'd walk out and speak to the crowd. She would go first and introduce me. I held her hand and asked, "Are you nervous?"

"No," she answered. "Are you?"

"No," I said. "We know what we have to do."

Hours later when we got back to our hotel room, I burst out, "Holy shit! I can't believe what we just did." We both laughed hard. We could finally allow ourselves to admit our nervousness.

When Hadassah went out on stage, there were thousands of delegates holding up signs that said simply "Hadassah" and chanting her name. She was very emotional because throughout her life, people were always mispronouncing her unusual name. Hadassah looked beautiful and spoke with her customary sincerity and passion. Now, it was up to me. A week earlier, when we began to work on my speech, I remember asking Jon Sallet, "What do you think should be the organizing principle of my acceptance speech?"

"You are the organizing principle," he answered.

He was right. It was an autobiographical speech, but ultimately it was about America as an opportunity society, a country where someone like me could run for the second-highest office in the land. I began that speech with the words, "Is America a great country, or what?" and ended with the words, "Only in America."

My favorite lines in between were:

> We have become the America that so many of our parents dreamed for us. But the great question this year is what will we dream for our country—and how will we make it come true.

I went on to praise the Clinton-Gore record, described Al as the gifted and good person I knew him to be, and talked about our plans to continue the progress and prosperity. I also described Al's strong record on defense, his support of our troops, and his vote to authorize the Gulf War of 1991. I compared our program to the very different promises of the Republican ticket, and I criticized Governor Bush's record in Texas, focusing on his shortcomings on health care and the environment. I began each sentence that was critical of Bush with the same words: "I'm sad to say." The phrasing reflected the advice President Clinton had given me about how to treat our opponents, and also was a comfortable way for me to fulfill my vice-presidential responsibility to distinguish Al and me from our opponents. That acceptance speech to the convention was a thrilling personal experience, and worked for our campaign. The delegates were exuberant and the media reaction was very positive.

On Thursday evening, the convention ended with an inspiring speech by Al. The delegates loved it and so, it seemed, did the American people. He praised Bill Clinton as "a leader who moved us out of the valley of recession and into the longest period of prosperity in American history." And he rang some New Democratic bells by saying that he and Bill Clinton had "changed things

to help unleash your potential, and unleash innovation and invest-
ment in the private sector, the engine that drives our economic
growth." I thought those were important steps forward. "And," he
added, "now we turn the page and write a new chapter." Al spoke
about himself, his life, his family, and their values, and then about
the programs he pledged to enact if elected. And, he effectively
responded to Bush, saying he would restore honor to the White
House by redefining the word "honor" to mean caring for people
who needed help, like families seeking better education or health
care for their children.

The convention ended with justified optimism among Democrats.
The public opinion polls turned in our favor. Bush's double-digit
lead had evaporated. We had actually moved ahead.

Later in August, I spoke at Reverend Wendell Anthony's Fel-
lowship Church in Detroit, addressing the important role faith
had played and should play in American life. It was the first time I
had flown on my own campaign plane, a DC-9 adorned with the
Gore-Lieberman logo painted in red, white, and blue. The plane
was chartered from Spirit Airlines, so we called it The Spirit—which
led to my telling the largely African American congregation that
"The Spirit has brought me here."

My message was the same as I had given repeatedly over the
years, including at the National Prayer Breakfast earlier that year,
which President Clinton had remembered. My basic point was that
our Constitution wisely promised freedom of religion, not freedom
from religion. President Washington himself had warned future
generations of Americans not to assume we would have a good
and just society without the moral influence of religion. That, like
so much else in our society, had to begin with our leaders, setting
an example that gave religion and its values a respectful place in
American life.

I quoted Michael Novak: "Americans are starved for good conversations about important matters of the human spirit. In Victorian
England, religious devotion was not a forbidden topic of conversation. Sex was. In America, today, the inhibitions are reversed."
I talked that Sunday morning about the positive, progressive role

religion had played in American history, motivating those who were anti-slavery abolitionists in the nineteenth century, social welfare and human rights advocates in the early twentieth century, leaders of the civil rights movement in the 1950s and 1960s, and environmental protectors in our time.

The reaction of the Detroit congregation was over the top. I was thrilled . . . until I left the sanctuary and went to a holding room in the church where my campaign manager, Tom Nides, was waiting.

He looked pained, and he quickly shocked me with the reason why: "The speech you just gave was crazy. You can't do that again. You went much too far and got much too religious.

"I couldn't believe what I was hearing," Tom shouted at me.

I thought he was crazed, but instead of saying that, I quietly told him the speech I gave was what I believed. It was what I had been saying and writing for years and, I thought, one of the reasons Al Gore had asked me to be his running mate.

The next day, the Anti-Defamation League, an organization founded by Jewish Americans to combat anti-Semitism, criticized me: "Religion does not belong on the campaign trail." At the same time, the Catholic League said, "Senator Lieberman should be commended, not criticized, for discussing the public role of religion."

I remembered President Clinton's counsel to me on the day my selection was announced. And I also remembered a remarkable incident eight years earlier in 1992, when Bill Clinton was selecting his running mate. I was in the senators' restroom adjacent to the Senate chamber when Al Gore came in. The media were reporting that Gore was on Clinton's short list, so I said to Al what I truly felt: "I've been reading about the vice-presidential speculation and I hope you get it. I think you'd be fantastic."

"Thanks," Al said. "I want to tell you an interesting story. Warren Christopher came and talked to me as part of the vetting process, and at the end, he said, 'Is there anyone else you would recommend that we think about?' I want you to know that I suggested you."

I was surprised and honored. Then Al added, "I want you to know, Joe, that Chris asked me, 'Do you think voters in Tennessee would support an Orthodox Jew for vice president?' And I told him I didn't think it would be a problem because Tennesseans are very religious. They're mostly Baptists, and they will identify with someone who is religiously observant."

"Besides," he added, "the Old Testament is real to the people in Tennessee, so I think there will be a connection, because Joe lives through the Old Testament and so do they."

Al's words about the Baptists in Tennessee reminded me of Con O'Leary's words before my 1988 Senate election about the Roman Catholics in Connecticut. Both stories spoke to the broad respect for religious observance in American life, and to the growing affinity between religious Christians and Jews. I left Rev. Anthony's church in Detroit understanding that Tom Nides's outburst reflected thinking in parts of the Democratic Party—and probably in parts of the Nashville campaign headquarters—but not a majority of Americans.

As September began, we were in the lead. You could see the difference in the campaigns. Al Gore was impressive and seemingly indefatigable. Together, he and I campaigned for twenty-four hours straight on Labor Day, visiting varied sites and workers in several important states. We began on Sunday afternoon and didn't stop until Monday night. Governor Bush, on the other hand, seemed testy and off-balance. He made gaffes in his speeches and looked like he was trying to find excuses for not debating Al.

Then, as September was ending, Bush broke out of his daze and changed his favorite target from Bill Clinton to Al Gore. Instead of focusing on restoring honor and dignity to the White House after Clinton, the Republicans began to target Al Gore as a big-spending liberal and an "Old Democrat." And Bush said in speeches: "The vice president was seated right behind Bill Clinton at the State of the Union when the president declared, 'The era of big government is over!' Apparently, the message never took."

The Bush campaign thought they had found a vulnerability in the Democratic campaign. Earlier in the year, Nashville had decided to have Gore counter Bush's inexperience and vagueness on issues with a series of recommendations for new governmental programs. Now, Republicans were using all those programmatic pledges to portray Gore as a big-spending, big-taxing liberal. At the same time, the Republican campaign and Bush were moving to the center. He repeatedly described himself as a "compassionate conservative," not just a conservative. In effect, the Republicans were making the argument that Bush, not Gore, was the centrist in the race.

By the end of September, we had fallen behind in the polls again, and there was great anxiety in our campaign. In the meantime, I kept up a torrid campaign schedule (except on Saturdays) visiting two, three, or four states a day, drawing good crowds, getting good local press, and sometimes national press, and staying on Nashville's message of the day while adding my own New Democratic flourishes.

The Vice-Presidential Debate, the third big moment in a vice-presidential campaign, was scheduled for the evening of Thursday, October 5, at Centre College in Danville, Kentucky. In 1992 and 1996, Bill Clinton and Al Gore had set a new standard for debate preparation, and naturally I was expected to meet that standard. I had started more than a month before with big briefing books read on the plane between campaign stops and debate prep when time could be blocked out. On Sunday evening, October 1, with four days to go before the debate, I left the campaign trail for intensive pre-debate training. The campaign had rented an old mansion near Danville, and Hadassah and I moved into a motel nearby. My advisers and I agreed on my goals in the debate:

1. Remind voters of all the accomplishments of the Clinton-Gore years and make the argument that Al Gore and I were logically the best choice to continue the prosperity and progress;
2. Stress the commitment Al Gore and I had to traditional family and moral values; and
3. Defend against Cheney's attacks on Gore by describing Al's record and his independent-minded leadership.

A week before the debate, Al called me and asked how my preparation was going. I told him I was working hard to get ready and had a first-rate team to help me, thanks to him.

"You know what Cheney is going to focus on during the debate, don't you?" Al asked.

"What do you think?" I answered.

"Me," he said. "He's going to attack me. I hope you're ready."

Once again, a devilish impulse went rogue in my brain. "You mean at this big moment of my public life in a vice-presidential debate with millions of people watching, I have to spend all my time defending you?" A second of silence, and then a big Gore laugh.

"Yes," I said. "I will be ready to defend you from Cheney's attacks, and it won't be difficult."

But a funny thing happened on the way to the vice-presidential debate. On Tuesday evening, October 3, the first presidential debate occurred. I thought Al was very impressive and much better prepared than Bush. But the media focused on the fact that Al sighed audibly during a few of Bush's answers and seemed condescending to his opponent. The next day, Bush's campaign began running an ad called "Trust" which portrayed Bush as a man who keeps his word and Gore as a man who does not. The basis of this attack was minor misstatements Gore had made in the debate. The rule of expectations was at work. The media had low expectations of Governor Bush, and so—because he didn't make a major mistake in that debate—they heralded his performance. On the other hand, they and the Republicans were holding Al to very high standards. Small discrepancies and personal mannerisms, like sighing, were seen as major flaws.

The next day, the "A" team of Nashville consultants flew into Kentucky to work with me on my final debate preparation. Two of them were old friends—Stan Greenberg and Carter Eskew. And two I knew, but not well—Bob Shrum and Tad Devine. They brought a surprising message. In overnight polling, it was clear that the public thought the presidential debate had been too contentious and personal. They advised me to put away all the plans we had to attack George Bush's record in Texas and Dick Cheney's right-wing votes in Congress. They urged me to be positive, but to be ready to rise to the defense when and if Cheney attacked Gore.

"So, I shouldn't bring up any of those awful votes Cheney cast while in Congress?" I asked. "Please don't," they said.

After the campaign, I read that Dick Cheney received the same advice from Matthew Dowd, the Bush campaign pollster: "What about Gore's lack of credibility?" Cheney apparently asked. "I wouldn't go personal," Dowd advised.

So, Dick Cheney and I were liberated by public opinion about the first presidential debate to have a great debate of our own in which we disagreed on most questions, but in a civil, mutually respectful way.

I accomplished everything I hoped to that evening, and I would guess the same was true of Cheney. It was a win-win. The media reaction was very positive. The *Washington Post* called the debate "serious, well-informed, substantive, and grown-up." The *New York Times* wrote: "What viewers did see was both the seriousness and dry wit that define both men." And, most important to me, Al and Tipper called right after the debate and cheered over the phone: "You did just great; you did everything I could have wanted. I couldn't have been prouder of you."

So, I had finished the three vice-presidential national spotlight moments—the announcement, the convention acceptance speech, and the debate. There was a month left until Election Day, and we were not where we wanted to be in the polls. It was time to step back and reflect on how I could best help our ticket in the time remaining.

At the end of every week, Tom Nides would brief me on the latest campaign polling, usually on board our plane. We were still doing well on specific issues like health care, prescription drug costs, the environment, and education, but we were doing badly on defense and values. It was clear the Republicans were making progress at portraying Al as a big-spending liberal. The head-to-head polling had us behind, one poll by double digits, but most by three to five points.

In conversations with Tom Nides and Al From, who had come on board my campaign plane for the last month, we decided to refocus. Al, Paul Orzulak, and I redrafted my standard stump speech. We had three goals for the last month.

Our first was to undercut the Republican attack on Al as a big-spending liberal, which was coming from Bush and Cheney as well as an expensive Republican ad buy in seventeen important states that accused Al Gore of "proposing three times the new spending President Clinton proposed." I would base my response for Al on the Clinton-Gore record. America had the smallest government in forty years, a federal government surplus, and welfare rolls that had been cut in half. Al Gore and I would continue that record of fiscal responsibility and good government management.

Second, the polls showed how strongly voters felt that America had "lost its moral bearings" and trusted Bush more than Al to get us back on the right track. That was infuriating to me because I knew Al as a man of the highest honor and best values. I appealed to Tom Nides, Carter Eskew, and Stan Greenberg:

> This election is still so close in spite of the fact that we are
> so far behind on values. Let's do some television ads that
> remind people of Al's character and stress the commitment
> that he and I have to family values.

Tom, Carter, and Stan convinced the campaign to make such a commercial. I thought it was brilliant. I knew it would help. But the campaign never ran it. When I asked why, I was told that the focus group netted good reactions to the values message, but not as good as other ads on single issues. I still think that was a big mistake. Sometimes you can run ahead in polls on particular issues, but still fall behind on the overall concerns—the mega issues—that decide how people vote.

I was disappointed but resolved to do everything I could to make the case for Al Gore and me on values. In every stump speech and television interview I could squeeze it into, I spoke of the New Democratic values of opportunity, responsibility, and community, and of Al Gore's personal faith and values. I did so as someone who had worked with him and known him well for fifteen years. I also accepted an invitation from Notre Dame University, the great Catholic university in South Bend, Indiana, to give a speech on the important role of faith in America's public square. It embraced the same themes that I spoke of in my National Prayer Breakfast and Detroit church speeches. Now, I related those themes to the election:

> Vice President Gore and I want to bring truth to power. The truth of faith and the power of values that flow from it. We cannot cure our moral ailments from Washington. This we know. But we can exert leadership from our public pulpit and exhort the American people to realize their best ideals in their lives and in the life of the American community.

The speech received surprisingly good national media coverage. This time, unlike my church speech in Detroit, Tom Nides watched on television in Nashville and called right after to say, "Beautiful job, Senator." Not even the Anti-Defamation League had a negative word to say this time.

The third big policy challenge I took on in the fall of 2000—the economy—should never have been an issue in doubt because the Clinton-Gore record was so extraordinary: twenty-two million new jobs in eight years, four million new businesses. It was arguably the strongest economy in American history. And Al Gore and I knew a lot better than our Republican opponents how to keep it growing. In my speeches, I would add that "Al Gore and I know that government didn't create the prosperity, the American people did. Government shouldn't get in the way of what the private sector does best. But there are things that we can do to expand opportunity, but not expand the government." And then I would quote my law school classmate and friend, the late Senator Paul Tsongas, who often said: "You can't be pro-jobs and anti-business, because its business that creates most of the jobs."

Meanwhile, our national campaign was reverting to the populist "people vs. the powerful" rhetoric. The campaign management did this because the race was very close, we were still behind, and they worried that Ralph Nader's third-party populist candidacy could take enough votes from us to elect Bush and Cheney. I believe they misread America's voters. Ours is a country where people want government to protect them from businesses that are unfair to them or break laws. But most Americans are not anti-business, and they are rarely against people who have made their way to the top of the economic ladder. Most people want to earn their way up that ladder themselves.

Jacob Weisberg later wrote about this turn in the campaign: "Notwithstanding a successful centrist presidency and the best economy in memory, Gore adopted an angry populism as the tone of his campaign." Then he quoted Michael Kinsley's characterization of this message as: "You've never had it so good and I'm mad as hell about it."

One early morning during the campaign, I had breakfast with a group of firefighters in Florida, all members of the International Association of Firefighters (IAFF) union. The delicious meal was prepared by a couple of the firefighters in their kitchen. When I asked them what they talk about on a typical morning, they responded, "the stock market."

Those firefighters and millions of other working Americans don't think of an America in which the people are arrayed against the powerful. They want to own a piece of the pie, and a lot of them do. I worried that the populist, "us against them" rhetoric that had grown louder in our campaign during October missed that reality about working, middle-class American families. So, I spoke for and to them. I felt that I was closing strong, wrapping the campaign's goals in centrist principles and vocabulary. I had promised to do the best I could to get Al Gore elected president, and in October 2000, I felt I was keeping that promise.

I was in Miami, Florida, for the last Sabbath of the campaign. I knew I needed all the prayer and rest I could get. Our internal polling showed us continuing to gain on Bush. We were only a couple of points behind. That was within the margin of error. It was effectively a dead heat, but momentum seemed to be on our side. The Democratic base was fired up. Independents and moderates seemed increasingly concerned that Bush was not the "compassionate conservative" he claimed to be. His poor record on health care and the environment as governor of Texas was bothering unaffiliated voters.

As soon as Sabbath ended on Saturday night, I went to Little Havana in Miami for a campaign event and had a cup of strong Cuban coffee, which gave me a great start on an around-the-country, three-day campaign swing, during which I got a total of six hours of sleep. The tour went west, north, east, and south back to Tampa, Florida, early Tuesday morning, Election Day, for one more cup of Cuban coffee, a sunrise rally, and national television shows with Al Gore.

Then I flew to New Haven to vote and back to Nashville to get some rest before the returns came in. But when I landed in Nashville, our campaign chairman, Bill Daley, called and said the race was still too close to allow me time to rest. I needed to go straight to headquarters to do live radio and television interviews with stations in secondary markets in competitive states. One was with a radio station in Palm Beach, Florida, whose host told me her listeners had been calling to say they worried they had been confused by the ballot and might have voted for Pat Buchanan instead of Al Gore and me. That was the beginning of the thirty-six-day saga of highs and lows that ended on December 12, with a terrible US Supreme Court decision in the case of *Bush v. Gore*. Al Gore and I lost the 2000 election by a vote of 5–4.

We had won the popular vote by more than 544,000 votes.

Al conceded from the vice president's office in an eloquent and gracious speech on the evening of December 13. It was one of his best ever. Early the next morning, I went right into my Senate office, which was my characteristic reaction to defeat and disappointment. Shortly after I arrived, Bob Dole called me. "Good morning, Joe. I am calling to offer you membership in a very exclusive club," he said. "Only people who have lost national elections can join. Congratulations. You now qualify. And, incidentally, I'm the leader of the club because I've lost more national elections than anybody else."

What a great way to begin the morning after. It made me laugh and was also reassuring because after his defeats, Bob Dole continued to be a productive public servant. Bob finished the call with these kind words: "Joe, you've got a lot to be proud of and you're back in the Senate. You were so wise to run again."

A short while later, I walked over to the Senate floor to give my personal concession speech. I began with congratulations for Governor Bush and Secretary Cheney and an appeal for unity based on shared values:

> Whether you are happy or sad with the results of the 2000 election, I do think every one of us should be grateful this morning that here in America, we work out our differences not with civil wars but with spirited elections. We resolve our disputes not through acts of violence but through the rule of law. We preserve and protect our system of justice best when we accept its judgments that we disagree with most.

For that, Al Gore deserves more credit than he has ever received. On Tuesday night, December 12, Al called me at home to tell me the United States Supreme Court had just ruled against us but had left open a door for us to go back to the Florida Supreme Court and ask for a statewide recount. Did I think we should? My answer:

> Of course, I am hurt and angered by the Supreme Court decision but I haven't read it, so you have to allow for that in my answer to your question. As a former state attorney general, who has always believed that if you have a plausible legal argument you should make it and let the courts decide, my reflexive response is that we should go back to the Florida Supreme Court. There is a lot on the line for our country in the outcome of this election, and the Supreme Court has apparently said we have a right to go back to the Florida court, so I think we should.

Al said he would think about it, and called me back about an hour later. "Joe, I have decided to end this. We are a little more than a month from inauguration of the next president. An appeal and recount in Florida would probably take that long if not longer, and would result in a Constitutional crisis and serious questions about continuity of our government. This decision is difficult for me and I know it is for you, but I believe it is right and best for our country."

I had counseled him otherwise, but Al Gore's decision *was* the right one for our country.

When people ask me how I feel about the 2000 campaign, I often joke: "I loved every minute of it . . . until election night." That is the truth. It was a wonderful experience. I saw the American people from coast to coast, and I loved what I saw. They could not have been more welcoming and accepting to Hadassah and me. My religion was the focus of public attention when Al Gore chose me, because it was a "first," but it was hardly mentioned at the end of the campaign—which is just the way we hoped it would be. The bigotry some feared never materialized. We faced no anti-Semitism. That justified the confidence in the American people that gave Al Gore the courage to break that barrier and open the door wider for every other American. That may be one of the most lasting, positive effects of the Gore-Lieberman 2000 campaign.

During the campaign, I had moments of disagreement with some of the strategic and policy choices the team was making. And they caused me to worry that the Democratic Party was moving away from the centrism of the very successful Clinton-Gore years. But the reality is that Al Gore and I got 544,000 more votes than George Bush and Dick Cheney, more total votes than any Democratic ticket in American history and more than any ticket of any party except the Reagan-Bush ticket in 1984 up to that year. And the votes, as my Connecticut mentor John Bailey would say, are what counts, or should.

On our twenty-four-hour tour of America on Labor Day 2000, I stopped in a minor-league ballpark in Pennsylvania. A man told me he had given Bill Clinton a lucky Irish coin during the 1992 campaign and told him that if he carried it with him every day, it would bring him to victory. Now he was going to give me another lucky Irish coin with the same instructions and prediction. Of course, I carried it every day for the rest of the campaign.

I told this story to Bill Daley after the US Supreme Court decision, and asked him—as an Irish American—why he thought it didn't work.

"It did work," Bill said. "You and Al got the most votes. The problem was nobody told the coin it also had to carry the Electoral College."

LESSONS FOR CENTRISTS

1. A political campaign is a campaign is a campaign. A national political campaign is bigger than a state or local campaign—but not that different. In all campaigns, your goals are to convince more people to vote for you than your opponent(s) and then to do your best to make sure the voters who prefer you actually vote. You have to raise money to pay for media which can help you achieve both of those goals. And you have to be effective at conveying your message in so-called "free media."

2. In my very first campaign for the Connecticut State Senate in 1970, I learned that you can't be both the candidate and the campaign manager, even though that is the instinct of most candidates. There is just too much to do. The relatively limited scope of a state campaign, however, allows the candidate to be involved in many campaign decisions—but hopefully not too many.

    In the 2000 national campaign, the scope was enormous. There were too many states to visit, too many media stops and calls to make, too many fundraisers for the Democratic National Committee to attend. For me, the 2000 campaign was the one where I applied the lesson I had learned thirty years before in my first state senate campaign. I spent almost all my time campaigning and almost none managing. That was smart, even though it was also frustrating for me because I brought a lot of political experience. I tried a few times to alter some aspect of policy or politics in the campaign, but it wasn't easy for two reasons, I think:

a. The big value I could add to the campaign was as candidate and that alone was a sixteen-to-twenty-hour-a-day job.

b. The vice-presidential candidate arrives after the presidential campaign has been going for months or years. It is like arriving at a party when it is almost over. Relations have already been formed. Al Gore was, of course, there from the beginning, but he too was mostly and wisely the candidate, not the campaign manager.

This lesson about not trying to be the candidate and manager of a political campaign will probably be more helpful to candidates for state and local political offices. For that small group of Americans who is fortunate to be nominated to run for president or vice president, I urge you to try harder than I was able to in 2000 to shoulder your way into strategic campaign decisions. But not too often.

3. I cannot and should not resist sharing one other lesson learned in the 2000 campaign.

We need a constitutional amendment repealing the Electoral College. It is undemocratic and unfair. In the greatest democracy in the world, a majority of the voters should decide who their president and vice president will be, just as a majority of voters decides who will fill about every other elected government position in our country.

4. The difference in the way Al Gore and Donald Trump handled their respective post-election grievances in 2000 and 2020 is stark, instructive, and deeply relevant to centrist ideals.

In 2000, the conflict over the outcome was limited to one state, Florida, where the votes in controversy between the Democratic and Republican tickets—votes that would determine which candidate would have the Sunshine State's electoral votes—were always less than 1,000. In 2020, President Trump objected to results in several states where the cumulative vote difference was much larger. He acted to have the outcome overturned in fifty different lawsuits in courts all over America. That was his right, but none succeeded. In 2000, the litigation was all in Florida where Al Gore and I ultimately prevailed in the State Supreme Court. Then the case was surprisingly taken up the by the US Supreme Court, where we were defeated. Throughout the post-election litigation, Trump refused to accept the judgments of the courts, which was not his right in our rule-of-law country. He kept saying he had won by a landslide, which had been taken away from him by fraud.

Gore and I knew it was close in Florida, but we were confident we had won and that the courts would agree. When the US Supreme Court ruled against us, we and millions of our supporters felt aggrieved and angry, but Gore decided "for the sake of our unity as a people and the strength of our democracy" to concede. He understood that we are a country that abides by the rule of law, and we had lost in our country's highest court of law. Even though its decision seemed profoundly unjust to us, we were honor bound to accept it.

Trump, on the other hand, refused to respect the Constitutional order or the decisions of the courts of law that had ruled against him. He continued to declare that he had been cheated out of a landslide election victory by corrupt state and local election officials of both political parties, and that their corruption had been upheld by federal judges appointed by presidents of both political parties (including Trump himself). He went beyond disrespecting and demeaning the electoral process ordained by our Constitution and the rule of law— and he called on his supporters to come to Washington on the day the electoral votes from the states were finally to be counted in Congress for a protest rally that his political committees paid for and he addressed. He urged his supporters to march on the US Capitol, where they committed the most violent attack by Americans on our government and Constitution in our nation's history.

The centrist ideal that is the theme of this book is based on a foundational belief that the national interest is more important than partisan or personal interest. That is why centrists in both political parties understand that the perfect cannot be allowed to be the enemy of the good, and so they compromise to serve the common good. Leaders who put their partisan or personal interests first do not believe in that centrist ideal. They serve their personal interests first, not the interests of the nation and its values.

In all of American history, there is not a more flagrant and destructive abuse of putting country ahead of personal interest by an elected national leader than the reckless behavior of President Donald Trump in 2020.

I hope and pray that America will never again experience anything like it.

9

BIPARTISAN CENTRISM UNDER BUSH 43

In 2001, the presidential inauguration fell on a Saturday, our Sabbath. Despite our feelings about how the election of 2000 ended, Hadassah and I knew we had a responsibility to be there, just as Al and Tipper Gore would. We lived four and a half miles from the Capitol, and I do not drive or ride in a car on Friday night or Saturday in order to protect the day as a Sabbath of prayer, rest, and reflection. There are exceptions to this prohibition if, for example, driving or riding is necessary to protect public or personal health and safety, or the well-being of the community. But we didn't think attending an inauguration qualified, so we made reservations to spend the Sabbath at the Phoenix Park Hotel on Capitol Hill, an easy walk to the inauguration on Saturday morning.

When we checked into the hotel on Friday afternoon, we realized we had overlooked something obvious. The hotel was packed with Bush-Cheney revelers, having a great time and making a lot of noise. We didn't belong there, so we packed up, checked out, returned home, and asked our neighbors and dear friends, Shelly and

Mindy Weisel, if they had room for two more for Sabbath dinner. We said we would bring wine.

The next morning, we made the long walk from home to the Capitol with a Capitol Police detail. It was a cold but clear day. Across from the White House, we passed St. John's Episcopal Church where the Bushes and Cheneys were attending the traditional Inauguration Day services. Hadassah and I smiled because we knew that if Al and I had been able to take office, that would have been an interfaith service. As we came close to the Capitol, we heard the thunderous sound of thousands of protesters. They turned out to be ours. When they saw Hadassah and me walking by on the street, they were very surprised and began to cheer and chant our names. It was definitely therapeutic and much appreciated.

Our police detail finally found a way through the crowds to get us into the Capitol. The Senators had already taken their seats on the platform, but the ceremony had not yet started. Hadassah and I walked alone down the red-carpeted ramp, stopping along the way to say hello to friends, including General Colin Powell, who was about to become Secretary of State. With that big Powell smile, he looked at his watch and said, "Why is it that you couldn't get here on time on this important morning, Senator Lieberman?"

"I'm surprised to hear that question," I responded, "from a guy who grew up in the Bronx with a lot of religious Jewish neighbors."

Colin made a quick recovery: "Of course, of course. Forgive me. Good Shabbos, Senator and Mrs. Lieberman. And thank you for making a special effort to be here on Shabbos."

We laughed and thanked him.

After the ceremony, Hadassah and I stopped for a coffee at a gathering in the Capitol, hosted by the Democratic Senate Leader Tom Daschle. As we left Daschle's office, President George W. Bush was coming down the hall toward us. I had not met him before that chance meeting. He was coming from the President's Room, a beautiful and ornate space a few steps from the Senate Chamber where presidents since Lincoln have come to sign important legislation and every newly inaugurated president since Reagan has gone to sign formal documents. I extended my hand and said,

"Congratulations, Mr. President." He thanked me and said, "Congratulations to you, Senator. You ran a great campaign. You're the one who made it as close as it was."

"Thanks," I responded, "but I am sure it was more than me. Anyway, that's history now. Hadassah and I will be praying for you and Mrs. Bush. We wish you well and will help if we can."

He thanked me and, with a characteristic Bush half smile, said, "I bet we can find some ways to work together." Just a few days later, the White House called to say that on Monday, January 29, the president would be going to the largely African American Anacostia neighborhood in Washington to announce his program for making more faith-based organizations eligible for federally funded social programs, a goal that they knew I shared. I had worked on a similar initiative, also supported by Al Gore, in the Senate. In fact, the Welfare Reform Bill of 1996, sponsored by Clinton and Gore, had a "Charitable Choice" provision Bush had used as Texas governor to allow faith-based organizations to compete for money from federal block grants to the state.

I knew that some Democrats would be upset to see me in public with President Bush so soon after the election, but the president and I agreed on this policy and it would not be right to say no just for partisan political reasons. On the morning of January 29, I rode in the presidential limousine with President Bush and my Republican colleague and friend, Senator Rick Santorum of Pennsylvania, to the Fishing School, a faith-based afterschool mentoring program in Anacostia, DC.

Bush was relaxed and conversational on the way over. He had graduated from Yale four years after I had, and we talked about some friends we had in common. When I asked him if he had been back to the Yale campus recently, he said he had not been back for years because of the way they treated his father. I was puzzled.

"What did they do to him?"

He said that once when his father was president and spoke at Yale, the students booed him. In the year after our conversation that morning, Rick Levin, president of Yale, mended fences between President Bush 43 and his alma mater, and Bush's daughter, Barbara, went to Yale. That little exchange we had in the car showed me how deeply the Bush family valued loyalty to one another. I admired it.

At the Fishing School, the president announced he had issued two executive orders. The White House had briefed us before the event, and I agreed with them both. One created a new White House Office of Faith Based and Community Initiatives to promote cooperation between religious and social service organizations and federal government programs. The other directed five cabinet departments to establish similar offices within their departments.

Bush had these words for strict church-state separationists whose opposition he anticipated:

> Government, of course, cannot fund and will not fund religious activities. But, when people of faith provide social services, we will not discriminate against them.

The president also announced that he was sending a set of proposals to Congress to create new tax deductions for contributions to charitable organizations and new federal grants for those organizations which could be worth $24 billion over ten years.

Rick Santorum and I agreed to cosponsor legislation that would enact the new tax credits and authorize the new funding. In 2001, the House had a Republican majority and the Senate was split 50–50, but Vice President Cheney made it a Republican Senate. Some people in the White House and in the media saw this initiative as a way for Bush to show he really was a compassionate conservative. Others speculated that he chose this faith-based proposal as his first domestic policy initiative because he and Al Gore had supported it in the campaign. Therefore, the White House thought, the odds were that it would be enacted with bipartisan support.

It wasn't. The White House learned that they were not in Texas anymore, where Governor Bush often had bipartisan support for his programs. In Washington, it would be harder to build the necessary coalitions in the political center and they couldn't make another mistake like this one. President Bush stressed there would be limits and qualifications in the proposed legislation to guarantee it would not violate the Constitutional separation of church and state, but it struck a nerve with separationists, civil libertarians, some liberals, and partisan Democrats who did not want the new Republican president to succeed on his first legislative initiative.

In the summer of 2001, two things doomed the faith-based initiative. Senator Jim Jeffords left the Republican Party that June and joined the Democratic caucus, giving Democrats a majority, 51–49. In July, the *Washington Post* reported that someone in the White House had promised the Salvation Army that the administration would exempt faith-based organizations that accepted federal funding from laws protecting people from discrimination based on their sexual orientation. All hell broke loose. The White House quickly promised that there would be no such exemption, but the damage had been done. To make it worse, the Republican-controlled House rushed ahead to pass a hardline, faith-based initiative bill which was very different from the one Santorum and I introduced in the Senate.

The lines of suspicion and division were hardening, making the president's proposal unacceptable in the now Democratic Senate. I worked with the administration on a compromise that greatly reduced the tax incentives for contributions to faith-based charities in the original bill and promised "equal treatment" for religious organizations in the awarding of federal social service funds. The president endorsed the compromise in an Oval Office event on February 7, 2002, with Santorum, a few other senators, and me in attendance. We worked on that compromise for the rest of 2002, but could never get enough votes to pass even a watered-down version in the Senate.

In the November 2002 elections, Republicans won back a majority of seats in the Senate, but the White House, Senator Santorum, and I agreed there still wasn't enough support to pass our legislation. So, we introduced a third version of the bill that passed both chambers and was signed by the president in April 2003. It provided new tax incentives for contributions to charitable organizations without any reference to religious groups.

When Democrats and some in the media chided President Bush and his team for making mistakes that led to the failure of their first legislative proposal, the administration's response was that funding had been increased for faith-based social programs under existing law and that the president had made some changes in regulation which helped those organizations. But it was not the legislative success President Bush (and I) had hoped for.

However, Congress did pass and Bush signed two other major domestic policy proposals in the first two years of his presidency: first, a big tax cut enacted in the spring of 2001, which I voted against because I thought it was an unfair budget buster; and second, comprehensive education reform called "No Child Left Behind," which I strongly and actively supported. It was the most significant bipartisan, centrist domestic legislation introduced by President Bush that passed during the eight years of his presidency.

It was also a great personal experience, because I worked closely with Ted Kennedy, who was the "Master of the Senate" during my time there. An unabashed liberal Democrat, Kennedy nevertheless had a great record of working productively across party lines and with his committee's conservative Republicans like Orrin Hatch, Mike Enzi, or, in the case of the No Child Left Behind legislation, Judd Gregg of New Hampshire. Kennedy had a wonderful personality topped by an explosive laugh that filled not only the room he was in, but the corridors outside. He was ideological, but when he wanted to get something done, he could be very pragmatic.

I called his method the Kennedy Strategy. In negotiating a major piece of legislation, Ted would suggest to leading Republicans on his committee that together they make a list of all the issues involved in that bill and divide them into three categories: 1) those that they agreed on and could pass; 2) those they could never agree on so they would just take them off the table; and 3) those that both sides believed they might be able to negotiate to a compromise agreement. They would concentrate on that third group. In a remarkable number of cases, the Kennedy Strategy worked to produce constructive compromises, solve problems, and enact important legislation with bipartisan support.

That's why I believe that although Ted Kennedy was definitely a very liberal Democrat, he was also a very effective centrist senator when he chose to be. He came to the center and brought others from both parties with him to get good things done.

He did exactly that on the No Child Left Behind Act in 2001, with President Bush and New Democrats like me. We had overlapping goals. Kennedy wanted to reauthorize the Elementary and Secondary Education Act and increase funding for public schools. President Bush wanted to refocus federal education programs on outcomes by testing students as he had done in Texas. Bush also wanted to help low-income children in failing public schools go to private or faith-based schools.

My interest in public education reform went back to the 1970s when I was a state senator and fought for more funding for the schools in my district, only to find that too many low-income students, usually African Americans and Hispanic Americans, were falling behind and dropping out of school at alarming rates. They were not receiving the equal education they had a right to. There was a focus on how much money I and others could bring back to the schools in New Haven and West Haven, but very little attention to the output. Were the children getting a good education? The answer clearly was no, so I changed my approach. I continued to fight for more money for the schools, but insisted on accountability for the quality of education the children got for the money we were investing.

When I reached the Senate in 1989, I joined with my Republican colleague, Senator David Durenberger of Minnesota, to cosponsor the first federal legislation supporting charter schools, which are quasi private schools that receive a charter and support from the local public school system. That charter is renewed or terminated based on testing of the students in the school to see if they are learning.

One day in 1995, I visited the Catholic Schools of Bridgeport, Connecticut, at the invitation of Archbishop Edward Egan, who was later elevated to cardinal in New York. I was impressed by how well those schools were educating low-income minority children, most of whom were not Catholic. But they were constantly in financial trouble. I returned to Washington and joined with my Republican colleague Dan Coats of Indiana to sponsor legislation to award scholarships to low-income children to enable them to attend private and faith-based schools. It was a way to help parents who, if they had the money, would take their children out of failing public schools and put them into better private or faith-based schools, just as wealthier parents do all the time.

Unfortunately, I was never able to convince more than a handful of Democratic senators to vote for the amendments Dan Coats and I introduced. Public-school unions, particularly the powerful teachers' unions, opposed allowing any money to go outside the traditional public-school framework. To me, helping these poor children get a better education was the kind of anti-poverty and civil rights reform Democrats should have supported. When Al Gore asked me to be his running mate in 2000, my backing of school choice pilot programs was the reason why the teachers' unions were unhappy.

Early in 2000, I worked with the DLC and Senator Evan Bayh to develop and introduce education reform legislation. We got only a few votes in the Senate but a lot of thoughtful and respectful consideration. The goal of our proposal was to invest in reform and insist on results. "We want to give states and local districts the resources they need (and) . . . we want to hold them accountable for better educating our children," Evan and I had said in 2000. When we introduced it for the second time in January 2001, we hoped it could be a bridge builder, because it "brought together the best ideas of both parties to form a new approach to federal education policy, one that refocuses our resources and our resolve to raise academic achievement." We added, "It is simply unacceptable that twelfth-grade Black and Hispanic students read and do math on average at the same level as eighth-grade white students."

Our hopeful conclusion was that "President Bush has articulated a set of priorities that overlap significantly with our New Democratic proposal," and there was "a lot of room for collaboration: with

Senator Kennedy." From the beginning, the outline of a potential agreement was clear—more federal money for education for Kennedy and New Democrats, and more accountability through testing for Bush and us New Democrats. But there was a lot of work to be done to get there.

I was impressed by how personally committed to education reform President Bush was. He also had a lot of work to do to convince Republicans in Congress to support a larger financial and educational role for the federal government in local public schools than they wanted. In fact, at the Republican National Convention in 2000, some Republicans had tried to put a plank in the platform that called for the abolition of the US Department of Education. The Bush campaign rushed in and stopped it. But some of those Republicans were in Congress.

On our side, we'd have to convince Democrats to accept testing of students, which might put pressure on ineffective teachers and was opposed by the teachers' unions.

Sandy Kress, a lawyer who had been chairman of the Dallas School Board and Governor Bush's adviser on education, was drafted by the president to come to Washington to work on educational reform. President Bush enjoyed pointing out to Kennedy, Bayh, and me that Kress was a Democrat and a member of the DLC. Kress played an important part in the passage of "No Child Left Behind," building rapport with all involved, strategizing, negotiating, and offering and accepting compromises. He also helped see to it that the bill did not get hijacked by Republicans on the Right or Democrats on the Left, the way the president's faith-based initiative was.

The main negotiations were between:

- Kress for the Bush administration;
- Kennedy and Gregg for the Senate;
- John Boehner of Ohio—the Republican chair—and George Miller of California—ranking Democrat on the House Education Committee—for the House; and
- Evan Bayh and me for the DLC Democrats.

Most often, we would meet in Kennedy's "Hideaway," a big room on the top floor of the Senate side of the Capitol with plenty of comfortable chairs, Kennedy family pictures on the walls, and a beautiful view of the National Mall out the window. As a bonus, Kennedy would often be accompanied by his friendly and some-times noisy Portuguese Water Dog, Splash. When one of us became excited and raised our voice, Splash would bark loudly. Kennedy's response to this canine violation of Senate decorum was grandly apologetic and clearly delighted.

The president made the first big compromise in the negotiations. Although he had recommended a private-school choice option in his bill, he believed that would probably kill overall educational reform. I had supported private-school choice for low-income children, but I also agreed to put it off for another day. Evan Bayh and I had a compromise in our bill called "public school choice." It would allow parents to move their children from a public school that was judged to be failing into another better public school. It was eventually accepted by all concerned and was in the final bill.

In the Senate and the House, there were lengthy, complicated debates about how the testing of students would work and what the response would be if the tests did not show that students were making "AYP"—Adequate Yearly Progress. Another contentious issue was whether to aggregate the test results or disaggregate them according to the income, race, or ethnicity of the students. We in the DLC fought hard for disaggregation alongside the Bush admin-istration, because we believed that separate data was necessary if we were going to achieve our main goal of closing education gaps between rich and poor children. The proposed bill also said that every child must have "highly qualified teachers," and there was naturally much debate about how to define that term and enforce it.

Kennedy continued to focus on more funding for education. In the end, he got much more—from $42.2 billion in fiscal year (FY) 2001 to $55.7 billion in FY 2004. Funding that gave special support to students with disabilities was raised from $6.3 billion in FY 2001 to $10.1 billion in FY 2004. President Bush and we New Democrats were successful in requiring that every public school in

America receiving federal funds had to administer standardized tests every year to all students, and if AYP was not achieved, specific remedies, options for parents, and ultimately the closing of failing schools were imposed.

When the bill reached the Senate floor, all of us who supported the bipartisan proposal promised to oppose all amendments, even if we would normally have voted for one of them. This was similar to the promises made on other controversial bipartisan agreements (such as the Clean Air Act of 1990) in which the participants all accepted less than they wanted in order to get something done. If they were free to vote for amendments embracing their "perfect" desires on the Senate floor, the agreement would disintegrate and no good would be done. The promises were kept and, on June 14, the bill passed the Senate with overwhelming bipartisan support, 91–8.

In the House, John Boehner was the new chair of the Education Committee. He was a proud and grateful graduate of a Catholic school in Ohio and a strong supporter of school choice programs, but his first priority on education reform in 2001 was to secure a victory for the new Republican president. He calculated that about forty Republican House members would only support the testing Bush wanted if vouchers stayed in the bill, but he also knew that most Democrats wouldn't support the bill if vouchers were in. So, to help his president, Boehner took the vouchers out and worked with George Miller to get the Democratic votes he needed.

On the House floor, a Republican attempt to put vouchers back in was defeated by a strong bipartisan vote. Another amendment—this one strangely bipartisan—was offered by liberal Democrats and conservative Republicans to remove testing of students. Again, the center held, and that amendment was defeated. The bill passed the House overwhelmingly, 384–45.

Now, the House and Senate bills had to go to conference to create one bill to send to the president. I was very happy to be appointed to that Conference Committee. I was not on the Education Committee, which meant that my appointment had to be "cleared" by Ted Kennedy before it was made by Tom Daschle. Our staffs estimated that there were 2,750 differences between the

House and Senate bills, but the two were very similar on the big issues of accountability and funding. Throughout the summer of 2001, the Conference Committee members and our staff met daily to resolve differences and respond to interest groups who wanted to add to or subtract from the bill—or to kill it. By early September, many of the issues in contention had been resolved, but some big ones remained.

Then, on September 11, America was attacked by terrorists. Ten days later, the president invited the education bill conferees to the White House and appealed to us to finish our work on No Child Left Behind. He said that after the attacks of 9/11, it would mean a lot to the country if we could work across partisan lines to pass a bill that would improve educational opportunity for all of America's children.

A lot happened that fall, including the beginning of war in Afghanistan and anthrax attacks on Senate offices. But the differences on education reform were resolved and the Conference Report was passed during December in both chambers, 87–10 in the Senate and 381–41 in the House. President Bush signed it on January 8, 2002. It was the biggest reform in the federal government's role in our nation's schools since the Elementary and Secondary Education Act was enacted in 1965. It was also a textbook case of how government can and should work for the benefit of our country. The president and Congress, Republicans and Democrats, had ideas they shared on education reform, but there were also some we did not share. We came to the center and negotiated and compromised to enact the bill. As a result, many more of America's children have received an equal education than before. It is also true that there is still a lot more work to be done to achieve universal equal educational opportunity.

The story of how No Child Left Behind was enacted in 2001 is the best guide to how to finish the job.

LESSONS FOR CENTRISTS

1. The failure of President Bush to enact his faith-based initiative taught him and his White House staff a lot about legislating in Washington. It is a partisan place, and it was particularly so after the disputed ending of the 2000 election. Most Democrats would only endorse Bush administration proposals that clearly agreed with positions they already supported. Faith-based legislation was just not a priority for most Democrats in Congress. Either the White House would have to work hard to give Democrats a reason to support the president's proposals, or face defeat. They never came up with a persuasive reason. The Bush administration also made some avoidable mistakes, most notably when someone in the White House seemed to assure a religious organization that it could receive funding under the president's proposal while continuing to discriminate based on sexual orientation. That might have been the result of the early Bush White House still being disorganized but, whatever the reason, it was the end of any chance to adopt the president's proposal.

2. President Bush and his team applied those faith-based legislation lessons they learned in proposing and enacting the No Child Left Behind (NCLB) Act. First, they brought a Democrat, Sandy Kress, up from Texas to work full-time on educational reform legislation—mediating disputes, finding common ground, facilitating compromises, and avoiding self-inflicted setbacks.

    Second, they engaged with Ted Kennedy, the leading Democrat on education, and with Evan Bayh and me, because we had introduced a New Democratic Education Reform proposal. Like the Bush White House legislation, ours was focused on imposing accountability on American education by requiring regular testing of students in schools receiving federal aid to determine whether that aid was working to educate students.

Kennedy's priority was different but not inconsistent with the priorities the Bush administration and we New Democrats had. Teddy wanted to increase funding for public schools.

The compromises necessary to enact a bill were clear. Bush would have to accept the higher funding levels Kennedy wanted and drop private-school choice, which many conservative Republicans strongly supported. Kennedy would have to accept testing of students, which the teachers' unions opposed. Bayh and I thought that was a constructive compromise and offered our proposal for public-school choice to sweeten the agreement. That is how the most significant reform of American education in four decades was enacted by bipartisan majorities at an increasingly partisan time.

3. You don't have to be a moderate to be a centrist. Kennedy was one of the most liberal Democratic members of Congress. Bush was a conservative Republican, albeit one who had added the adjective "compassionate" before "conservative." They both wanted to adopt an education bill, so they (and we from the DLC) met in the center to talk, negotiate, compromise, and enact a law that achieved a large percentage of the objectives we all had, and, most important, improved the educational opportunities of millions of America's low-income children.

10

UNITING IN THE CENTER
AFTER 9/11/01

hree days after the terrorist attacks against America on 9/11/2001, President Bush traveled to New York City to visit Ground Zero and meet with families of some of the victims. He kindly asked the senators from New York, Connecticut, and New Jersey to travel there with him on Air Force One. When we arrived at the World Trade Center site, where I had been several times before the attacks, I was disoriented. I couldn't place myself in the context of what I had seen there in the past. It was like the war zones I had visited in Kuwait, Bosnia, Kosovo, and Afghanistan. But this was New York, the Big Apple, the financial and entertainment capital of the world. Ground Zero still smelled of the fires, and some buildings were still simmering with smoke.

I was right at the foot of the heap of rubble that the president climbed with a New York firefighter and issued his famous warning to our attackers that we were coming after them. When the president came down, a group of public officials and clergy of all faiths were gathered together and Cardinal Edward Egan was asked to offer a prayer. President Bush was standing next to me as we bowed our heads and the cardinal prayed. When we had all said "Amen," I told the president his strong words to the terrorists were unifying and inspiring. He thanked me. "And Cardinal Egan's prayer was moving," I added.

"It was," the president said, "and it gave me a chance to appreciate your echoes." I was puzzled. "My echoes, Mr. President?" I asked respectfully. "Yes, your shoes, your ECCOS. They're great, aren't they?"

"Oh, my ECCOS. Yes, indeed. They are great." And, warming to this surprisingly relaxed moment after all the stress the president had been through during the previous three days, I added, "And I bought them at Barrie's in New Haven," the campus shoe store of choice for generations of Yale students.

"Barrie's," Bush smiled. "Now that brings back a lot of good memories."

The president went on to his next event, personal meetings with the families of people who had been killed in the World Trade Center. I went to our home in Connecticut for Sabbath with my family, and for post-9/11 public events on Sunday. On Monday morning, Hadassah, our thirteen-year-old daughter Hani, and I returned to Washington. I had become chairman of the Senate Governmental Affairs Committee just a few months before in May 2001, when Senator Jim Jeffords left the Republican Party and joined the Democratic caucus—giving us a majority and making every ranking committee Democrat, like me, a chairman. As fate would have it, long before the 9/11 attacks, I had scheduled a hearing of our committee for Wednesday, September 12, to discuss the vulnerability of America's critical infrastructure to cyber-attack by terrorist groups and hostile nation states.

Senator Fred Thompson of Tennessee (and sometimes of Hollywood) had been our committee chairman before Jim Jeffords switched sides and was now the ranking Republican member. Fred and I worked well together. For someone who had spent some of his life acting in movies and television, Fred was not a "showboat" in the Senate. He focused on issues like the better management of our government, rather than other topics more likely to interest the media. After the attacks on 9/11, he and I agreed to move forward with our hearing on September 12.

In my opening statement that morning, I said this would undoubtedly be "the first in what we expect to be a series of hearings and investigations on a problem that is today even more important to us than it had been before . . . the vulnerability of our homeland to unconventional enemy attack." Our committee had previously discussed whether we needed a new government department committed to homeland defense, based on the earlier recommendation from a bipartisan commission co-chaired by our former Senate colleagues Warren Rudman and Gary Hart. We moved quickly after 9/11 to answer that question. On September 21, we convened a hearing with Senators Rudman and Hart to hear their commission's proposals. In introducing them, I said that my personal response to the terrorist attacks of 9/11 was probably no different than theirs or most Americans':

> I have gone from shock to anger to remorse to determina-
> tion that we must together do everything we can to be as
> certain as we possibly can that nothing like what happened
> on September 11 happens again.

There was a lot that our committee could do, and I am proud to say that we did most of it.

In the Rules of the Senate, the Committee on Governmental Affairs was given authority over "the organization and reorganization of the executive branch of the government," which meant that we had the jurisdiction and responsibility to act to fix what made America vulnerable on 9/11. "Bold organizational change is demanded of us now, given the events of September 11," I said at the hearing on September 21. "This committee can lead the Congress to that change. I hope and believe we will."

Senators Rudman and Hart reminded us that in their report, issued in January 2001, they had predicted that "a direct attack against American citizens on American soil is likely over the next quarter century." That is why their commission had recommended the creation of a National Homeland Security Agency (NHSA) to coordinate all the government's homeland defense activities. Now, I thought their recommendation needed to be taken a big step further. America did not just need a new agency—we needed a new Department of Homeland Security with its own fully empowered and focused secretary.

I asked my staff to begin drafting legislation that would accomplish that. I also began to look for a Republican co-sponsor. There was nothing partisan about the attacks on 9/11, and there should have been nothing partisan about Congress's response. Fortunately, in the end there wasn't; but there was a lot of disagreement and tension between Congress and the Bush White House. It was caused not by partisanship, but by fear of partisanship, which led to defensiveness in the White House.

My working relationship with the Bush White House on post-9/11 legislation was very different than it had been on No Child Left Behind. President Bush had led the effort to reform our schools by demanding accountability. On the three major post-9/11 homeland security legislative initiatives—creation of the Department of Homeland Security, establishment of the independent 9/11 Commission, and adoption of the commission's recommendations to reform America's intelligence agencies—Congress took the lead and the president and his administration had to be pulled into the changes. Why? The president's aides had apparently convinced him he should be worried about Democrats in Congress "blaming" him for the 9/11 attacks.

Leaders of the executive branch agencies also resisted changes to their status quo and what they saw as probable loss of power and independence if a new department was created. It may have been a coincidence, but on the night before our committee was to hear Senators Hart and Rudman's recommendation to establish a new homeland security agency, President Bush appointed Governor Tom Ridge of Pennsylvania to a new position in the White House: Homeland Security Advisor to the president. I had great respect for Governor Ridge, but I felt strongly that simply appointing an advisor in the White House would not do what was needed to protect our homeland after 9/11.

The reluctance and resistance of the Bush administration is probably why my natural first choice of a Republican co-sponsor for the Homeland Security Department bill, Fred Thompson, told me he was not ready to step out front. My second choice was Arlen Specter, a Republican from Pennsylvania, who had served with Hart and Rudman and praised their report and recommendation when it was issued. Arlen also brought his past experience as the district attorney of Philadelphia, and as chairman of the Senate Intelligence Committee. I was delighted when he said yes. He was an excellent lawyer and legislator, and I knew he would contribute greatly to the bill's drafting and credibility.

On October 11, 2011, exactly one month after 9/11, Senator Specter and I announced at a press conference that we were introducing the Department of Homeland Security Act of 2001. It eventually led to the creation of the Department of Homeland Security and the consolidation of more than twenty existing agencies and offices to strengthen our country's ability to prevent another terrorist attack like 9/11. During the rest of 2001 and into 2002, the Governmental Affairs Committee held nineteen hearings to spotlight America's homeland security vulnerabilities and to hear expert testimony about how to fix those problems. We were methodically building our case.

The Bush administration continued to oppose the creation of a new department, but some Republicans in Congress came on board. Meanwhile, the media increasingly supported our proposal, and a surprising new force gave the most effective support we could have had. It was the families and friends of people who had been killed by the al-Qaeda terrorists on 9/11. They had taken their grief and turned it into powerful lobbying of Congress and the White House for reforms, including the creation of a new Department of Homeland Security. That was the way they would honor the memories of their loved ones and protect every other American family from suffering this grievous loss. They testified at public hearings. They went to congressional offices and the White House.

They made it personal, and were hard to resist. Turf protection and defensiveness yielded to their losses and pleas. The three big legislative responses to 9/11 (the new Department of Homeland Security, the 9/11 Commission, and the enactment of its major recommendations for intelligence reform) became law as a result of genuine negotiations, compromises, and non-partisan support from Congress and the administration.

But they would not have passed without the support of the 9/11 families.

The families' support was especially important to the bill John McCain and I introduced in December 2001 to create the National Commission on Terrorist Attacks upon the United States (known as "the 9/11 Commission"). That legislation was born on a Sunday morning in the Green Room at the NBC Studios on Nebraska Avenue in Washington where John and I were waiting to go on *Meet The Press*. We were talking about how congressional committees and the Bush administration were already jousting over who could best investigate how the al-Qaeda terrorists could have attacked the US so devastatingly on 9/11. We both agreed that these questions were critically important to our national security, but they couldn't be answered credibly by either Congress or the administration, who were rapidly descending into a partisan fight. John and I knew that there was a better way—to create an independent, non-partisan commission, with a co-chair from each party, and an equal number of members from each party.

Early in December 2001, we introduced a bill to create such a commission. It was blocked by the Bush White House. In a book on the commission and its work that was published more than a decade later, Michael Allen, who worked in the Bush White House, described why the administration first opposed the commission. It is exactly what we assumed, but did not know for a fact at the time:

> A commission to investigate the attacks posed a dilemma
> for the White House. On the one hand, it was politically
> dangerous in the short term to be seen opposing such an
> inquiry, especially with a highly visible group of victims'

family members . . . But, in the longer term, the White House worried the inquiry could be turned into a political instrument against the president . . . Speaker Hastert had pulled the president aside in a White House meeting and warned that the commission could be "a very good set-up by the Democrats to pin the whole issue on you" . . .

Tom DeLay declared . . . "We will not allow our president to be undermined by those who want his job . . . "

These arguments carried the day. The president chose to fight in Congress.

That showed how much partisan paranoia had filled Washington so soon after the 9/11 attacks. In this case, the paranoia was truly baseless. Neither the 9/11 families, nor Congressman Tim Roemer (Democrat of Indiana) who led the fight for an independent commission in the House, nor John McCain and I had any partisan motives for our commission. It was exactly the opposite. We wanted to create an independent commission so there could be a non-partisan and therefore credible investigation of the 9/11 attacks. We banded together and fought back against the administration. It was slow going but we were making progress. A lot of congressional Republicans who wanted to support our bill were holding back because of the White House pressure.

As we headed into the summer of 2002, a large number of 9/11 families attended a Washington rally on the Capitol grounds where many of us spoke. Later that afternoon, I invited the leaders of the 9/11 families to my office and was able to convince Nick Calio, who was Assistant to President Bush for Legislative Affairs, to meet with them. Nancy Pelosi, the Democratic leader of the House, joined us. Calio was respectful and empathetic, but he could not convince any of us that an independent commission was unnecessary. A woman who had lost her husband on 9/11 rose to speak to Nick. She spoke personally, passionately, and finished her remarks in tears. There was silence until Calio, clearly moved, closed the file in front of him, stood up, and said he would go back to the White House and convey the families' message.

Unfortunately, the White House was unmoved, but Congressman Roemer and a small group of Republican members of the House were. On July 25, Roemer introduced the commission bill as an amendment to the Intelligence Authorization bill. The roll was not called until 2:00 a.m., and it passed by one vote. Twenty-five Republicans joined 193 Democrats and one independent to achieve a majority. It was a great victory and, despite continued White House opposition, the wall in Congress began to collapse.

McCain and I looked for a Senate vehicle to which we could attach our 9/11 Commission bill. We found it on September 24, on pending homeland security legislation, and it passed 90–8—a wonderfully strong bipartisan vote which led the administration to throw in the towel and begin to negotiate a few amendments with us. The bill passed as part of the Intelligence Authorization Act, which President Bush signed on November 27, 2002. The 9/11 families were ecstatic. Their voices had created an independent investigation of the terrorist attacks that had taken their loved ones.

There is one more story that shows that not all the opponents of the commission had given up, and also illustrates how persistent and non-partisan John McCain could be for a bill he believed in, no matter who opposed him. At the end of 2002, after most members of Congress had gone home, the two chambers stayed in session to pass remaining bills—but only if there was unanimous consent; in other words, if no member objected. John and I were chatting on the Senate floor when our staffs told us that Speaker Hastert had put a hold on the bill that appropriated funds for the 9/11 Commission we had just created. Without that money, the commission could not start its investigation.

"I will take care of this," McCain said. "Come with me."

We went into the Republican Cloak Room off the Senate floor. "Get me Denny Hastert," McCain ordered the clerks.

John's side of the ensuing phone conversation with the Speaker went like this:

> Denny, I understand you are holding the bill to appropriate money to the 9/11 Commission. I also know you have a lot

of House bills that need to pass the Senate without objection before the end of the session. Let me put it to you straight, pal. Until that 9/11 bill passes the House and goes to the White House, not another fucking House bill will pass the Senate because either Joe Lieberman or I will be here twenty-four hours a day and we will kill every one of them.

With that, John hung up the phone. What could I do but laugh like hell and give him a hug? Within a half hour, the funding bill passed the House and was sent to the president for his signature. And McCain and I could leave the floor to allow all those other pending House bills to pass the Senate without objection.

The creation of a new US Department of Homeland Security was, unfortunately, similar to our journey to enact the 9/11 Commission: Congress initiated; the administration resisted; the 9/11 families and opinion leaders supported us; bipartisan congressional support grew until the administration yielded; we negotiated and reached an agreement; and the Department of Homeland Security was created.

On October 12, 2001, I chaired a hearing of the Governmental Affairs Committee on the bill Arlen Specter and I had introduced the day before. I was glad to announce that a bipartisan companion bill had been introduced in the House by Republican Congressman Mac Thornberry of Texas and Democratic Congresswoman Ellen Tauscher of California. We would work closely with them.

At another Committee meeting, six months later on April 11, 2002, I responded to the continuing argument by the Bush Administration that White House Homeland Security Advisor Tom Ridge was doing the job as it needed to be done. After expressing my admiration for Tom Ridge, I said, "We must still ask, six months into Governor Ridge's appointment, whether we are any better positioned to defend ourselves against another terrorist attack . . . Governor Ridge, I am sure, has done everything within his power . . . But . . . he lacks the necessary authority to overcome the bureaucratic obstacles that always get in the way of major change in the way government conducts its business."

I was also very critical of the White House for refusing to allow Ridge to testify before our committee: "Given the bearing of his work on the lives of every man, woman, and child living within our borders, he needs to work with Congress (in public) to fully explore these issues."

The Bush administration's refusal to even talk about a new Department of Homeland Security was increasingly upsetting to Democratic leaders like Senate Majority Leader Tom Daschle and the "Dean" of the Senate, Robert C. Byrd. They began to chastise the administration in speeches on the Senate floor.

It was the spring of 2002, a little more than six months after 9/11 and the anthrax attacks that followed. The American people were still suffering from post-traumatic stress and polls showed they strongly favored the creation of a new Department of Homeland Security. I sat down with Senator Daschle and we decided to force the issue in my committee to see if any of the Republicans were ready to break from the administration—and, if not, to put more pressure on them and the White House. On May 22, our committee took up the basic bill Arlen Specter and I had introduced back on October 11, 2001, amended in response to the expert opinion we had received in the twenty hearings our committee had held on homeland security since then. The bill was reported out of committee favorably but unfortunately on a straight party line vote. Every Democrat voted in favor. Every Republican voted against, even though some of them had told me privately that they wanted to support it but couldn't on orders from the White House.

But the Bush White House was under increasing pressure from Senate Republicans. It was an election year. They knew that Senator Daschle controlled the floor schedule and would undoubtedly bring up the Homeland Security Department bill, which would put them on the unpopular side of the big problem of our time. The response of the White House was to begin work in secret on their own proposal to create a Department of Homeland Security. A few months later after it became public, I said in a Senate floor speech:

Somebody once said that it's common in Washington to see people change their positions but rare to see them change their minds. And I would like to think that's exactly what happened in the White House. The president and his assistants changed their mind about the desirability of a Department of Homeland Security.

The White House apparently told its anxious agency heads that they would just have to learn to live with the new department. It was now unstoppable.

On the evening of June 6, 2002, in a televised address to the nation from the White House, President Bush announced his support for a Department of Homeland Security:

> After September 11, we needed to move quickly and so I appointed Tom Ridge as my Homeland Security Advisor. As Governor Ridge has worked with all levels of government to prepare a national strategy and as we have learned more about the plans and capabilities of the terrorist network, we have concluded that our government must be reorganized to deal more effectively with the new threats of the twenty-first century. So tonight, I ask Congress to join me in creating a single permanent department with an overriding and urgent mission: securing the homeland of America and protecting the American people.
>
> . . . Only the United States Congress can create a new department of government. So, tonight, I ask for your help in encouraging your representatives to support my plan.

I had to laugh at this presidential rewriting of history, which ignored the fact that his administration's opposition had been the major roadblock to quicker adoption. However, I was encouraged because the president's announcement meant that we would finally create a new department to protect America from another 9/11 attack.

On June 18, President Bush sent his legislative proposal to Congress. It overlapped our committee bill and the Thornberry-Tauscher bill (which had passed the House) on at least 90 percent of the issues involved. We worked out those remaining differences in relatively short order, and our committee reported out a bipartisan bill in July that was taken up in the Senate in September. Then a truly awful, petty, and unnecessary partisan issue was raised, for which I blame someone in the White House or the Republican congressional leadership. It resulted in a new split in the Senate on post-9/11 homeland security along party lines, meaning there were not enough votes to break a filibuster and take up the department bill we had all just agreed on before the November elections.

The proposal as reported out of our committee—with bipartisan support—contained a routine provision extending to employees of the new department normal civil service protections and the same limited, collective bargaining rights as other federal employees. Republicans in the Senate seized on this provision and argued that giving collective bargaining rights to employees of the new department would interfere with their ability to protect the American people from terrorists. This partisan political argument ignored two facts: 1) employees of some of the security agencies being brought into the new department already had collective bargaining rights and civil service protections, and there was no evidence presented that this had ever interfered with their work; and 2) police departments across America were unionized without any adverse effect on law enforcement.

We argued vigorously against these baseless contentions and tried hard to find a compromise. Three of the Senate's great centrists— John Breaux, Democrat of Louisiana; Ben Nelson, Democrat of Nebraska; and John Chafee, Republican of Rhode Island—came up with a sensible bipartisan compromise on the union issue, but the Republican leadership refused to budge. Five times they refused to allow a vote on the bill they had supported or on the compromise bipartisan amendment.

Senator Daschle was moved to give a furious speech on the Senate floor. He was totally justified. The White House had even begun to question the patriotism of Democratic senators for supporting that non-controversial provision. In the re-election campaigns of two Democratic incumbents, Max Cleland of Georgia and Jean Carnahan of Missouri, Republican political committees sponsored television commercials attacking Cleland and Carnahan for, as the ads claimed, knuckling under to union bosses instead of standing up to protect their constituents from terrorists. This was, of course, a grotesque lie and the tawdriest form of political campaigning. Both Cleland and Carnahan had been early supporters of the Homeland Security Department, and Cleland was a decorated Vietnam War veteran. On Election Day, both Cleland and Carnahan were defeated and the Republicans regained control of the Senate, 51–49.

In November, after the election was over, the Senate came back into session and back to bipartisanship. President Bush wanted the Homeland Security bill passed, as did we Democrats. We adopted the compromise amendment that had been offered before the election by Senators Breaux, Nelson, and Chafee, and the bill passed the Senate, 90–9. It then passed the House unanimously and President Bush signed it on November 25, 2002. It was the largest federal government reorganization since the Department of Defense was created in the National Security Act of 1947, bringing together twenty-two different agencies and offices—from border and transportation security, to emergency preparedness and response, and information and cyber security, infrastructure protection, and science and technology. President Bush quickly nominated Tom Ridge to be the first secretary of Homeland Security, and he was unanimously confirmed by the Senate on January 22, 2003.

Governor Ridge once said to me that being the first secretary of Homeland Security was like being a pilot who was asked to fly a plane while it was still being built. But he did a great job at launching the new department, one that has so improved the protection of the American people from so many different kinds of threats. The creation of the Homeland Security Department started in Congress with bipartisan sponsorship in the Senate and the House, but the opposition of the Bush administration made it partisan and delayed its establishment much longer than necessary.

What made the administration finally support the idea? It was in part because of the persistence of those of us in and outside of Congress who advocated for the new department. Maybe we even convinced the president and others that we were right. Sometimes the road to a centrist solution is long and winding. The birth of the Department of Homeland Security was one of those times.

At the end of 2002, Fred Thompson retired from the Senate. We remained friends and would see each other regularly until he passed away in 2015. After he left the Senate, Fred practiced law and acted in the successful television series *Law & Order*. At dinner one night with John McCain and me, Fred said he spent 90 percent of his time practicing law and 10 percent acting, but his income was 90 percent from acting and 10 percent from law.

Next in seniority among Republicans on our committee was Susan Collins. She and I had worked well together on the committee and on other issues. She is a centrist Republican. Both of us were eager to get things done and not at all hesitant to work across party lines to do so. We developed real trust in one another, including a "no surprises" understanding. If one of us didn't think we could agree on an issue or work together, perhaps for political reasons, we would tell the other quickly. Those disagreements happened rarely, and never had an effect on our relationship.

Susan was chairman of our committee from 2003–2007 and I was chair from 2007–2013 when I retired from the Senate. At the committee's first public hearing after I became chair in 2007, I remember saying that the only thing that would change was our titles. I promised to work with Susan as fairly and openly as she had with me when she was called "chair."

Together, Susan Collins and I got a lot done, much of it because our colleagues, party leaders, and outside interest groups knew that our goal was not partisan gain, but problem solving. They also knew we were both resolute—perhaps even stubborn—once we had a goal.

The Governmental Affairs Committee was historically the Senate's major investigative committee, and Susan and I took on and completed some important investigations—including one in 2005 into why our government failed in its response to Hurricane Katrina. That led to introduction and enactment of comprehensive, bipartisan legislative reform of the Federal Emergency Management Agency (FEMA). In 2009, we conducted a major investigation into the killing of thirteen people at Fort Hood in Texas by a Muslim American Army doctor who had become an extremist and terrorist, and in 2012, another investigation into the murder of the US Ambassador to Libya at Benghazi. Both of those investigations included findings about why such violent acts against Americans succeeded and what should be done to prevent them from happening again.

The first big legislative project Susan Collins and I worked on together after she became chair of the Senate Governmental Affairs Committee was to manage the Senate's response to the report of the 9/11 Commission, which was issued in July 2004 after nearly two years of intensive work. The Report of the Commission was as non-partisan as John McCain and I hoped it would be—the opposite of the partisan attack the Bush White House feared. The 9/11 Report was also comprehensive. It made recommendations that, under the Senate rules, were arguably in the jurisdiction of several different Senate committees. That would make it hard to adopt the recommendations of the 9/11 Commission quickly.

So, the majority leader, Bill Frist of Tennessee, worked with the Democratic leader, Tom Daschle, to give exclusive jurisdiction to our committee. Frist argued that the rules gave our committee jurisdiction over the organization and reorganization of the federal government, which the Report called for, and also said that he had confidence that Susan Collins and I would carry out this assignment in a non-partisan way. He asked only that we consult with the leadership of the other committees regarding policy decisions that would normally fall under their jurisdiction. Senators Frist and Daschle also urged us to move as quickly as we could to enact the recommendations of the 9/11 Commission, because almost three years had passed since the attacks.

When the Senate went into summer recess in 2004, Senator Collins and I stayed in Washington and on July 30, 2004, convened the first of what I described as "rare summer recess hearings" on the Commission Report. By early September, when our colleagues returned to Washington, we had conducted eight hearings on the Report, and were preparing to go to a bill "mark-up." The 9/11 Commission had been chaired by Tom Kean, the former Republican governor of New Jersey. His vice-chair was Lee Hamilton, the former Democratic leader in the House. They and their members worked vigorously and cooperatively. The commission interviewed more than 1,200 witnesses, reviewed millions of documents, held twelve public hearings, and produced clear findings and recommendations in a compelling narrative that was published and became a surprise best-seller.

The Report indicted the status quo in America's intelligence and law enforcement communities and recommended major changes. As Rep. Hamilton said, "A critical theme that emerged throughout our inquiry was the difficulty of answering the question: 'Who is in charge? Who ensures that agencies pool resources, avoid duplication and plan jointly? Who oversees the massive integration and unity of effort to keep America safe?' Too often the answer is no one."

That led to a withering analysis that agencies of our government had information telegraphing the attacks of 9/11, but the terrorists were not stopped because no one "connected the dots." Great agencies like the CIA and FBI were harshly criticized for their failure to collaborate. The commission made two recommendations to end this administrative chaos: creation of a National Intelligence Director to lead and coordinate all of America's intelligence operations; and establishment of a National Counter Terrorism Center, where representatives of all the agencies of our government with authority to help stop terrorist attacks on our homeland would be located in one space, all day every day, sharing information and the most advanced technology. There were forty-one recommendations in the Commission Report that went beyond intelligence reform to cover subjects such as border and transportation security, information sharing, privacy, and outreach to the Muslim world.

If enacted, the 9/11 Commission's recommendations would be transformational. The case the commission made for them was compelling and non-partisan. This time, the response from the White House and the majority of members of both parties in both chambers of Congress was also non-partisan. There were disagreements in Congress about different parts of the commission's recommendations, but, significantly, they were based on turf protection or ideology, not party affiliation.

Republicans and Democrats, White House and Congress, fought side by side against attempts to weaken the commission's proposals. In the House, the Republican Chairman of the House Armed Services Committee Duncan Hunter, urged on by Secretary of Defense Donald Rumsfeld, fought long and hard to protect the independence of the intelligence activities of the Pentagon from any influence or oversight by the new National Intelligence Director. Congressman Jim Sensenbrenner, the chairman of the House Judiciary Committee, wanted to do more in the bill than most others did to tighten our immigration laws. The White House worked hard to mollify Hunter and Sensenbrenner with different language. Speaker Hastert's chief of staff, Scott Palmer, also tried, but when he concluded the two Republican chairmen were not going to compromise, he worked directly against their desired changes. He had the support of the Republican chairman of the House Intelligence Committee, Pete Hoekstra, and Jane Harman, the ranking committee Democrat.

Senator Collins and I introduced legislation in early September 2004 that would enact all forty-one recommendations in the 9/11 Commission Report. We then brought it before our committee, where it was debated, amended, and unanimously approved. On September 27, the Senate began debate on our committee bill. It was a good debate with a few amendments passed and the bill was adopted 96–2. The House ultimately passed a similar bill.

Now, both bills would go to a conference committee of senators and representatives who would have to agree on a common text of the bill that could be taken up by the House and Senate and, if passed by both, sent to the president.

In conference, Congressmen Hunter and Sensenbrenner fought hard to change and weaken the bill. Collins, Hoekstra, Harman, and I held strong for the commission's recommendations, which meant opposing Hunter's efforts to shield the intelligence activities of the Pentagon and Sensenbrenner's attempts to turn this 9/11 bill into comprehensive, hard-line immigration reform legislation.

But then there was a House Republican caucus in which a majority of members voted with Hunter and Sensenbrenner. That led Hastert to stop the process because, according to what had become known as the Hastert Rule, he would not bring to the House floor any measure that was not supported by a majority of his caucus, even though there were more than enough votes to pass the bipartisan commission bill from Republicans and Democrats on the House floor. That was one more rule of Congress that worked against bipartisan centrist compromises.

In November of 2004, after President Bush was re-elected, he and Hastert appealed to Sensenbrenner and Hunter to accept a compromise: the president also asked Rumsfeld to pull back from the fight. New wording was agreed to and the House passed the bill on December 7. The Senate followed on December 8, 89–2.

In a grand ceremony at the Andrew Mellon Auditorium in Washington, on December 17, 2004, President Bush signed the bill with Bill Frist, Tom Kean, Lee Hamilton, Pete Hoekstra, Jane Harman, Susan Collins, and me clustered happily and proudly around him. From the Commission's Report to the president's signature, only five months had elapsed. It was the biggest reform in America's intelligence organizations since 1947. That, of course, was appropriate. In the late 1940s, the Cold War with the Soviet Union had just begun and required new agencies to meet the challenge. In its Report, the 9/11 Commission wrote, "As presently configured, the national security institutions of the US government are still the institutions constructed to win the Cold War." But the Cold War had ended more than a decade before. Now, we needed new institutions, constructed to win the war on terror, and that's what the bill we passed in 2004 did.

It was a wonderful bipartisan centrist accomplishment in which the national interest prevailed over lesser interests that could have divided and defeated us. As I look back at my twenty-four years in the Senate, my work on this law and the earlier ones to establish the Department of Homeland Security and create the 9/11 Commission are the accomplishments that I am proudest of—because I believe they have meant the most to our country, and they were all possible only because they had bipartisan support.

LESSONS FOR CENTRISTS

1. Is there any force great enough to overcome the deepening partisan divisions in Washington? Yes, there is. We learned after the terrorist attacks on America on September 11, 2001, that a national catastrophe can break through the partisanship. But even then, it will not happen automatically, as we also learned after 9/11. It took work to keep bringing our discussions in Congress back to the attacks of 9/11, and what we all wanted to do to prevent such a thing from happening again.

   The Bush administration spent months opposing the increasingly bipartisan movement in Congress after 9/11 to create a Department of Homeland Security (DHS). The resistance seems to have been caused by bureaucratic opposition within the administration by agencies and offices that would be combined into the new department. They liked their autonomy. Another factor was a reflex reaction of conservative Republicans to the creation of a new department and therefore a bigger government that would cost more money. But neither of those responses comprehended the terrible and unique trauma the nation had endured on and after 9/11.

   The administration's opposition to the creation of an independent commission to investigate how 9/11 could have happened, however, was caused by partisanship—more accurately, by fear of partisanship. In the Bush White House and among Republicans in Congress, there was great anxiety that the independent commission proposed by John McCain and me would be taken over by Democrats and would ultimately "blame" the Bush administration for the 9/11 attacks. That was the opposite of why McCain and I introduced our bill. We believed that investigations by congressional committees would become partisan and an investigation by the administration would lack credibility and appear self-protective.

It took months, but eventually we overcame the administration's opposition to both the new DHS and an independent 9/11 commission. That happened because the nation and the media were demanding real government reforms in response to 9/11, and the victims' surviving family and friends formed organizations that made the awful human losses of that infamous day painfully real. The families forced members of both parties in Congress and finally the Bush administration to rise above their partisanship to enact both bills by strong bipartisan majorities. President Bush signed both.

The report and recommendations of the 9/11 Commission were comprehensive and transformational, but their consideration and adoption in 2004 was surprisingly not impeded by partisanship. The obstacles were bureaucratic turf protection by the Department of Defense, represented by Duncan Hunter, chairman of the House Armed Services Committee, and an opportunistic attempt by Jim Sensenbrenner, chairman of the House Judiciary Committee, to force broad, ideologically conservative immigration reform onto the 9/11 Commission Report legislative train. That was a familiar tactic in Congress, but this time a bipartisan majority would not allow it for fear that it would delay or even block that train from reaching its destination.

A lot of Republicans had their priorities in order— and strong backbones. They stood up to Hunter and

Sensenbrenner, two of the most powerful Republican leaders in the House.

The result was comprehensive intelligence reform, which deserves a lot of the credit for the fact that the US has not experienced another attack like 9/11 since then.

11

MY CENTRIST PRESIDENTIAL CAMPAIGN IN A PARTY MOVING LEFT

In January 1989, my first month in the US Senate, I went for a haircut at the Senate Barber Shop, which was located in the basement of one of the Senate office buildings. When I returned home later that day, I proudly told Hadassah that it only cost me $4.00. She looked at my head and said dryly: "You got your money's worth." That was the last time I went to the Senate Barber Shop, but my conversation with the barber has remained with me. He greeted me warmly as a new senator and asked about my first impressions. I said that I was thrilled to be a senator. It was a personal dream I had no reason to assume I would realize. "I am living my dream."

"That's great," the barber said. "You mean you don't want to be president?"

"Me? President? No way. I am lucky to be a senator!"

"That's interesting because, based on all the senators who sit in this chair, I thought ninety-nine of the 100 senators want to be president."

I laughed and naturally asked, "Who's the one who doesn't want to be president?"

"Senator Rudy Boschwitz," the barber said. "He can't run for president because he was born in Germany."

I laughed again. But the barber had the last laugh.

In January 2003, I declared my candidacy for president of the United States. Early in February 2004, after failing to win any of the eight primaries I participated in, I ended my candidacy. I have surprisingly positive memories from that campaign, perhaps because I always viewed it as an unexpected opportunity—a bonus above and beyond the realization of my dream to be a US senator. It is also true that I enjoyed "retail" campaigning around the country, which was more intimate than during my vice-presidential campaign, and the people I met were warm and responsive. That naturally influences my memories.

But in terms of my devotion to centrism, my campaign for president was a troubling experience. The Democratic Party was no longer Bill Clinton's New Democratic Party. It had moved left back to where it had been during the twenty-four years from Nixon's election in 1968 to Clinton's election in 1992, when Republicans won every presidential contest—with the exception of Jimmy Carter's post-Watergate Democratic victory in 1976.

During my presidential campaign of 2003 and 2004, I was offering a centrist platform that most Democrats who voted in primaries that year no longer wanted. I was also supporting a war that most Democrats no longer supported. I didn't abandon my beliefs or my voting record. I didn't change who I was to pick up more votes. I ran as a Kennedy-Clinton Democrat—progressive on social issues, pro-jobs and pro-business on economic issues, internationalist on foreign policy, and strong for national defense. I am glad that I kept the faith, but it wasn't the path to the Democratic nomination in 2004.

I couldn't have rationally thought about running for president in 2004 if Al Gore had not asked me to be his running mate in 2000. That is why I told Al in 2001 that I would not make a decision about seeking the presidency until he decided whether or not he wanted to run again. I told him I hoped he would run and, if he did, I would of course support him. In the meantime, I began to talk with my advisers about the decision and I visited New Hampshire and Iowa more frequently just in case—ten days in New Hampshire and three in Iowa during 2001 and 2002.

Other Democrats began their presidential campaigns as I awaited Al Gore's decision. Howard Dean, the former governor of Vermont, was the first to declare on May 31, 2002. John Kerry, my Senate colleague and friend from Yale, was the next major candidate to enter, on December 2, 2002. During November of 2002, Al and Tipper Gore published two books about the importance of American families and began a nationwide book tour. Al had also campaigned for congressional candidates in November 2002 and began appearing again on the television talk shows, condemning the Bush administration policy on Iraq and offering ideas for health-care reform. Political analysts thought it was the preface to another presidential run. I had no idea.

On December 15, in an appearance on *60 Minutes*, Al announced that he would not seek the presidency in 2004. "I personally have the energy and drive and ambition to make another campaign, but I don't think it's the right thing to do," he said. I quickly discussed possible next steps with Hadassah, our children, my mom, Sherry Brown, my closest political allies in Connecticut and around the country, and my national political brain trust, including Carter Eskew, Stan Greenberg, and Al From.

The consensus among them was that with Gore's exit, the field was wide open and I had as much of a chance as anyone else. As a DLC Democrat, I would be more moderate or conservative on the issues than most of the other probable Democratic candidates. It would not be easy, but I had a credible opportunity to run for president, so why turn away from it? I agreed. I knew why I was running, and I believed that it was possible I could be nominated and elected. So, on January 13, 2003, in the auditorium of my high school in Stamford, I declared that I was a candidate for the Democratic nomination for president.

> We must rise above politics and restore independence to the White House, not compromise our economic or environmental or health security for political contributors or extreme ideologues . . . We must rise above partisan politics and stand up for our values here at home because family and faith and responsibility matter more than power and partisanship and privilege . . . I intend to talk straight to the American people and to show them I'm a different kind of Democrat.

The CNN story on my announcement described me as "perhaps the most conservative of the Democrats who have so far announced plans to run," citing my support of "limited experimental use of vouchers," my "pro-business voting record," and my co-sponsorship of the Senate resolution authorizing President Bush to use our military to disarm Saddam Hussein's Iraq. In response to the last, I said, "This is one of those times where you have to rise above partisanship and put your country's security first."

The *New York Times* said I opened my campaign with "sharp criticism of President Bush's performance on both domestic and foreign issues," and was good enough to add that I had "gained a reputation as an independent thinker and a legislator who works across partisan and ideological lines to find common ground." The *Times* also said that I had taken positions that put me "to the right of many of his Democratic colleagues."

My message was not likely to raise the passions of partisan Democrats, but I hoped it would earn support among centrist and moderate Democrats in the primaries and show that I was the most electable Democrat in November.

From my high school announcement, we went to my mom's house (my dad had passed away in 1986) for a series of media interviews. They went well. It was, after all, opening day. Two of the most surpsising questions came from national reporters who were Jewish Americans:

First: "If you are elected, you will be America's first Jewish president. Would you continue the tradition of having a Christmas tree in the White House?"

Before I could answer, the second reporter jumped in and asked:

"And what about the Easter egg hunt on the White House lawn?"

At the time, I found the questions silly and irritating, but I'm glad that I gave serious answers:

"The White House belongs to the American people. The president and his family are temporary residents. If I become president, the White House will continue to observe and respect the religious and patriotic traditions of our country, including the Christmas tree and Easter egg hunt."

In the polls taken early in 2003, I was ahead. The NBC–*Wall Street Journal* Poll in January 2003 had me favored by 25 percent of Democrats, followed by Dick Gephardt at 17 percent, and John Kerry at 14 percent. Howard Dean was at 3 percent. I knew my lead was mostly a hold-over in visibility and emotion from the 2000 election and its aftermath. Nonetheless, it was a good place to start. Now, there was a lot of work to do.

Sherry Brown did not want to run this campaign, the first without her at the helm since I was elected attorney general in 1982. I hired Craig Smith, a political consultant who had come to Washington from Arkansas in 1992 with Bill Clinton, as my campaign manager. Carter Eskew and Stan Greenberg would continue to be available for consultation, but neither had the time to work for the campaign. They were already committed to other campaigns or corporate clients. I asked Mark Penn to become my pollster and strategic adviser, and Mandy Grunwald to be our media consultant. Both were veterans of Bill Clinton's campaigns and White House, and Mandy had worked with Hillary Clinton in her successful campaign for the US Senate from New York in 2000. They worked hard and served me well. To paraphrase authors, responsibility for the failure of that 2004 campaign is mine, not theirs.

At our first campaign staff meeting in a suite in a Washington hotel, I remember asking whether it made sense for me to skip Iowa and New Hampshire, the first caucus and primary states, because the Democratic primary voters there tend to be more liberal. Maybe I should enter the battle in more moderate states holding primaries on February 3, including Arizona, Delaware, Oklahoma, and South Carolina. Carter Eskew immediately responded: "You can't do that. You have to run in Iowa or New Hampshire or both, because history shows that if you don't do well in one of those you are probably out; and if you win both, you are probably the nominee." Carter was right again. In 2004, John Kerry won both Iowa and New Hampshire and never stopped from there to the nomination. We decided that I would go into Iowa and New Hampshire and reserve the right, depending on how I was doing, to drop out of one—most likely Iowa—before the votes were cast.

We needed to start building political organizations, with local leaders and campaign staff, in Iowa, New Hampshire, and the seven states that would hold primaries on February 3, 2004. Although I was now running for president of the United States, the campaign began just as my campaigns had in Connecticut: with person-to-person outreach, on the phone or during visits to the states. I started with people I knew from my time as attorney general of Connecticut, US senator, or candidate for vice president. I moved on to the recognized Democratic leaders in the state who I did not know but needed to.

The case I made for my candidacy was that I had the best chance to defeat President Bush because I could stand toe to toe with him, based on my record in the two areas where he was strongest: national security and values. I could also present a clear alternative to Bush on taxes, fiscal responsibility, environment, and social issues. It was the "left-right" campaign I ran against Senator Weicker in 1988. And it was what I believed. But this time I was in Democratic primaries, not a general election against a Republican. Even though the 9/11 attacks had only recently happened and a war in Iraq was about to begin in March 2003, the sentiment in the Democratic primaries became increasingly anti-war and isolationist.

My strong record on security and continued support for the Iraq War was losing its appeal.

Nevertheless, during 2003, I was able to assemble a wonderful group of supporters in the early caucus and primary states. Many of them, I am proud to say, have gone on to higher public office since then. But it took time to build support—particularly in Iowa and New Hampshire—where the activists had been through it many times. They were not in a hurry. The local Democratic elected officials, past elected officials, party leaders, and citizen activists expected to be asked, even courted, more than once before they decided who to support. That seemed particularly true in New Hampshire, where people understood the decision they made would be important to their party, their country, and possibly to themselves.

I remember attending a fundraiser that a lawyer friend hosted for me in Manchester, New Hampshire. There were about twenty-five people there, three of whom had the title "ambassador." Those three had chosen to support Bill Clinton in the 1992 primary and stuck with him through the Gennifer Flowers storm. When Clinton made it to the White House, they became US ambassadors.

My favorite response to my requests for support around the country came from Mike Turpen, the former attorney general of Oklahoma. He and I had been state attorneys general at the same time. After I finished describing my platform to Mike and why I thought I had the best chance to be elected in November, he said: "Joe, I have listened to what you have said and I have made up my mind. I will support you. I will support you because you know something none of the other candidates know."

"That's great, Mike. Thank you very much. But what is that thing that I know?"

"You know my name!"

In Iowa, another former colleague and friend, Attorney General Tom Miller, the dean of state attorneys general, agreed to support me, and recommended Kevin McCarthy, a rising star in Iowa Democratic politics, to run my campaign there. Kevin later became the Iowa House Democratic leader. He was at the center of one of my favorite "Only in America" stories from the 2004 campaign.

I attended the famous Iowa State Fair in August 2003 with Kevin and a bunch of our supporters. It was a beautiful, sunny day, and the Iowans were very welcoming. I spoke from the special soapbox/stage for political candidates and visited the refrigerated barn where I saw magnificent sculptures made from Iowa butter, including the legendary, life-sized Iowa butter cow. Walking along the fairway, I noticed a lot of people eating something on a stick that I didn't recognize. So, I asked Kevin what it was. "That's pork on a stick, Senator, but don't worry, I know Jews don't eat pork so I'll protect you."

About a half-hour later, a local television crew interviewed me. After asking some good, serious questions, the reporter—with the camera still going—said, "Senator, there are so many great and unusual things to eat here. Are you going to try something different today, like a . . . deep-fried Twinkie?"

I blurted out, "I can't wait to have a deep-fried Twinkie." Mostly I was relieved that he had not asked me about whether I was going to go for the pork on a stick. With that, Kevin ran across the fairway and back. I had no idea why. "The Twinkies are okay for you," he whispered to me. "I just checked. They're fried in Iowa soybean oil, not meat fat. Let's go and get a couple of them."

As I said, "Only in America."

As we walked over, I thanked Kevin, an Irish Catholic, for becoming an expert on the Jewish dietary laws, which was not part of his job description. That deep-fried Twinkie was the only one I have ever eaten in my life. It was not only Kosher; it was delicious.

In New Hampshire, my campaign was run by Ray Buckley, a smart, personable local Democrat with a great sense of humor. Ray later became chairman of the New Hampshire Democratic Party, and vice chair of the Democratic National Committee. I was fortunate to have Dick and Katrina Swett as the leaders of my New Hampshire campaign. I had met Dick when he served in Congress in the early 1990s. Later, from 1998–2001, he was America's excellent ambassador to Denmark, one of the three ambassadors at that event in Manchester. Katrina Swett was the daughter of my congressional colleague and global human rights leader Tom Lantos. In 2004, she was national co-chair of my presidential campaign. Later, Katrina became president of the Lantos Foundation for Human Rights, which has done important work around the world.

I was also grateful to have the support of Chris Pappas, whose family owned and operated the Puritan Backroom restaurant in Manchester for three generations. Hadassah remembered going there for ice cream during summers when she worked as a counselor at a camp nearby. Chris Pappas had just graduated from Harvard College in 2002 and was a great help to me. In 2018, I am proud to say, Chris was elected to the US House of Representatives, the first openly gay congressman in New Hampshire history.

In Delaware, my centrist Senate colleague and dear friend Tom Carper came to my side and brought with him a great group of Democratic leaders including Chris Coons, then a county executive, later a US senator after Joe Biden became vice president in 2009; John Carney, then lieutenant governor, who later served in Congress and as governor; and Jack Markell, then state treasurer and later governor. With this great team working for me, it was no wonder that Delaware was the state primary in which I did best, coming in second on February 3, 2004. Although my campaign never made it to Virginia, I am proud to say that the leader of my supporters there was the former mayor of Richmond, then lieutenant governor, Tim Kaine, who was later elected to the US Senate and chosen by Hillary Clinton to be her vice-presidential running mate in 2016.

I also had to start raising money for the presidential campaign, mostly from people who had given to me before. At the end of the first quarter, I reached $3 million (more than I raised in my entire 1988 Senate campaign). John Edwards was first that quarter with $7.4 million, John Kerry was a close second with $7 million, and I was third with $3 million. Howard Dean was fourth with $2.6 million. In the second quarter, Dean jumped to first with $7.5 million. Kerry was second with $6 million, I was third with $5 million, tied with Edwards.

As 2003 went on, the big fundraising and political story was Howard Dean. His populist rhetoric and opposition to the war in Iraq caught fire. That was reflected in the results of an online poll, apparently the first ever conducted by the new liberal, anti-war website, MoveOn.org. In June 2003, 317,000 people "voted." Dean got 44 percent of the vote, anti-war Congressman Dennis Kucinich 24 percent, and John Kerry 16 percent. Dean also had begun to raise unprecedented amounts of money online in small contributions. It was not just the ideology of the Democratic Party that changed in 2004. Political fundraising had also changed, moving out to the grassroots via the internet. And in the short term, that also meant moving left.

I was much more impressed by the democratization of political fundraising than I was by the leftward ideological movement of my party. By the beginning of 2004, Howard Dean's campaign had brought in an impressive $40 million, and he was rising in the polls. Debates among the Democratic candidates began early and went on a long time. I thought they were more substantive than many political debates and showed the range of opinions among the nine candidates, although often I was not on the popular side of the range.

The first debate was at the University of South Carolina in Columbia on May 3, 2003. Gallup took a poll the week before the debate, showing me as the first choice of 23 percent of Democrats nationally. John Kerry was second at 17 percent, Dick Gephardt had 13 percent, John Edwards 9 percent, and Howard Dean 5 percent. The debate, which was broadcast by ABC News and moderated by its anchor, George Stephanopoulos, was six weeks after the invasion of Iraq that had overthrown Saddam Hussein. That was where Stephanopoulos started his questioning of John Kerry, Howard Dean, and me. Our answers to that first question of the first debate foretold what would follow in every other debate and, in some ways, predicted the outcome of the campaign for the Democratic nomination.

Kerry was asked first whether he supported the invasion of Iraq. He said he would have preferred that President Bush give diplomacy more time, but he was glad Saddam Hussein was gone. Governor Dean said it was "the wrong war at the wrong time," and that Kerry was trying to have it both ways since he had voted for the war. I was next and said I strongly supported the war because Saddam was a threat to the US and a threat to his regional neighbors, who were our close allies, as he had shown when he invaded Kuwait in 1990. I also said that he had brutally repressed the human rights of the Iraqi people and used chemical weapons against them. He also supported terrorist groups like those who had attacked us on 9/11: "We did the right thing in invading Iraq and overthrowing Saddam." I added that no Democrat who cannot convince the American people he or she will protect their security at least as well as George Bush can defeat him in 2004. Support of the war in Iraq will be a major test of that, I argued.

Kerry, Dean, Edwards, and I continued our disagreements on Iraq in every debate that followed. They became more intense and divisive as the reality on the ground in Iraq changed from the triumph over Saddam to the chaos that engulfed post-Saddam Iraq. I joined my opponents in criticizing the Bush administration's failure to have an effective post-war plan for Iraq. But when the president asked for $87 billion to continue to fund the war in Iraq, I voted for it to support our troops. Kerry and Edwards voted against it; Dean and General Wesley Clark (who had entered the campaign in September) both said they would have voted against it if they had been in Congress.

At a debate at the Fox Theatre in Detroit on October 26, I said I voted for the $87 billion to support the 140,000 American troops in Iraq, and I criticized Kerry and Edwards for their inconsistency. "How can you have supported the war," I asked, "and now oppose funding for the troops who are fighting the war that was authorized by the resolution you voted for?" I also began to broaden my arguments based on my opponents' waffling on the war. In a debate at the Orpheum Theatre in Phoenix on October 9, I said that four of the candidates—Dean, Kucinich, Al Sharpton, and Carol Moseley Braun—and I had opposite positions on the war. I was clearly and consistently for it and they were against it clearly and consistently, but I respected them for that. On the other hand, Kerry, Edwards, and Clark had flip-flopped for and against the war. Then, I tried to take that argument to issues other than the war:

> Integrity is on the ballot next November. George W. Bush promised he would grow and protect the middle class. The fact is he has squeezed and shrunk it. We will not get those middle-class voters back unless we convince them we will be more honest in saying we will protect them.
>
> I believe strongly that I am the Democratic candidate who can beat George Bush because I can take him on where he's supposed to be strong, but is not, on defense and values, and then beat him where we know he is weak on his failed economic policies and his social agenda that is so right wing it has left the rest of America, including the middle class, behind.

There were many times in the debates and during the campaign when I had opportunities to talk about the more "left" parts of my "left-right" positions on issues such as the environment, particularly climate change, civil rights, human rights, immigration reform, health-care reform, and labor law reforms, but they didn't get much attention. At a debate on September 7 at Morgan State University, for example, I discussed my involvement in the civil rights movement in the 1960s and declared that the struggle for racial equality in America was a long way from being over. As president, I promised, I would do everything I could to realize the Dream that I heard Dr. King describe at the Lincoln Memorial in August 1963. But there was little or no media coverage of the more Democratic positions I took in the campaign, and not much resonance among Democratic primary voters either, as my poll numbers fell throughout 2003.

I also took some centrist positions that other candidates had previously taken but simply abandoned during the 2004 campaign. One example was the No Child Left Behind Act (NCLB), which had passed with strong bipartisan support only a couple of years before. In our ninth debate at the Maytag Auditorium in Johnston,

Iowa, on January 4, 2004, we were asked about NCLB—which continued to be opposed by the American Federation of Teachers and the National Education Association, the two big teachers' unions.

Howard Dean said he was strongly opposed to NCLB. John Edwards went so far as to say his vote for NCLB was a mistake. The others waffled. I was the only one of the candidates to defend the law, reminding everyone that it was not just George Bush who supported NCLB, but Democrats like Ted Kennedy and George Miller who helped write and pass it. That should not be a surprise, I said, because the NCLB provided billions of dollars more for local education, particularly for schools that low-income children attended. The accountability standards were all about doing a better job giving equal educational opportunity to those children which, I argued, had always been a priority for the Democratic Party.

In a few of the debates, there were questions about trade policy, and there again I was dismayed as some of my primary opponents apparently "forgot" fair-trade votes they had cast under President Clinton, which had helped grow the economy so impressively in the years he was president. At one of the debates in Iowa, I made my case in local terms:

> Several of the candidates on stage have taken very protectionist positions in this debate that would hurt agriculture in Iowa and around the country. One-third of cash receipts of Iowa agriculture are from exports . . . We can't create jobs by building walls of protectionism. One-fifth of manufacturing jobs in Iowa are dependent on trade. The top two markets for goods from Iowa are Canada and Mexico. If you break NAFTA, as some of the candidates here have said they would do if they were president, you will kill tens of thousands of jobs in Iowa. I thought that was a lesson Bill Clinton had taught us.

I embraced the Clinton New Democrat legacy often throughout that presidential campaign, but never more emotionally than in the debate in Durham, New Hampshire, on December 9, moderated by Ted Koppel. Earlier that day, Al Gore had endorsed Howard Dean. At the debate, Koppel asked some of the candidates to respond to Gore's endorsement. John Kerry said he was surprised by the endorsement "especially because Joe Lieberman showed such loyalty to Al Gore in saying he would not get into this race until Al decided whether he was going to run." Then Koppel said to me that he assumed Gore's endorsement of Dean was a punch in my "solar plexus" and a real setback for my campaign.

Of course, it did hurt me personally, but I was too proud to acknowledge that publicly, so I began by saying it might actually help my campaign if all the supportive calls coming into my offices were an indication of the public responses to Gore's endorsement. I added that I was raised to respond to setbacks by doubling my determination to succeed and that is what I would do now. Then I counterpunched:

> This campaign is about whether we are going to build on the transformation of the Democratic Party that Bill Clinton began in 1992 and carried out during his administration. Some of the candidates this year—and now maybe Al Gore—are leaving that great legacy behind and seem to want to take our party back to the left populism where we don't win elections. I am fighting not just for this nomination but to keep the Democratic Party on the path that will take us to victory over George Bush in November.

In fairness to Al Gore, by that point in 2003 my campaign was fading. In early September, Howard Dean vaulted into first place in the NBC–*Wall Street Journal* poll with 17 percent. I had dropped from 25 percent in July to 16 percent in September. In November, Dean was at 15 percent, Gephardt at 12 percent, and Kerry and I were tied at 11 percent.

In September, declining poll numbers in Iowa led us to withdraw from the Iowa caucuses in order to concentrate on the New Hampshire primary, which would be held on January 27, and on the seven primaries in the moderate states a week later on February 3.

On December 22, Hadassah and I actually moved into an apartment in Manchester, New Hampshire, for the remaining weeks of the primary campaign. We soon rented another apartment in that same complex for my eighty-eight-year-old mother and other family members.

I spent a lot of time on retail campaigning that month in New Hampshire, at open town hall meetings, diners, bars, and Main Street walks. The response was warm and encouraging, notwithstanding the falling poll numbers. On January 1 and 2, 2004, Hadassah and I visited a number of sports bars to watch the college football bowl games, including one of our favorite saloons, Billy's Sports Bar & Grill in Manchester.

I also spent time visiting New Hampshire's newspapers and editorial boards, and I was honored to be endorsed by the *Union Leader*, the state's largest newspaper, and most of the other papers in the state. In fact, I received the most endorsements of any 2004 Democratic primary candidate from newspapers around the country, leading one of my campaign aides to quip that if editorial boards determined nominees for president, I would have won the Democratic nomination in a landslide.

But it is voters who choose nominees, and the Democratic voters were not following the editorial boards. In the Iowa caucuses, which were held on January 19, the polls suggested a close contest between Howard Dean, who continued to rise, and Dick Gephardt, who was from neighboring Missouri and had won in Iowa when he first ran for president in 1988. The two front-runners, Dean and Gephardt, naturally attacked each other. That is one reason why Kerry and Edwards went right by them. Kerry was first with 26 percent of the vote, and Edwards a surprisingly close second with 23 percent.

Dick Gephardt finished fourth with 18 percent and withdrew from the race. I admired Gephardt even more after the campaign than before. He stayed true to positions he had previously taken, including his support of the invasion of Iraq. Although that led me to appreciate Dick Gephardt, it was not cause for optimism about the future of my campaign. Campaigns are often about whether candidates meet expectations. Going into the Iowa caucuses, Dean was expected to win. He finished third with 20 percent, only 3 percent behind Edwards and 6 percent behind Kerry, but that was behind expectations—and he suffered. On the night of the caucuses, Dean let loose the most famous scream in American political history.

He'd finished third, and while rallying his supporters for the upcoming primaries, he began excitedly listing states to come, ending with, "And then we're going to Washington, DC, to take back the White House. Yaaaaaay!" It became arguably the first viral moment in American politics.

Having been in similar situations a few times, I was empathetic—even though I never screamed like he did. I assumed Howard's scream was the result of both a desire to rally his troops in New Hampshire and an uncontrollable expression of his disappointment about not having done as well as he was expected to in Iowa. The media and the primary voters had a much different response. They heard the scream, which was replayed over and over on television and the internet, as evidence that Howard Dean was an unhinged extremist who could never beat Bush. His campaign never recovered.

John Kerry and Howard Dean were both from states that neighbored New Hampshire, so they came into the primary there with good recognition. Kerry now also had momentum from Iowa. That left John Edwards, Wes Clark, and me in a battle to finish third in New Hampshire, which our campaigns and the media said was important.

After Clark entered the race in October 2003, he surged to first or second in the polling. We viewed Clark as a problem, because as a retired Army general, he brought national security credibility to challenge my own. He had the look of a centrist candidate who could take votes from me among the bloc of Democrats who self-identified as moderates. But Clark soon began to wobble on Iraq and other issues, which may help explain why he also stayed out of the Iowa caucuses and was in the battle for third in New Hampshire.

Small movements in the numbers can make big differences in a campaign, particularly when you are struggling to stay alive as a candidate, as I was by then. A day before the New Hampshire primary, on January 26, 2004, Gallup announced a New Hampshire poll that had Kerry in first with 38 percent, and Dean second at 25 percent. In the race for third, I had "jumped" ahead with 12 percent. Clark was at 10 percent, and Edwards at 9 percent.

Later that day, I did an interview from New Hampshire on CNN with Wolf Blitzer, who asked how I felt about the good Gallup poll results. Naturally, I said I was excited by our jump up in the polling and felt my campaign now had "Joementum." I do not remember whether I coined that phrase or a staff member did, but it turned out to be a contribution to America's political vocabulary that lived on, although not with the best ending for me. Years later, it worked much better for Joe Biden. On primary day, which was brutally and characteristically cold in New Hampshire, Kerry won with 38 percent of the vote. Dean got 26 percent, and, in the fight for third place, Clark and Edwards each got 12 percent and I got 9 percent.

One of my local campaign team members said that night that if Clark had not run, and the major candidates were Kerry, Dean, Edwards, and me, the center would have been open to me and I probably would have come in a strong third with 15–20 percent of the vote. Maybe, but "ifs" don't determine campaign results. Votes do. For me, the 2004 campaign was effectively over.

The next day, I spoke to supporters in the states that would hold primaries on February 3 where we had strong organizations—Arizona, Delaware, New Mexico, Oklahoma, and South Carolina—and the consensus was that I should stay in. Those were also more "moderate" states than Iowa and New Hampshire.

But John Kerry was on a roll. On February 3, he carried Arizona, Delaware, New Mexico, and South Carolina. Clark and Edwards finished with 30 percent in Oklahoma, and Kerry was second with 27 percent. My strongest finish was second place in Delaware, thanks to Senator Tom Carper and his team.

Even there, the exit polls told the story. Over 80 percent of the voters in the Delaware primary in 2004 said they now opposed the decision to go to war in Iraq, and over 50 percent said they were "angry" with the administration of President Bush. I was for the war and opposed Bush, but not enough for Democratic voters. In 2004, that meant there was no state Democratic primary I could win, no matter how moderate—or even Republican—the state was likely to vote in the November general election. Regardless of the state, Democratic voters everywhere were against the Iraq War and against Bush.

That night at a hotel in Arlington, Virginia, before a crowd of supporters and with my family and congressional colleagues from Connecticut—Senator Chris Dodd and Congresswoman Rosa DeLauro—I ended my presidential campaign:

> Am I grateful for the support I received from you and so many people around the country? Yes, I am deeply grateful. Am I committed to continuing the fight for the causes we campaigned for? You bet I am.
>
> I offered a mainstream voice, and I still believe that is the right choice and the winning choice for our party and country.
>
> Dear friends, a campaign ends but life goes on. So tomorrow when I wake, the first words I will say are the first words I say every morning. I will thank God for blessing me with another day of life. And I will pledge . . . to serve the Lord with as much gladness and purpose as I can to improve the world around me.

Wes Clark left the race a week later on February 13. Howard Dean followed on February 18, and John Edwards on March 3. John Kerry had won the Democratic nomination for president in 2004.

I have a lot of respect and affection for John Kerry and his life of service. In the 2004 campaign, he gave Democratic primary voters what they wanted. I did not. As I said, the Democratic Party was no longer where it had been under Bill Clinton. The war in Iraq brought the lingering anti-war sentiment in the Democratic Party to the surface. But the party had also changed in other ways from the Clinton years. It was no longer a party that was pro-trade, fiscally responsible, and believed that the "era of big government was over." The Bush campaign exploited and attacked all those differences as well as Kerry's changing positions in the general election campaign that year. President Bush was re-elected.

After my campaign ended in February, I spent part of every day for a few weeks calling people around the country who had helped me to say, "thank you." In my thank-you conversation with Ray Buckley, who managed my campaign in New Hampshire, I said:

> Ray, one of the puzzles to me about the New Hampshire primary is how great a reception I received as we campaigned around the state, but then I didn't do well on primary day. How do you explain that? Were people just being nice?

Ray's answer was surprising, funny, and undoubtably true:

> You know, Senator, I have asked myself the same question. I don't think they were just being nice. I think they did support you. But I think that a lot of the people who greeted you so warmly and supportively were *Republicans*. They *couldn't vote* in the primary.

Ray delivered those last two sentences with ascending volume and laughter, in which I joined. At the time, I did not appreciate that Ray Buckley's insight would play a large part in my re-election to the Senate in 2006.

LESSONS FOR CENTRISTS

1. American political parties change their policy priorities all the time. If you want to be the nominee of a political party whose priorities have changed, you better alter your policies or you are not going to be nominated. That, in a nutshell, is the obvious lesson I learned in my 2004 campaign for the Democratic nomination for president, but it didn't seem so obvious at the beginning of the campaign.

   The striking part of that lesson was how quickly the Democratic Party had changed. In 2000, one of the reasons I was chosen by Al Gore to be his vice-presidential running mate was that I was a Clinton-Gore New Democrat, which tied Al Gore and me closer to the impressive accomplishments of the Clinton administration. By 2004, supporting most of those centrist positions was no longer a winning path in the Democratic presidential primaries.

   And there was a big new factor, of course: By the beginning of 2004, the Democratic Party, most of whose members in Congress had voted to authorize the war in Iraq in 2003, turned against it. The party that had in the previous decade initiated wars in Bosnia and Kosovo to stop aggression and genocide by the totalitarian government of Serbia, now wanted to retreat from Iraq as quickly as possible—no matter how vulnerable, repressed, and impoverished that would leave the Iraqi people.

   This rapid change of opinion among Democrats was in part because the president was no longer a Democrat, Bill Clinton, but a Republican, George Bush. That was a difference that I concluded was not as important as my opinion about the war. I had been a centrist JFK-Bill Clinton Democrat all my life and couldn't suddenly change my position on Iraq with a straight face—and with my self-respect intact.

2. I also learned a strange personal lesson from my 2004 presidential campaign. I could run a losing campaign and still enjoy it. Why? Because I really liked seeing America again during my second national campaign. As I traveled across the county, I thought of Mark Twain's Huck Finn and Jim, and how much they enjoyed riding their raft down the great river that was America.

I also had a sense of purpose in that 2004 campaign, even though it became clear I was not going to be the Democratic nominee for president. I was holding the centrist banner high, sticking to the policies that had worked so well for President Clinton and hoping they would again soon for another Democratic candidate for President. The possibility and pressure to win ended. Instead, I took pleasure in holding the centrist banner high, sticking to what had recently worked so well for Bill Clinton and Al Gore, and hoping it would again soon for another Democratic candidate for president.

12

HOW I BECAME A THIRD-PARTY CANDIDATE

After the 2004 election, I was surprised to find myself with a "crossroads in life" decision to make.

It began with a call from Andy Card, President Bush's chief of staff: "The president would like you to think about whether you would become our ambassador to the United Nations if he nominated you."

That was a surprise. I was honored and intrigued by the possibility, as I told Andy. But it was not an easy decision because it meant that I would have to leave the US Senate, where I had become a senior member and had a lot of goals I wanted to accomplish. On the other hand, America's role in the world had been a priority for me since I arrived in the Senate. Representing the US at the UN would give me a new opportunity to pursue that priority. I was in general agreement with the Bush foreign policy, so I was comfortable with the idea of representing our country and the administration in the UN.

I asked Andy if I could take a few days to think about it. "Of course," he answered. "President Bush told me to urge you to take some time to think about it because he knew it would not be an easy decision for you. He also wanted me to tell you that he has asked Condi Rice and Steve Hadley to be available to discuss this possibility with you."

Rice had been national security advisor in Bush's first term and was about to become secretary of state. Hadley had been her deputy and would replace her as national security advisor. I told Card I appreciated that and would definitely talk with both of them.

"I am sure you will understand that our conversation should be kept confidential," Andy added.

"Of course," I responded.

"One more thing I need to say. The way this works is that the president is not formally saying now that he will nominate you, but I can tell you that he is not currently considering anyone else for the position and he hopes very much you will accept it if he offers it."

A few days later, I met with Condi Rice in the White House office of the national security advisor. It was quite small but very well placed in the West Wing. Condi was thoughtful and warm, and said she hoped I would accept it. She said as secretary of state she would involve me in policy formation and, when appropriate, implementation. She added that it would be great to have a Democrat on the administration's foreign policy team because that would send a message of bipartisanship to the American people, Congress, and the rest of the world.

I also had a very good discussion with Steve Hadley in the even smaller office of deputy national security advisor—also well-placed in the West Wing. He said he hoped I would accept and that he was confident we would work well together, as we had in the past. I thanked him and asked whether the UN ambassador had typically been involved in policy-making decisions. His answer was important to me:

> Condi and I would always welcome your input and try to make use of your skills in relating to other ambassadors at the UN, but I don't want to mislead you. In the years I have

been deputy NSA, the UN ambassador has occasionally come to Washington for NSC meetings, but he has stayed in New York most of the time and therefore has not naturally been in the flow of decision-making here in Washington.

Hadassah and I had long talks about this possibility, and we ultimately decided that there was more I could accomplish in the Senate. I called Andy Card to give him my decision and asked him to thank the president for the honor of his consideration. A day later, I was in Connecticut in my car between stops, when President Bush called.

"I appreciate all the thought you gave to the possibility that Andy Card called you about, and I understand why you made the decision you have," he said.

The conversation ended with mutual expressions of respect and shared confidence that we would find other ways to work together. I have never regretted my decision, but I have often thought of how different my life would have been after 2005 if I had left the Senate to go to the UN.

Now, I return to the story of my previously scheduled life, which also contained some big surprises that required me to make big decisions.

On a sunny weekday morning in December 2005, my campaign team came over to our house in the Georgetown section of Washington to hear the results of the benchmark poll Stan Greenberg's firm had taken for my 2006 re-election. Stan was traveling, so his partner, Al Quinlan, presented the numbers. Sherry Brown had flown down from Hartford for the meeting, and Clarine Nardi Riddle was also there. She was my Senate chief of staff and had worked with me on and off since 1978, when she joined me as deputy counsel when I was state senate majority leader. She went on to be my deputy when I was state attorney general and succeeded me as attorney general when I went to the Senate. My media consultant since 1988, Carter Eskew, was naturally also with us.

We sat around our kitchen table and listened to Al Quinlan tell the story his poll numbers told. It was not good news. My support had dropped substantially among Connecticut Democrats, and it was clear from the poll that it was because of my continuing support for the unpopular war in Iraq. I should not have been surprised. It was exactly what I had seen in my presidential campaign. But I was taken aback, to be honest, because I thought Connecticut Democrats would react differently from Democrats around America. They had known me and supported me for years. We agreed on most issues. They knew how hard I had worked for our state, and how much I had been able to accomplish: job-creating contracts for Connecticut's defense companies; environmental protection for Long Island Sound and the Connecticut River; increases in federal support for our schools, highways, and bridges; and even Connecticut's first national park site. Would the war in Iraq cancel all that out?

Al Quinlan has a naturally raspy voice, but that morning he tried to convey the bad news in softer tones, like a doctor speaking to a very sick patient. Carter Eskew suggested a treatment he thought would be a cure:

> These polling numbers are really disappointing and unfair to you, but they are undoubtedly accurate. Senator, I am going to say something now that I definitely did not expect to say this morning. Looking at these numbers, I think there is a very real possibility that you will lose the Democratic primary in Connecticut next year, but I also think that you can and will be re-elected if you run as an independent. Although your support has gone way down among Democrats, it remains very high among independents and Republicans and you still have a solid minority of Democrats with you. Together, they will re-elect you. So, I ask you to seriously consider skipping the Democratic primary and running as an independent. In some very important ways, it is who you are and what a majority of voters want in their elected officials today.

I was stunned by Carter's suggestion, but I was not angry because I knew he wanted me to be re-elected. We talked a lot about the pros and cons of the strategy. In the end, I said it was too big a change of heart and head for me to make. My decision that morning was: "I have been a Democrat all my life. I joined the party when JFK was president. If Democrats don't want me anymore as their candidate, let them vote me out in the primary. But I will not run away from my record, my party, or this fight."

My decision was both cerebral and visceral. I am sure it was, in part, because I was very surprised and emotionally defensive about how much support I had lost among Connecticut Democrats based on this one issue. I wanted to prove that I could turn it around. I also wanted to show that in my home state, Democrats would nominate a centrist, even one who supported the Iraq War. And finally, I wanted to prove what I had been taught at the beginning of my political career, and believed ever since: if voters trust you and generally agree with you, they will not vote you out of office because of differences on one or two issues. That political belief has always also been fundamental to centrist problem-solving politics and government. It enables elected officials to take political risks by going to the center to solve problems. In 2006, it did not prevail in the Connecticut Democratic primary. But in the end, it did in the general election.

As I look back at that morning in December 2005, I understand that there were at least two other possible responses. First, I could have changed my position on the war in Iraq. Many Democrats in Congress had supported the war-authorization resolution in 2002 and long since changed their positions. Some explained the change by saying that the Bush administration had lied about the Iraqis having weapons of mass destruction and therefore their vote was based on a false premise. The second option was to follow the others who said the Bush administration had made a terrible mess of post-Saddam Iraq by firing all the Iraqi military and civil servants because they had been members of Saddam's Ba'ath Party, thus depriving the country of people with experience to maintain order and run the government. It therefore no longer made sense for our military to stay in Iraq, risking their lives for a lost cause and costing our country billions of dollars.

My problem with these two arguments was that I did not believe them. On the first, there was very credible evidence on the public record—that has never been refuted—that Saddam had chemical and biological weapons. He did not have nuclear weapons, but he had an infrastructure to develop them when he thought the time was right. On the second argument—failure of the Bush administration's post-war policy in Iraq—I agreed with the criticism, but strongly disagreed with the response. I thought if the US retreated from Iraq in defeat, it would be a disaster for the people of Iraq who would be threatened immediately by Iran, Islamist terrorists, and possibly even the return of Saddam Hussein. An American retreat would also be devastating to America's credibility in the world, which was the foundation for regional, global, and American stability, prosperity, and freedom. Our allies would lose confidence in us and our enemies would be emboldened.

I had a history of concern about Iraq and Saddam Hussein that began long before the 2003 Iraq War and my 2006 re-election campaign. In 1991, I was one of only ten Democratic senators to vote to authorize President George H. W. Bush to go to war to push Saddam's army back out of Kuwait. I feared then that Saddam would become a regional and global menace if we allowed his invasion of Kuwait to stand.

After our military achieved that goal in only 100 hours, President Bush stopped our troops from going to Baghdad to remove Saddam. However, he did call on the Iraqis to rise up and overthrow the dictator. When the Shias and Kurds tried, the US did not support or protect them. Saddam's helicopter gunships took to the air and slaughtered his defenseless Iraqi opponents. I was infuriated by what was happening and went to the floor of the Senate on April 11, 1991, and warned:

> I did not speak out and vote for the use of force against Saddam Hussein in January only to remain silent in April while Saddam's murderous rampage goes on. I believe that the United States must pursue final victory over Saddam. We

must use all reasonable diplomatic, economic, and military means to achieve his removal from power.

Eventually, the US declared the largely Kurdish Northern Iraq region to be a no-fly (by Saddam's airplanes) safe zone. A Kurdish regional government was established and thrived under US protection. But the rest of Iraq, particularly its Shiite majority, continued to be repressed and brutalized by Saddam's government. He also hosted conferences in Iraq of anti-American Islamist terrorists and gave them financial support, presumably as a threat to us and our allies in the Middle East. And he built more chemical and biological weapons while keeping the structure and personnel in place to develop nuclear weapons when he could.

During the 1990s, leaders of Iraqi exile groups that opposed Saddam's rule began to visit Washington. Because I had continued to speak out against Saddam, they asked to talk with me. I was glad to do so. They were an ethnically and religiously diverse and impressive group. I had no idea whether they could succeed in overthrowing Saddam, but I was convinced that if they or we did, Iraq would be much less a threat to us and its neighbors, and also hopefully more democratically governed. The Iraqi exiles talked to other senators and congressmen of both parties and a plan of action emerged.

In 1998, Senators Trent Lott, Bob Kerrey, John McCain, and I—two Republicans and two Democrats—introduced the Iraq Liberation Act (ILA), which declared that the policy of the United States was to change the regime in Iraq, support a transition to democracy, and authorize some financial assistance to Iraqi groups who were opposed to Saddam. A similar, bipartisan bill was introduced in the House. In February of 1998, President Bill Clinton, in an address at the Pentagon to the Joint Chiefs of Staff and Department of Defense personnel, recounted the promises Saddam made to end the Gulf War of 1991 and how they had repeatedly been broken, including pledges to disclose his chemical, biological, and nuclear weapons inventory, and the missiles he had to deliver those weapons. President Clinton then declared:

Saddam has built up a terrible arsenal . . . [and] he has used it not once but many times . . . against combatants, against civilians, against a foreign adversary, and even against his own people.

Despite Iraq's deceptions, UNSCOM inspectors . . . have uncovered and destroyed more weapons of mass destruction capacity in Iraq than was destroyed during the Gulf War.

This includes nearly 40,000 chemical weapons, more than 100,000 gallons of chemical weapons agents, forty-eight operational missiles, thirty warheads specifically fitted for chemical and biological weapons, and a massive biological weapons facility at Al-Hakim equipped to produce anthrax and other deadly agents. Over the past few months . . . they have come closer and closer to rooting out Iraq's remaining nuclear capacity . . .

President Clinton concluded:

If we fail to respond today, Saddam and all those who would follow in his footsteps will be emboldened tomorrow by the knowledge they can act with impunity, even in the face of a clear message from the United Nations Security Council and clear evidence of a weapons of mass destruction program.

Those were the words of President Bill Clinton in February 1998, not of President George Bush in 2002 or 2003. The Iraq Liberation Act passed the House on October 5, 1998, by a strong vote of 360–38. Two days later, it passed the Senate unanimously. President Clinton signed the bill into law on October 31. It was then the official bipartisan policy of the United States to support regime change in Iraq; in other words, to remove Saddam Hussein from power.

Four years later, on September 12, 2002, President Bush went to the UN General Assembly to ask the Security Council to vote to enforce the resolutions regarding Iraq that Saddam Hussein had persistently violated. The next day I spoke in the Senate in praise of the president's UN speech and declared, "If Saddam does not comply, and the United Nations proves itself unwilling or unable to take decisive action, then the United States surely can and must assemble and lead an international military coalition to enforce the UN resolutions and liberate the Iraqi people, the Middle East, and the world from Saddam Hussein."

Bush's actions constituted the leadership I had been calling for against Saddam Hussein for more than a decade. I went right to work with Senate colleagues in both parties and the White House to draft a resolution authorizing the president to use military force in Iraq. Senator John Warner and I introduced the resolution, as the two of us had in 1991 for the Gulf War. But this time, as a welcome sign of the broad bipartisan support that existed for defeat of Saddam, our resolution was blended into one introduced by the bipartisan leaders of the Senate, Tom Daschle and Trent Lott. It recited the many evils of Iraq under Saddam and said this authorization followed the US policy enacted in the Iraq Liberation Act.

The resolution passed the Senate on October 11, 2002, by a vote of 77–23, with twenty-nine Democrats voting "aye" and twenty-one against. In the House, the same resolution, introduced by Dennis Hastert and Dick Gephardt, was adopted by a vote of 296–133 with eighty-one Democrats in support and 126 opposed. Five months later, on March 19, 2003, President Bush ordered the American military to invade Iraq. They were joined by troops from the United Kingdom, Australia, and Poland. Their purposes, as Bush and Prime Minister Tony Blair said in a joint statement that day, were "to disarm Iraq of weapons of mass destruction, to end Saddam Hussein's support of terrorism, and to free the Iraqi people."

After our troops captured Saddam's home city, Tikrit, less than a month later on April 15, he went into hiding. On May 1, President Bush declared an end to major combat operations. It was another spectacular victory for the American military. Then all the post-war troubles began.

In the months and years that followed, I visited Iraq regularly as a senior member of the Senate Armed Services Committee, usually in the company of John McCain and Lindsey Graham, who had been elected to the Senate from South Carolina in 2002. On one trip, General David Petraeus called the three of us the "Three Amigos," and it stuck. When we came back to the US, I usually reported in op-eds for newspapers, in speeches in the Senate, or at think tanks in Washington about what we had seen and what we thought had to be done to achieve victory in the post-war conflict in Iraq.

For example, in April 2004, I delivered a speech at the Brookings Institute in Washington in which I pleaded with Democrats and Republicans to remain as united in post-war Iraq as we were when we adopted the Iraq War resolution in October 2002. I particularly appealed to Democrats, most of whom already seemed to be for the earliest possible withdrawal from Iraq, to think how "catastrophic" it would be if the US and coalition forces retreated before the new Iraqi military was ready to take over.

On November 29, 2005, after my fourth trip to Iraq in seventeen months, I wrote an op-ed for the *Wall Street Journal* entitled "Our Troops Must Stay." I reported that I had seen "real progress there," in the military conflict and in rebirth of the country. People were living better lives and certainly were more free. Eighty million Iraqis had turned out to vote in the election of an interim national government. I wrote,

> None of these remarkable changes would have happened if coalition forces, led by the US, had not overthrown Saddam Hussein. And I am convinced, almost all of the progress in Iraq and throughout the Middle East will be lost if those forces are withdrawn faster than the Iraqi military is capable of securing the country.

Ned Lamont, a businessman from Greenwich, Connecticut, said he decided to challenge me in the Democratic primary in 2006 after he read that op-ed in the *Wall Street Journal*. I later heard that his decision-making was more complicated than that, but I assume the op-ed was part of it. I have no regrets. I wrote about what I saw in Iraq and what I believed and had been saying about Saddam and Iraq for a long time. I would not change my position to gain political advantage in the Democratic primary.

At that pivotal meeting at our home in December 2005, Carter Eskew was not asking me to change my beliefs, just to change my party. I also refused to do that because I saw it as running from a fight which I thought was larger than Iraq, and really about whether the Democratic Party would be a center-left party or move further to the left where it had not won national elections.

Early in 2006, Sherry Brown called me in Washington and said, "I've been thinking, Boss, and listening to people here. I totally understand and respect your decision to go ahead and fight for the Democratic nomination and not run as an independent. But I think we ought to at least know what the Connecticut law says about running as an independent. So, with your permission, I want to ask Dan Papermaster to begin to research the law and let you and me know. It will be totally secret, and we can even give it a codename, if you want."

"That makes sense," I said. "Please ask Dan and let me know what he reports back. And, Sherry, thanks."

Dan Papermaster was a prominent, young, Hartford attorney. His family and ours had been friends for a long time. After I was first elected to the Senate in 1988, Dan took a leave of absence from his law firm to come to Washington with me for a few months to help with my transition. He had previously worked with my old friend and new colleague, Chris Dodd, and knew his way around the Capitol. In fact, the day before I was to be sworn in as senator, I said, "Dan, I just realized I don't know how to get from my office here in the Hart Building to the Senate Chamber in the Capitol tomorrow so I can be sworn in as a senator."

On January 4, 1989, Dan showed me how to get to the Senate. In 2006, he showed me how to stay there by running as an independent. To run in Connecticut as a third-party candidate, I had to gather at least 7,500 signatures on petitions. That was not simple, but certainly manageable. Dan also reported that Connecticut law would allow me to seek the Democratic nomination, which he knew I wanted to do, and, if I was unsuccessful at that, stay in the election as an independent.

The political problem was timing. The law required me to file those 7,500 signatures on the day after the Senate Democratic primary. The primary was on August 8. The signatures needed to be filed by the close of business on August 9. There was no way we could get 7,500 signatures in one day. That meant if I wanted to keep the third-party option open, I would have to announce the petition drive weeks before primary day, which would be politically awkward and might be damaging in the primary. Sherry put Dan Papermaster's memo in a safe, and we agreed we would return to it if the reality of the campaign required us to.

Although Ned Lamont did not declare for the Senate until March 13, 2006, it was clear by the end of 2005 that he was running. The anti-war movement apparently had also been polling in Connecticut and had seen my sinking numbers among Democrats. All they needed was a candidate. One of the people they first asked was Lowell Weicker, who later told reporters he was too old and banged up to run again, but he knew a young businessman in Greenwich, named Ned Lamont, who might be interested.

Lamont had served on municipal government boards in Greenwich but had never won an election. In the Connecticut Democratic Primary in 2006, none of that mattered. It was all about my support for the war in Iraq. The anti-war movement, energized by what was being called the "netroots" (as contrasted with the grassroots in earlier political generations), had found their candidate. On January 13, 2006, in an interview on a website called "myleftnutmeg.com," Ned Lamont was reported to be "dismissive" of the notion that the war (in Iraq) is just one issue of many for voters to consider:

> I hear people say, "Well, Joe's good on everything else," and
> my response is, "Other than that Mrs. Lincoln, how did you
> like the play?

I took Ned seriously. We knew from our polling that my vulnerability among Democrats was my position on the war. And Ned and his wife were very wealthy and prepared to put a lot of their money into his campaign. As is now the standard for senators, I had started raising money for the 2006 campaign, slowly but early, in 2001. I set that aside in 2003 and 2004 because I had to gather support for my presidential campaign. In 2006, I knew I needed to intensify my fundraising for the Senate campaign. Thanks to a lot of generous friends, I did. But Lamont kept up with me by raising some money over the internet and making up the rest with his family money.

This pattern continued until primary day in August, and right through election in November. Both of us would have enough money to run the campaigns we wanted to run. In fact, we both probably had too much money. I ended up with a surplus after the election because of an outpouring of support after Lamont won the primary. I thought Ned spent too much on television advertising in the fall campaign without a consistent or effective theme in the ads. One of my friends said he imagined Lamont's media consultants wearing masks and pointing a gun at Ned because they were really stealing his money.

For me personally, those first months of 2006 were an emotional roller coaster. The low points were when longtime friends in the Democratic Party or in political organizations told me they could not support me this time because I wouldn't change my position on Iraq, although they agreed with me on most everything else, and they were very grateful for everything I had done for them or for their organizations.

The worst of these moments was the call I got from the president of the Connecticut International Association of Machinists (IAM) union, which represented thousands of employees at the jet-engine-producing Pratt & Whitney Company. I had worked very hard and successfully for them and the company. After the union president told me they were going to support Lamont, I told him I was shocked and hurt—after all, I had helped deliver for his workers at Pratt. His response was:

> Believe me, Senator, this is one of the hardest calls I have
> ever had to make. You could not have done better for us
> than you have. It has meant thousands of jobs for my mem-
> bers. But I am acting at the direction of the national leader-
> ship of my union, which told me we could not support you
> because our national union is for getting out of Iraq now.

At the time, that call angered me too much to appreciate the
comedic irony of a defense industry union opposing me because I
was supporting our military at war.

There were some very high points, however. I greatly appreciated the loyalty of the Democrats and independent organizations
that stuck with me. Most of the Democratic Party leaders in and
outside of Connecticut continued to support me in the primary,
even if they disagreed with me on the war in Iraq. Apart from
the IAM, every other union stuck with me in the primary. After
I lost the primary, the American Federation of State, County, and
Municipal Employees (AFSCME) and the United Auto Workers
(UAW) switched to Lamont, but all the other unions continued to
support me through the election.

The day after I lost the primary, I received a call from Harold
Schaitberger, the president of the International Association of Firefighters (IAFF), who wanted me to know that his national union
and his Connecticut firefighters were sticking with me.

The words he used in that call should be in a book of inspira-
tional thoughts for people who believe in bipartisan centrist politics
and government. Harold said:

> Senator, I am calling to assure you that we are supporting
> you today as strongly as we did in the primary yester-
> day, because you are the same person with the same great
> record on so much that matters to firefighters today as you
> were yesterday. The only thing that has changed is the
> name of your political party. Big deal. We are with *you* all
> the way.

I was very grateful to the diverse group of organizations that supported me in that campaign, before and after the primary—including, for example, the Humane Society, Defenders of Wildlife, Human Rights Campaign, US Chamber of Commerce, National Association of Realtors, and Planned Parenthood.

From my first campaign in 1970 for state senator, through my campaign in 2004 for president, I had always enjoyed meeting people along the way—on the streets, in diners, at town hall meetings. The primary campaign of 2006 was different. The reactions were decidedly mixed. Many were as warm and conversational as ever, others were unfriendly, uncivil, or angry.

Lamont was waging an active television, radio, and social media campaign mostly about the Iraq War, but also about my alleged closeness to President Bush, who was deeply unpopular among the Democrats. My support for the war was portrayed as support for Bush, even though I had been against Saddam and for the liberation of the Iraqi people long before George W. Bush became president. My concerns about Saddam went back to 1990 when President Bush 43 was still an executive of the Texas Rangers baseball team. I backed the war not to support President Bush, but to defeat Saddam Hussein.

Bush and I happened to have had the same goals in Iraq, but I wasn't going to change my position because he was a Republican and I was a Democrat. Lamont's focus on portraying Bush and me as two peas in the same unpopular pod was caricatured to an extreme by what his campaign called "The Kiss."

After the president finished his State of the Union speech in January 2005, as he exited the House chamber, he stopped along the way and shook hands or hugged members of Congress. I was one of those who got a hug, but—I can attest because I was there—not a kiss. It was naturally filmed and available to the Lamont campaign in 2005, and they used it repeatedly in the media. They were so excited by "the kiss" that they had someone make two life-size, papier-mâché sculptures of Bush and me embracing, and put them on the back of a pickup truck that was driven to all my public events throughout the rest of the campaign. The driver was a very unpleasant gentleman. I thought Lamont's focus on this was shallow and silly. But it seemed to be influencing Democratic primary voters. In both private and public polling, Lamont was rising.

On February 16, a month before Lamont declared his candidacy, the Quinnipiac Polling Institute had me at 68 percent to Lamont's 13 percent. It also showed very strong disapproval of the Iraq War. Four months later, however, after Lamont had bought a lot of media time hammering at me and tying me to Bush, it was much closer. I was at 55 percent and he was at 40 percent. The Quinnipiac poll director, Douglas Schwartz, said Lamont was also probably helped by his "surprisingly strong showing at the State Democratic Convention, which gained him a lot of headlines." That made sense. Lamont was supported by 35 percent of the delegates at the convention in May, more than twice as many as he needed to qualify for a primary without having to get 15,000 signatures. For me, the convention was an eerie and difficult experience. It was like going to a family reunion where about a third of the people there either wouldn't talk to me or yelled at me about Iraq and President Bush.

In that troubling June 8 Quinnipiac poll, there was a big burst of sunlight beneath the dark headline. They asked all the voters in the state about how they would vote if I ran as an independent in November. Eight percent said they would vote for the Republican candidate, Alan Schlesinger; 18 percent for Lamont; and 56 percent for me. A week later, Lamont started running commercials in which he said he would endorse me if he lost the primary and challenged me to do the same if I lost. Instead, we decided to implement Dan Papermaster's legal memo.

On July 3, at a press conference in front of the state capitol, I announced that my supporters would begin circulating petitions to qualify me to run as an independent in November. I said I still hoped to win the Democratic primary, but if I didn't, I wanted to give everyone the right to decide whether I would continue as their senator, because I had always felt it was my responsibility to serve all the people of Connecticut, regardless of party.

The 2006 primary campaign was the first statewide campaign of mine that Sherry Brown did not manage. She was a recent breast cancer survivor and didn't want the stress of this campaign. I had told her I understood completely, but now I asked her if she could lead the petition effort. Thankfully, she said yes. She had about a month to get 7,500 signatures that had to be certified as valid by the state to get me on the ballot as an independent. She got many more than that.

The next Quinnipiac poll was published on July 20, just ahead of the August 8 primary, and it showed how right we were to begin circulating those petitions. Lamont had pulled ahead of me for the first time, 51–47. I still had a solid lead in a three-way race in November: 51 percent to Lamont's 27 percent, and 9 percent for Schlesinger. Sixty-eight percent of the voters disapproved of President Bush's job performance, and 70 percent were against the war in Iraq. I was running commercials on Connecticut media that touted my record of accomplishment for the state, protecting Long Island Sound and the Connecticut River, saving the Submarine Base and thousands of jobs in New London, and portraying me as an independent-minded but effective Democrat.

Many national Democrats came into Connecticut to validate those messages for me, including my Senate colleagues Joe Biden, Barbara Boxer, and Ken Salazar. John Kerry stayed neutral in the primary and said he would support whoever won it. Hillary Clinton put out a statement of support for me but said she would back whoever won the Democratic primary. Some of my paid media campaign recollected my close working relationship with President Clinton, who was still popular in Connecticut. I was thrilled when he agreed to speak at a big rally in Waterbury, Connecticut, during the last week of the primary campaign. He could not have been better.

But on primary day, August 8, Ned Lamont defeated me, receiving 52 percent of the vote to my 48 percent. The *CBS–New York Times* exit poll told the story of a Democratic Party in transition, away from where it had been under President Clinton, and far, far away from President Kennedy's Democratic Party I had first joined.

Forty-three percent of the primary voters said they supported Lamont because they wanted the US to get out of Iraq, and 24 percent said they did so because they thought Ned would oppose Bush more than I would. That totals two-thirds of Lamont's voters. Seventy-eight percent of the voters were against the decision to go to war. Sixty percent of them said I was too close to Bush and 84 percent of them said they disapproved of the job Bush was doing as president. One small consolation for me was that 56 percent of the Democratic primary voters still thought I was doing a good job, which suggested I could hold a solid minority of Democrats in the November elections.

Receiving the returns on that primary night was the worst personal experience in my political career. We expected I would probably lose, but it still hit me hard. Defeat in an election is a personal rejection, no matter how much you expect it. But by the time I went out to address my supporters that night, I had pushed the hurt feelings down, and was ready for the next round. My speech was more like a rally speech beginning a campaign than a concession speech ending one. I was fired up and felt liberated to be carrying my campaign to all the voters of Connecticut, and so were my supporters.

The next day, even though the state office stopped counting at 7,500, we filed about 15,000 signatures to run as a third-party candidate. I was on the ballot in what would be a new and different campaign for me. The first thing I did was reach out to Sherry Brown and ask her if she could come back for three months to manage my independent campaign. From the 1982 campaign for attorney general to the 2000 campaign for re-election to the Senate, I was undefeated when Sherry was campaign manager. She agreed. I terminated the contracts of the outside consultants that had managed my primary campaign.

I also called my two longtime media and polling consultants, Carter Eskew and Al Quinlan (Stan Greenberg remained largely absent from the campaign), and told them I appreciated all their help, but I needed new campaign consultants for a new campaign. I think they were both relieved. Carter was mostly doing corporate work by then, and Al Quinlan and Stan, typical of the partisanization of all parts of our politics, were a strictly Democratic polling firm. They didn't work for Republicans or independents, and I guessed they had been under pressure from national Democratic leaders to get out of my campaign.

I had no idea who to hire in place of Carter and Stan. As far as I knew, there were no consultants who specialized in independent campaigns. Carter told me he had someone in mind who might be perfect because he had done the media for Mike Bloomberg's independent campaign for mayor of New York. His name was Josh Isay. That was a coincidence. Josh had gone to the same elementary school with our older children in New Haven. Josh and I met to talk. We clicked, and I hired him. He did great creative work for me in that campaign.

The choice of a new pollster was more roundabout. We put out a call for a Republican pollster who was prepared to work for a registered Democrat running as an independent. That led us to Neil Newhouse, a prominent Republican pollster. He was interested and we were impressed by his record, his personal style, and his commitment to my campaign. We hired him. Neil never missed a conference call, always produced accurate polling numbers, and gave me great strategic advice. One of my favorite lines from the 2006 campaign came from Neil after the election was over. That year, Democrats won both houses of Congress for the first time since the Gingrich Revolution in 1994. Neil said, "I never could have imagined at the beginning of this year that my most successful campaign would be for a Democrat."

It turned out that Neil Newhouse was not the only national Republican involved in my campaign. On the afternoon of the primary, I was waiting with a few family members and staff in my room at the Goodwin Hotel in Hartford where we were going to receive the returns and speak to my supporters that night. The phone rang and whoever answered was shocked: "Senator, it's Karl Rove calling from the White House. Do you want to talk to him?"

I had met Rove on Air Force One from Washington to New York three days after 9/11, when President Bush visited Ground

Zero. He and I had a few good conversations that day about 9/11 and the challenges ahead. At the end of the day, we exchanged email addresses and kept in touch from time to time. I took his call on primary day, 2006.

"How's it going Senator?"

"It's going to be close and could go either way."

"That's what we have heard. And that's why the 'Boss' asked me to call you and tell you that if you don't win today, he hopes you stay in as an independent. He thinks the country needs you in the Senate and knows that the political problems you are having are because you have stayed strong on the war in Iraq. So, he wanted me to tell you that if you lose today and run in November, we will help you in any way we can."

I was beyond surprised by the call and had no idea exactly what it meant. But I responded:

Karl, that means a lot to me. Please thank the president, and thank you too for this call.

Two days later, Fran Katz Watson, my longtime national fundraiser from Washington, called me. Her normally strong voice was quivering:

Senator, I just got a call from a man named Mel Sembler who told me he was calling me because *Karl Rove* asked him to. He lives in Florida and wants to do a big fundraiser for you. Do you have any idea what's going on?

I explained it all to Fran, which helped her better understand the several similar calls she received later. Connecticut's Republican candidate for the Senate in 2006 was Alan Schlesinger, the former mayor of Derby, Connecticut. His candidacy had been hurt earlier in the year when newspapers revealed he had been sued by casinos in Atlantic City for using a false name and not paying his gambling debts. When it looked like Lamont could win the primary, there was talk in Republican circles about finding a stronger candidate, but Schlesinger insisted on staying in the race—and Connecticut Republicans never mounted a strong effort to replace him.

I don't exactly know why, but there are several possible explanations. I was friendly with the Republican governor, Jodi Rell. She and I had worked closely together for the state, particularly in saving the New London Submarine Base. She stayed neutral. The one Republican congressman from Connecticut, Chris Shays, was a dear, personal friend of mine and my family in Stamford. Chris endorsed me. After the Rove call, it is hard to believe the White House didn't encourage Connecticut Republicans to stay out of the Senate race. Also, in a twist of fate, the chair of the Senate Republican Campaign Committee that cycle was Senator Elizabeth Dole, wife of Bob Dole. They were both close friends of ours. Elizabeth later told me proudly that her committee had given no support, financial or otherwise, to Schlesinger.

Polling showed I was receiving unprecedented backing from Connecticut Republicans. In the first Quinnipiac poll of a three-way race taken after the primary, I was ahead of Lamont 53 percent to 41 percent. Seventy-five percent of Connecticut Republicans said they planned to vote for me.

On the morning after the primary, I appeared on CNN's *American Morning* and the host, Soledad O'Brien, asked me what I would say if, as was rumored, the leaders of the Democratic Party asked me not to run in the general election. My answer was clear: "No, no, no."

> I am in this race to the end. For me, it is a cause. It is a cause not to let this Democratic Party that I joined with the inspiration of President Kennedy in 1960 to be taken over by people who are so far from the mainstream of American life that I fear we will not elect Democrats in the numbers that we should in the future. I'm carrying on because Lamont really represents polarization and

partisanship which are the last things we need more of in Washington.

Beginning on the night of the primary, most Democratic elected officials in Connecticut and nationally, including good personal friends and colleagues, rushed to endorse Lamont. Loyalty to one's political party has become a reflexive priority in American politics. The rush by my Democratic friends to Lamont's side was one more illustration of that. I understood. It hurt, nevertheless.

But let me stress the positive by mentioning my personal Democratic heroes who stuck with me after the primary. In Connecticut, that included Speaker of the House Jim Amann and Mayor Mike Jarjura of Waterbury. Among national Democrats, five of my Senate Democratic colleagues stuck by me publicly: Tom Carper of Delaware, Mary Landrieu of Louisiana, Ben Nelson of Nebraska, Mark Pryor of Arkansas, and Ken Salazar of Colorado. Why? They were centrists and friends. Both of those connections mattered to them and me.

From the US House of Representatives there were five or six Democrats who put out statements in support of me. One came to Hartford and spoke on my behalf, which touched my heart— Congressman John Lewis, the great leader of the civil rights movement and true American hero. Congressman Lewis talked of the times we had worked together in Congress and added that he could not forget that during the 1960s, I had come to the South to stand up for African Americans there. If I had the courage to do that, he said, how could he not stand with me in Connecticut now and ask the people of Connecticut to re-elect me. That endorsement from John Lewis meant everything to me. He was asked what he would do if I lost the primary. His wonderful answer: "I stick with my friends. Joe Lieberman is my friend."

Another of my Democratic heroes of that campaign was Congresswoman Rosa DeLauro from New Haven. On matters of policy, Rosa was probably the most liberal member of our Connecticut congressional delegation, which might make her the least likely to support me. But Rosa and I had grown up in New Haven

Democratic politics together. We were like family, and she is a loyal person. Rosa stayed out of the Senate general election campaign that year. I will never forget that.

From the Republican Party, my close friend and colleague, Senator Susan Collins of Maine, came in to campaign with me in Eastern Connecticut and brought a large check from her PAC, and a smaller but equally meaningful contribution from her mother. My friend Jack Kemp spent a day campaigning with me in Fairfield County. He was as personally warm and ideologically fresh as always.

Independent Mike Bloomberg hosted a "tri-partisan" fundraiser for me at his Manhattan home with former Democratic Mayor Ed Koch and former Republican Senator Al D'Amato as his co-chairs. It raised over one million dollars. Before the event, Koch said he wanted to help me in the campaign. We went to Grand Central Station and stood together at the gate to the trains taking commuters back to Connecticut. When one commuter complained about my support of the war in Iraq, Koch shot back at him, "Ok, but do you support Joe on most other issues?" That stopped the commuter. He thought for a few seconds, and then said, "Yes, I do." Koch was ready with his concluding argument: "Then you should vote for Joe. I always said to people in New York when I was running for Congress or mayor, if you support me on a majority of the issues, you should vote for me. If you support me on all the issues, you should see a psychiatrist." We all laughed at what might be called Ed Koch's centrist manifesto, and I might have picked up a vote.

After the primary, the campaign momentum flipped. Lamont was now an underdog in the general election. I had lost the primary, but now seemed on my way to re-election in November. Lamont kept putting his family's money into the campaign (ultimately about $20 million). Because the unpopularity of the Iraq War and President Bush were not enough to win in the general election, he attacked me in paid media for an endless succession of acts or votes, usually running an ad for a day or two and then changing the subject for the next day or two. It was as if he were throwing everything he had about me against the wall to see if anything stuck. Thankfully, nothing did.

After my loss in the primary, much to my surprise, I also became a cause. People were angry that I might not return to the Senate. They volunteered for the campaign or contributed large amounts of money—so much that I literally could not spend it all at the end, and was left with a surplus of about $2 million. That also meant that I had plenty of money for paid media, and Josh Isay did some great work with it.

My favorite Isay creation opened with a whiteboard with a thick, black chalk line down the middle and the word "Democratic" on one side of the line and "Republican" on the other. I am off screen at the beginning asking, "How do you protect Long Island Sound, and save thousands of jobs in Connecticut?" I walk into the picture, erase the line between the two parties, and turn to the camera to answer the question I had asked: "By standing up for what you think is right and working across party lines to get things done." That television commercial summarized my political vision and, for that matter, this book.

However, Josh Isay's most popular television ad was probably the one that dealt with our concern that as an independent, I was listed farther down the ballot, not up top with the Democrats and Republicans—where people were accustomed to finding me. This commercial began with a man walking his dog, a bloodhound, and saying to him, "Charlie, we're going to vote for Joe Lieberman. I might need your help to find him on the ballot." In the next scene, the man walks into a polling booth with Charlie, whose canine posterior is jutting out from between the curtains of the booth. The ad ended with me kneeling next to Charlie with my arm around him, saying to the camera, "You don't need a bloodhound to find me on the ballot, but I am in a different place this year. So take your time and please look for my name." Then I turned to my canine friend and said, "Thanks, Charlie."

In the days that followed, everywhere I went people asked, "Where's Charlie?" So, we retained Charlie, who was a paid professional, to go around with me for the last days of the campaign. He was a great hit. If he had been a politician, I am sure Charlie would later have argued that I couldn't have won without him.

I don't know whose idea it was but after Labor Day, as I campaigned around the state, I began to see more and more signs on lawns, buttons on clothes, and bumper stickers on cars and trucks that said "I'm stickin' with Joe." Those words captured the emotion a lot of Connecticut voters were thankfully feeling, and they gave me a great one-liner to use when I began speeches. I said some anonymous wise guy in my campaign had made a special button for my wife, Hadassah, that said, "I'm stuck with Joe."

Though the night I lost the 2006 primary was the most devastating experience of my political career, the night in November when I was re-elected to the Senate was the best. It was personal vindication and redeemed my faith that in our political system—people will vote for you even if they don't agree with you on every issue, so long as they agree with you on most and believe you're doing what you think is right. That belief is a precondition for centrist politics and government and for elected officials who are willing to stand up to interest groups or their own party for what they believe is right. The final vote on Election Day 2006 was 50 percent for me, 40 percent for Lamont, and 10 percent for Schlesinger.

Here's the other part that meant a lot to me. The exit polls showed that 66 percent of the voters were against the war in Iraq, the exact same percentage as disapproved of the way President Bush was handling his job. Sixty-three percent believed we should begin to withdraw our troops from Iraq. In other words, they were voting for me even though they disagreed with me on Iraq. That gave me then, and still gives me now, reason for hope regarding the future of independent centrism and bipartisanship in American politics. The exit polls said that I got 33 percent of the Democratic vote, 54 percent of the independent vote, and 70 percent of the Republican vote.

About a month after the election, Hadassah and I attended the annual holiday party at the White House for members of Congress and their families. Everybody gets to have their picture taken with the president and First Lady. It was the first time I had seen President Bush since the election. His face lit up when we walked through the door. He came over to me and gave me another hug (but again, no kiss) and said with a big smile:

"Liebie, you've got big cojones!"

I thanked him for that great compliment and for his help, and then turned to Hadassah and said, "Sweetheart, please consider using President Bush's kind words as the epitaph on my tombstone."

LESSONS FOR CENTRISTS

1. In 2006, my longtime bipartisan centrism earned me a Democratic primary in Connecticut, and I lost. It was a result that some of my advisors had foreseen a year before when they urged me to run for re-election as an independent. But I rejected that wise counsel because I could not believe Connecticut Democrats would vote against me based on one stand I had taken. We agreed on so much else. And I thought it was obvious that I was not opposing withdrawal of American troops from Iraq for political reasons or to support President Bush. It would have been much better for me politically if I had supported withdrawal.

   The difficult lesson I learned in 2006 is that my Democratic Party and American politics had changed. There were Democrats who felt so strongly against the war that they voted against me on that basis alone. I was hurt by that single-issue voting but I could ultimately understand it.

   What I could not understand or accept was the number of Democrats who voted against me because the Iraq War had become "President Bush's war" to them. He was a Republican. I was supporting the war. Therefore, I was no longer a good Democrat. It was more important to them that I be loyal to my political tribe than do what I thought was right.

That kind of twisted parochial reasoning by too many members of both parties discourages movement to the bipartisan center, without which gridlock in our government will not be overcome.

It has to stop.

2. Was one of the lessons learned in my 2006 Senate campaign that third parties are a good way to disrupt the partisan duopoly of Democrats and Republicans that has stymied our government?

American history (past and recent) doesn't support that conclusion. I was lucky that Connecticut is one of a minority of states that allows a candidate who has lost a party primary to run as an independent. In most of the states, the two major parties have foreclosed that second chance by law.

As a third-party candidate in 2006, I had some unusual advantages. I was an incumbent with high visibility in Connecticut and a centrist record that in previous elections had won me surprising support from Republicans and independents. When I was defeated in the Democratic primary, I became a "cause" for many independents and Republicans, and even some Democrats. For them, I was not the wrongdoer. I was the one who had been wronged.

My personal faith that voters would not turn away from an elected official who differed with them on only a few issues was crushed during the Democratic primary in 2006, but was thrillingly rebuilt in the general election.

The problem now is that centrists in both parties may have a hard time getting re-nominated in their party, and most also have no viable third-party option in the general election. Changing both parts of that political reality is one of the great challenges for American politics in the years ahead.

13

AN INDEPENDENT DEMOCRAT IN A REPUBLICAN CAMPAIGN

When I returned to the Senate in January 2007, I felt more independent than ever, and very grateful to the voters of Connecticut for sending me back to Washington that way. I also felt liberated because my presidential campaign of 2004 and Senatorial campaign of 2006 were over, which meant I could be a fully dedicated US senator.

There was another reason I felt so free, which I discussed only with my wife. I had decided I would probably not run for re-election in 2012. By then I would have been in elective office for forty years and in the Senate for twenty-four years. I had never wanted to spend all of my life in politics, and I certainly was not eager to go through another campaign like 2006. It was time for a new chapter for my family and me, and 2013 seemed—God willing—like a good time to start it. But it was only 2007, and I had time to make a final decision.

My non-partisan path back into the increasingly partisan Senate raised some unique questions, such as how my party affiliation should be described. I had been re-elected as an independent but remained a registered Democrat and, as I had said I would during the campaign, I rejoined the Senate Democratic caucus. I told anyone who asked that it would be most accurate to call me an independent Democrat. Some did, and some just called me an independent.

Because Democrats had regained the majority in the Senate, I became the chair of the Committee on Homeland Security and Governmental Affairs, and Susan Collins became the ranking Republican. As I wrote earlier, when Susan turned the gavel over to me at our first meeting in 2007, I said nothing had changed in our wonderfully bipartisan and productive relationship except our titles.

In that same spirit, Senator Claire McCaskill, a new member of the Senate and our committee, asked at one of our first meetings why Democrats and Republicans sit on opposite sides of the table, like a house divided. Why can't we sit side by side so the American people can see us working together? Susan Collins and I talked it over and quickly concluded, "Why not?" We mixed up the seating. It was one small step for bipartisanship and one giant leap forward for the US Senate.

During 2007, our committee held a series of hearings on the threat of domestic radical Islamic terrorism to the American people. We also continued to oversee and monitor the Department of Homeland Security, which our committee had originated in 2001 and 2002.

In 2007, John McCain and I introduced bipartisan climate change legislation for the third consecutive session. It would create a "cap and trade," market-based system to reduce greenhouse gas emissions in the US. Although John and I most often worked together on national defense and foreign policy, dealing with this greatest environmental challenge of our time had become very important to both of us.

Our work together began in 2001 when he said to me that during his unsuccessful 2000 campaign for president, people had asked him about global warming. He had given answers that he was not satisfied with because he didn't know much about the problem. He knew that I had been active in this area and said he wanted to work with me to learn more and see if we could get something positive done on climate change.

John and I and our staffs spent a lot of time in 2001 and 2002 talking and drafting a legislative proposal. We introduced the resulting "cap and trade" legislation in 2003 and again in 2005. In the end, we got a majority of votes for a resolution calling for a market-based system to regulate greenhouse gases, but not the sixty votes needed to break a filibuster to pass our proposal, which most Senate Republicans misrepresented as "cap and tax." In 2007, we were back to fight the good fight again. John and I also repeatedly challenged President Bush to drop his opposition to limits on greenhouse gas emissions.

From my seat as a senior member of the Environment Committee, I also continued my bipartisan work with Senator Mike Crapo, Republican of Idaho, to strengthen and adequately fund the Endangered Species Act.

In foreign policy, I accelerated my work with a very broad bipartisan group of colleagues to enact economic sanctions against the extremist, terrorist regime in Tehran that was expanding its influence in the Middle East through aggression into neighboring countries, including Iraq. I continued my support of our mission in Iraq, our new American commander there, General David Petraeus, and our new American ambassador, Ryan Crocker. That meant I continued to oppose attempts by Senate Democrats to cut off funding for our troops to force a retreat from Iraq.

In June of 2007, I visited Iraq and wrote once again in an op-ed in the *Wall Street Journal* that I had seen "hopeful signs of progress." I offered Anbar Province as evidence. When I had last visited Anbar with my two Amigos, McCain and Graham, in December of 2006, the US military would not let us go to the provincial capital, Ramadi. They said it was too dangerous. McCain had one hell of an argument with the military that day, which ended with him saying they better secure Ramadi soon so we could visit the next time we were in Iraq. They did. In June, we walked the streets of Ramadi. American and Iraqi troops, fighting side by side, had liberated the capital city from al-Qaeda control. One of Ramadi's leading sheikhs said to us: "A rifle pointed at an American soldier is a rifled pointed at an Iraqi."

In February 2007, McCain and I made our annual trip to the Munich Security Conference in Germany, co-chairing a bipartisan American delegation. Vladimir Putin came and delivered a tough, anti-American speech, often glowering at McCain and me who were seated in the first row right in front of him. So we, in true "boys will be boys" fashion, glowered right back at him. I had an opportunity to offer a more substantive response to Putin during a speech to the conference the next day:

> President Putin complained yesterday that there is "one single center of power" in the world today . . . But that power is not the United States (as Putin believes). That power is the power of freedom . . . and the totalitarianism of today, including Putin's in Russia, cannot defeat it.

In June 2007, Hadassah and I visited Prague, the city of her birth, to attend a conference of freedom fighters from around the world convened by Vaclav Havel and Natan Sharansky, two great fighters for freedom from the Soviet Communists. In my speech there I said the conference itself was "a testament to the transformative power of . . . brave people of principle to change history. Today, Stalin and Brezhnev are in the dust bin of history and Havel and Sharansky survive and flourish."

On April 30, I spoke at the University of Pennsylvania on the subject of "Civility and American Politics," discussing the harmful incivility in our politics which I had personally experienced in my Senate campaign the previous year. I also bemoaned the fact that both parties had become ideologically homogeneous. "Rockefeller Republicans and Scoop Jackson Democrats have become endangered species." Looking ahead to the presidential election of 2008, I said, "The challenge for the two parties is not just to appeal to their bases, but to reach out to the broad political center in America," so they can unite our country.

Later, John McCain challenged me personally to do exactly that. A few days after Thanksgiving in 2007, he called me and said he had a tough question to ask. He assured me that whatever my answer, it would have zero effect on our friendship. "Now," I said, "You have raised my interest. What's the question?" As was his nature, McCain set it out straight:

> My presidential campaign has come back from far behind where we were earlier in the year. Now it's going to be made or broken in New Hampshire. Independents can vote in the Republican primary there. You just got re-elected as an independent. You are now Mr. Independent in American politics. If you endorse me before the New Hampshire primary, I think it would make a big difference for me. So that's my tough question, Joey. Would you endorse me for president?

That was a tough question, but I told John it was definitely possible. I needed a few days to think about it. John and I had become the best of friends. Traveling to Iraq and Afghanistan (often with a stop in Israel), to Munich once a year, and to many other places around the world in between, we had time on planes to get to know each other very well. I greatly admired John, not only because of his heroism, but because of his willingness to stand up to his party and interest groups to get things done in Congress.

I knew the two Democratic presidential candidates in 2008, Hillary Clinton and Barack Obama, very well. Hillary and I first met when she was at Yale Law School way back in the early 1970s. We also saw a lot of each other during the two Clinton presidential campaigns, as well as the eight years of the Clinton administration.

When Barack Obama came to the Senate in 2005, a new program encouraged bipartisanship among incoming senators by asking each of them to choose a sitting senator from each party as mentors. Obama asked me to be his Democratic mentor. He didn't need much mentoring, but it was a great opportunity to get to know him. He was very smart, articulate, and personable, and he had survived and succeeded in the brass knuckles school of Chicago politics. I liked him and was impressed.

Later in 2006, Obama asked to see me in my Senate office. He told me he was thinking of running for president in 2008, and asked my opinion. I gave him my standards for such decisions. First, he needed to believe that he could do the job better than the other candidates, so he could convince the voters of that. And second, he needed to conclude that he had a chance to win, not that he would definitely win. I also told him that even if he ran and didn't win in 2008, he could set the stage for a later presidential campaign. He was a young man. After we talked a while, he asked me what I would do if I were him. I paused, thought, and then answered, "I would run."

By late 2007, Clinton and Obama had begun their campaigns. Neither of them had asked for my support and I understood why. I remained a controversial figure among the "netroots left," which was an increasingly important part of the Democratic base that Clinton and Obama needed in the presidential primaries.

Even though both parties were aware of how close McCain and I were, I knew that a lot of Democrats who were not in the "netroots" would be angry if I crossed party lines to endorse John. But, to me, it looked like an opportunity to erase that increasingly dark line between the parties that was becoming hurtful to our country, and to make a statement for independent-minded, bipartisan politics, instead of single-issue, litmus test politics. Although John and I agreed on almost every national defense and foreign policy issue, we disagreed on many domestic policy issues; but that never affected our trust in each other or our willingness to work together on climate change, closing the gun show loophole, and campaign finance reform.

I knew John was ready to be a strong, principled, unifying president. So, a few days later, I called him back and said I would be proud to endorse him. He was thrilled.

On Sunday afternoon, December 16, 2007, I flew to New Hampshire and joined McCain, Tom Ridge, and Steve Duprey, former

New Hampshire Republican chairman, for a pre-endorsement dinner at the memorably named "Common Man" restaurant in Concord. McCain had been rising in the polls in New Hampshire. A week before our dinner, he was in third place, close behind Rudy Giuliani, and Mitt Romney in first. Optimism filled the room at the Common Man that evening. It was one of the few times I saw John have an alcoholic drink, except for his annual schnapps at the Munich Security Conference.

The next morning, we went to the Veterans of Foreign Wars (VFW) Hall in Hillsborough, New Hampshire, for the formal endorsement. It was typically cold that day, and McCain, Ridge, and I each wore colorful sweaters under our winter sports coats. "I happen to think this guy is the best of all candidates to unite our country across political lines so we can begin to solve some of the problems America has," I said. "Political party is important, but not more important than what you think is best for the country."

McCain graciously thanked me and said he was hopeful that independents would be motivated to vote in the Republican primary in January. "Obviously, that can have a dramatic and significant effect on the New Hampshire primary," he said.

I visited New Hampshire to campaign with John before the primary and thought the public response to him was very positive. He continued to rise in the polls. On primary day, John won with 37.7 percent; Romney was second with 32.1 percent; and Huckabee was third with 11.4 percent. It was a great win and sent him on with real momentum to South Carolina, where George Bush had stopped him in 2000. This time, with the help of Lindsey Graham, McCain came in first; Huckabee was second. I was in South Carolina to campaign and celebrate with my two Amigos. John went to Florida and won there, too, on January 29. It was all over early. John McCain would be the Republican nominee for president in 2008.

McCain's people regularly asked me to join my friend on the campaign trail during the rest of the year, and I did whenever I could. He traveled around on a bus called the "Straight Talk Express," which was outfitted with an open living-room seating section in the back for John and the media traveling with him. There was no rest for the candidate . . . only constant repartee with the reporters. They loved it and he did, too.

Sometimes, surprise guests would arrive. One of them was the great baseball pitcher, Curt Schilling, who traveled with us one day on the bus around New Hampshire where he had become a hero during his years as a Boston Red Sox player. Between stops, Schilling regaled us with stories from his baseball career. On another occasion, I flew to Michigan in the evening to campaign with John the next day. It was about 10:00 p.m. when I arrived, and I asked the Secret Service whether John was there and awake. They said he was in his room with a guest, but I should go right in. I opened the door to find McCain and his guest, Clint Eastwood, who was in Michigan filming *Gran Torino* and staying at the same hotel. We had a wonderful conversation about John's campaign and Eastwood's movies.

In June, with the nomination clinched, John asked me to accompany him on a trip to Mexico and Colombia to highlight his foreign policy experience and his support of trade and immigration reform. We met the presidents of both countries, and visited some special local sites including the Basilica of Our Lady of Guadalupe in Mexico City, where we were hosted by a charismatic priest. At one point, the priest spoke with great passion and faith about the Virgin Mary. John must have worried I was feeling uncomfortable, because he interrupted the priest and said, "Monsignor, I don't know whether you know, but Senator Lieberman is Jewish."

"That's wonderful," the priest responded. "So was the Virgin Mary."

If we weren't in Mexico, I would have said, "Only in America"—but wherever, it was a memorable interfaith moment.

One day during the spring that year, Rick Davis, who was John's presidential campaign chairman and longtime political confidant, called me:

> "Senator, I have an interesting question for you. John wants to vet you for vice president. Are you okay with that?"

"Are you kidding, Rick?" I replied.

"No, I'm not kidding," Davis chuckled. "John is serious about considering you as his running mate."

I knew that presidential candidates sometimes vet someone for vice president as a thank you to that person to give him or her some favorable publicity, so my next response was, "John doesn't have to do this to thank me for supporting him. We are too close for him to have to do that."

"That's not why he wants to vet you."

"But," I continued in disbelief, "I don't know how he can do this. I got re-elected as an independent, but I am still a registered Democrat."

"He knows all that but I can assure you he is serious about considering you and he has his reasons. So, is it okay if we put you on the short list to be vetted?"

I was still in a state of disbelief, but I said, "I can't see how John can choose me, but if he wants to have me vetted, I will consent. It's okay."

"Great," Rick said. "You will be hearing from A.B. Culva-house who is chairing the VP vetting for us."

A few days later, I joined John on his campaign bus and before anybody else got on, I told him: "Rick called me and told me you wanted to vet me for vice president." I was totally surprised, and honored, "But, Johnny, I don't see how you could ever choose me."

"Why not?" he shot back.

"Because I'm a Democrat and you're a Republican."

"That's the point, Joey. People are fed up with all the partisanship in our government. Maybe a bipartisan national ticket is exactly what the people want and need."

I said,

I get it, I get it. And I admire you for thinking about the idea. It proves what a crazy maverick you really are. But please understand I don't expect this to happen so, as you said to me when you asked me to endorse you in the New Hampshire primary, whatever you do will have no effect on our friendship.

My best source inside the campaign was also my strong advocate and "Amigo," Lindsey Graham. He would call me regularly to tell me how I was doing among the McCain campaign leaders and advisors. Not surprisingly, there was a lively debate about my possible candidacy. First, it looked like Cindy McCain thought it was a good idea for John to ask me to run; another day, Steve Schmidt, the campaign manager, was reportedly on board. On another day, some others were arguing that if John chose me, there would be a rank-and-file Republican revolt against him—I had a pro-choice and pro-gay rights voting record.

Lindsey told me that someone had done a survey of Republican state chairs, and as many as a third of the delegates might walk out of the Republican Convention if I was nominated. Lindsey thought that would be great because it would prove to all the independent, swing voters in America that John McCain really was independent, and would be a bipartisan president. "And," Lindsey added, "Do you think those delegates and their followers will vote for Obama? No. They will vote for McCain no matter who is running with him." But the opponents apparently countered that while a lot of those Republicans might not vote for Obama, they might just not vote.

Meanwhile, I proceeded with the formal vetting process, answering all the questions and filling out all the forms. The process was thorough but not as demanding as the Gore campaign in 2000. That was probably because the McCain campaign knew I had already been vetted and had been through two national campaigns; teams of investigative reporters had also vetted me in their own way.

Later in July, McCain's chief vetter, A.B. Culvahouse, came to my home in Georgetown for a conversation. It was just the two of us, sitting at our dining room table. A.B. is a tall Tennessean and well-respected Washington attorney. He had come to Washington to work for Senator Howard Baker and gone on to be White House counsel for Presidents Reagan and Bush 43. In 2008, he was the Chairman of O'Melveny & Myers, the same national law firm Warren Christopher had chaired.

Culvahouse is a courtly Southern gentleman. That day in my dining room, he and I reviewed some of my answers on the questionnaire. The most fascinating new question was whether, if John selected me, and promised to serve only one term if elected, I would also make that pledge. A.B. explained that such a promise might help the campaign because John would be seventy-two years old when inaugurated—which would then make him the oldest person to become president in our history. Declaring he would serve only one term would also allow him to say he would only be focused on America's future, not his own political one. I told A.B. I thought that was a great idea and added, "This whole idea of John choosing me as his running mate seems like a fantasy to me, so it's very easy for me to say I would agree to only serve one term."

During August, I had a memorable phone conversation with Karl Rove. "McCain seems to want you to be his running mate," Rove said. "I know you two are great friends and I appeal to you as his friend to call him and tell him you don't want to be considered for vice president anymore. If he chooses you, he will destroy his candidacy and probably the Republican Party."

The strength of Rove's warning surprised me, but I knew he believed every word of it. I replied, "Karl, I have said to John from the first time Rick Davis and he told me they wanted to vet me for vice president that I didn't think he could ever choose me, but it's up to him. He's a grown-up and will make the decision."

A week or so later, Lindsey called to tell me that A.B. Culvahouse had said great things about me to John, but unfortunately it looked like the Republican Party leaders had convinced John he could not choose me. I told Lindsey I had always thought that would happen, and thanked him for being such a wonderful friend, supporter, and covert agent. After the campaign, Culvahouse told the media that John called him around this time in August and asked:

"What's your bottom line on Governor Palin?"

His answer: "High risk, high reward."

"You shouldn't have told me that, A.B. I've been a risk taker all my life."

During the last week in August, Hadassah and I went to her brother and sister-in-law's place on the beach in Amagansett, New York. John reached me there and told me that he was announcing his running mate the next day and, "Keep it quiet, Joey, but it's Governor Sarah Palin of Alaska." I promised to stay quiet. I also told him I didn't know anything about Governor Palin but, "You know John, I'm going to be with you 100 percent, and therefore with her."

I *was* with him 100 percent from the Republican Convention, through the dark days of the economic collapse of Lehman Brothers and the American economy, and campaigning right up until election night in Arizona.

In his last book, *The Restless Wave*, published in 2018 a few months before his death, John recalled that some of his campaign advisers and party officials had warned him in 2008 not to pick me as his running mate because my support for abortion rights and gay rights would split the Republican Party.

"It was sound advice that I could reason for myself," McCain wrote. "But my gut told me to ignore it, and I wish I had."

Since then, people have often asked me whether I think John and I would have won the 2008 election. We will never know for sure, but I doubt it. The American economy was too weak and Barack Obama was too strong. But it would have been a gutsy McCain attempt to break through the partisanship that was so clearly hurting our country.

In my 2006 Senate campaign and John McCain's 2008 presidential campaign, I came face to face with the partisanship in both major American political parties. The rising power of the so-called core constituencies in each party was dividing both from one another and from the American people, and it was making our national government dysfunctional.

In 2006, I lost in the Democratic primary but was able to take my case for centrism and bipartisanship to the general election, and was re-elected. In 2008, John McCain tried to do in his presidential campaign what had not been done since 1864, when Republican President Abraham Lincoln chose the Democratic governor of Tennessee, Andrew Johnson, as his running mate to unify the country that had been divided by the Civil War. In 2008, the core constituency in the Republican Party stopped John from leading a bipartisan ticket, just as the core constituency in the Democratic Party had defeated me in 2006.

If the centrists in both parties don't reassert themselves and reach across the aisle so that our government works again for our people, one day soon there will be the bipartisan national ticket John McCain aspired to in 2008—and, like Lincoln and Johnson, it might well win.

LESSONS FOR CENTRISTS

1. In politics, as in life, personal decisions and unexpected responses to them often lead to unforeseeable events which require other personal decisions.

   That is what 2008 looks like to me now. I never could have imagined that I would one day support a Republican candidate for president. However, the increasing partisanship in our politics and rising power of core constituencies of left and right in each party created new political realities that led me to support my close friend, John McCain, for president that year. My refusal to embrace a retreat from Iraq and my re-election to the Senate as an independent enabled me to do that. I mention Iraq not because John and I had the same position on the war, but because much of the base of the Democratic Party continued to view me as a party apostate because of the war. That explains why neither Senators Clinton nor Obama asked for my support. When John McCain did, I was free as a recently elected independent senator to give it and, looking back, I am glad that I did.

There is no question that my endorsement of McCain further alienated me from the base of the Democratic Party. Therefore, I cannot urge others to learn lessons from my endorsement of a Republican in 2008, without an obvious warning. There will be big political risks that come with doing something so bipartisan in an era that is so corrosively partisan.

But, if more political leaders endorse candidates in the other party when they believe it is the right thing to do for our country, then it would be very good for American politics and the American people. That was John McCain's vision in seriously considering me as his running mate. Republican Party leaders convinced him he was way ahead of political reality. I am sure Democratic leaders would have reacted the same way if a Democratic presidential candidate wanted to choose a Republican running mate then or now. But someday, if our politics don't find a way back to the bipartisan center, there will be a bipartisan, centrist national ticket.

14

CENTRISM IN SUPPORT OF PRESIDENT OBAMA

Hadassah and I started election evening in 2008 at John and Cindy McCain's beautiful apartment in Phoenix, and ended it a short ride away at the Biltmore Hotel where, on the Biltmore's great front lawn, John gave an uplifting and unifying concession speech and congratulations to president-elect Barack Obama. By Election Day, Obama's win was not a surprise. He had grown stronger as the year went on. When Lehman Brothers collapsed on September 15 and the economy rapidly fell into recession, the campaign was effectively over. America did not want another Republican president, even one as independent as John McCain. Although John's loss was expected, it naturally hurt him and all of us who supported him. He had worked tirelessly since at least 1999 for the opportunity to serve his country as commander in chief, but it was never to be.

When Hadassah and I returned to our room in the Biltmore and turned on the television, we saw Barack Obama with his family, speaking to an enormous crowd in a park in Chicago. He spoke eloquently of bringing the country together and working across partisan lines to solve America's most urgent problems. As I watched and listened, I felt pride and hope: pride that America had just elected an African American man as president because of the quality of his character and the great potential of his leadership, and hope for a better future for our country. It was the way I felt when John F. Kennedy was elected president in 1960, and more personally when Al Gore asked me to run for vice president in 2000. Another barrier had fallen. This barrier had been erected in racial slavery, maintained in legal racial segregation, and continued in racial bigotry. Now, as Jesse Jackson said to me in 2000, it had been broken—and the doors of opportunity would open wider for every other American. The American people had taken a giant step forward to becoming a more perfect union.

As I watched the president-elect that night, I recalled a memorable conversation I'd had with Barack Obama earlier that year in the Senate. He had just secured enough delegates to become the presidential nominee of the Democratic Party and had come back to the Senate because his vote was needed on an important bill. I congratulated him for winning the nomination. He thanked me and said: "I believe that one of the reasons I was able to win the nomination this year is because of what you did in 2000." Those words touched me. They were very thoughtful for him to say, especially since I was supporting his opponent, John McCain. "Thanks for saying that, Barack," I responded. "You are clearly the one who deserves the credit for winning this nomination and making history. But I would be very proud if my 2000 campaign made it even a little easier for you."

Early the morning after the election, Hadassah and I flew from Arizona back to Washington. She went home and I went right to my Senate office. One of the first calls that came in was from the Republican Senate leader, Mitch McConnell, who told me he had heard some Democrats were moving to take away my seniority and chairmanship because I had supported McCain. Mitch wanted me to know that I would be warmly welcomed in the Republican caucus and he would arrange good committee assignments for me. I thanked him and told him I was likely to remain in the Democratic caucus, unless my colleagues took punitive action against me. But if they did, I would get back to him.

The Democratic leader, Harry Reid, called a little later and asked if I would come to see him in his Capitol office the next morning. I always enjoyed being in Harry's office. I liked him, we worked well together, and there was a big, beautiful portrait of Mark Twain behind Harry's desk, which I appreciated. On that Thursday morning, Harry told me how angry the members of the Democratic caucus were that I had supported McCain and spoken at the Republican Convention. "Some of them even want to kick you out of the caucus. I won't allow that but, Joe, I have to ask you to give up your chairmanship of the Homeland Security Committee."

I responded strongly, "I can't do that, Harry. It is unfair. You know I have been a good member of the Democratic caucus, and I don't deserve to be treated that way."

Harry said, "I can probably give you the chairmanship of the Small Business Committee."

"You know that's a minor committee," I argued. If the caucus forces you to go forward with this, Harry, I will leave the caucus. Mitch McConnell already called me yesterday and told me they would welcome me in their caucus."

Harry said, "What's he going to do for you, Joe? He only has forty-one Republicans in the next session."

I responded, "McConnell will do for me whatever he can do for me. But I am not going to stay in the Democratic caucus if it demotes and humiliates me for something I did outside the caucus and the Senate for a friend."

Harry looked down and was silent for about ten seconds, which seemed like ten minutes to me. Then he looked up at me and said:

> I thought that was the way you would react. OK. Now let's talk about how we're going to get votes to defeat a motion in our caucus to take away your seniority and chairmanship. Who would lead such an effort for you?

First, I thanked Harry and assured him he would not regret having me in the caucus. Then I started to name some of the Democrats I was closest to: Chris Dodd, Tom Carper, Ken Salazar, Mark Pryor, Ben Nelson, and Mary Landrieu. Harry said,

> Ken Salazar would be the best one. I will call him and you should, too. But this is not a time when you should have to ask every member of the caucus. Your friends should make the calls and make the case for you.

Over the weekend, there were stories that President-elect Obama had told Reid it would be a mistake to take punitive action against me. It would undercut the message of unity and bipartisanship he wanted to bring into the White House with him. On Monday, in response to media requests, Obama's spokeswoman, Stephanie Cutter, released a statement that said, "President-elect Obama looks forward to working with anyone to move the country forward. We'd be happy to have Senator Lieberman caucus with the Democrats. We don't hold any grudges."

Ken Salazar was a proud Mexican American (whose Spanish ancestors had settled in America, believe it or not, about 400 years ago). He and I had a running joke, a conversation starter based on signs that some Hispanic delegates to the 2000 Democratic Convention had held high: "Viva Chutzpah." When I asked Ken to help me, that's what he said: "Viva Chutzpah." It captured the moment perfectly. Ken and his team of four or five other senators called every other Democratic senator. The responses were generally—but not universally—supportive and, of course, Barack Obama's statement was a big boost for me.

The Senate Democratic organizing caucus was traditionally held in the Old Senate Chamber on the third floor of the Capitol, which on most days is a place for tourists to visit. We convened there on December 18, 2008. No Democratic senator had yet declared that he or she would vote to punish me. All the vocal opposition was coming from the "Netroots Left"—which had begun a "Joe Must Go" petition drive after I endorsed McCain almost a year earlier.

At the caucus, Harry Reid and his deputies, Chuck Schumer and Dick Durbin, spoke for me. So did Ken Salazar, Chris Dodd, Tom Carper, and others. It was a closed door caucus, but I can say that Senators Pat Leahy and Bernie Sanders, both of Vermont, spoke against me because they announced that publicly. The final vote was forty-two for me to retain my seniority and chairmanship and thirteen against. Fortunately, I could never figure out exactly who the thirteen were, although it became a favorite guessing game among my staff.

Afterward, I told the media outside the Old Senate Chamber that I was grateful for the support of Senator Reid and the Senate Democratic caucus, and was looking forward to working with my colleagues and with President-elect Obama. Harry told the media he was happy with the way the caucus vote went. This was not "a time to walk out of here saying 'Boy, did we get even.'" Then, he added in classic Reid rhetoric:

"Lieberman is not some right-wing nut case."

I was sincerely grateful for the outcome. In a very partisan time, I had done something unusually bipartisan. A lot of people in my party in the Senate were predictably unhappy; but over the years, most of them had become my friends—and they knew I was a centrist Democrat they could work with, not, as our leader had said, a "right-wing nut case."

During President Obama's first term, I was able to play a constructive role in three of his major accomplishments: adoption of an economic recovery and stimulus plan in response to the Great Recession; enactment of comprehensive health-care reform; and repeal of the discriminatory "Don't Ask, Don't Tell" rules in our military. My record and experiences as a bipartisan centrist is what enabled me to be helpful on all three of these.

In his inaugural address on January 20, 2009, President Obama focused on the twin crises facing America—the worsening economic recession and the ongoing war with terrorists—and highlighted his hope for unity and bipartisanship in responding to both of those enormous challenges. "On this day," he said, "we gather because we have chosen hope over fear, unity of purpose over conflict and discord."

Even before he was inaugurated, Obama and his staff began to work on an economic recovery and stimulus proposal. With the help of his new chief of staff, Rahm Emanuel—who came to the White House after three terms in Congress—the president reached out repeatedly to the Republicans in the House and Senate. In the end, even though the recession had become the worst America had faced since the Depression of the 1930s, no Republicans in the House voted for the compromise stimulus plan that eventually emerged. Only three Senate Republicans did. Why did this happen?

Congressman Eric Cantor, the House Republican whip, gave this answer at the time:

"To his credit, the president reached out. The problem was there was never a reciprocal action from the speaker [Nancy Pelosi] . . . It's not about our being excluded [Cantor said he met with President Obama four times before the vote]. It's about the fact that the ideas we're proposing work."

In the House, everybody in both parties acknowledged that the economy was in serious economic trouble, but each party had a different solution to the crisis. Democrats wanted a combination of tax cuts and more spending, and Republicans wanted more and bigger tax cuts. It should have been possible to negotiate a bipartisan compromise in the House with, for example, less new spending and fewer tax cuts. Reporters covering the story predicted that in the end the compromise Senate plan (which achieved less new spending and fewer tax cuts) would be supported by ten or twenty House Republicans.

But Republican conservatives told their colleagues that they would face primaries in 2010 if they voted with Obama on the stimulus. A hardcore group of Republicans had already decided in January 2009 that their main goal was to defeat Obama when he ran for re-election four years later in 2012. In February 2009, after the stimulus was enacted, a group of the most zealous of those House Republicans organized a new movement called the Tea Party, which became a major factor in 2010 in nominating Republicans for Congress.

In the Senate, our government worked the way it is supposed to in a crisis as big as the recession—but it was only because of three centrist Republican senators: Susan Collins, Olympia Snowe, and Arlen Specter. Senator Harry Reid concluded early that he would need the support of every Senate Democrat and three Republicans to get to sixty votes and end the Republican filibuster that Mitch McConnell had already announced. Harry called me and said he needed my help with the three Republicans.

"I know they are your friends, Joe," Harry said. "I know you have worked with them on a lot of bipartisan stuff, and they trust you. I need you to help me and the president get their votes for a stimulus bill. You can tell them we are open to negotiating with them."

I told Harry I would be happy to help him. I knew it was urgent that Congress adopt an economic recovery and stimulus plan. Of course, I also owed him and the president for the way they supported me in my fight to remain chairman of the Homeland Security Committee. This was a very timely and comfortable way to repay them.

Harry was right about my relationship with those three Republican senators. The four of us were friends. We were all centrists who understood that the way to get things done was to work across party lines, and we often did that together. Susan Collins and I were the closest—since 2003, we had been the top Republican and Democrat on the Homeland Security Committee and had collaborated successfully on a wide range of legislation. Olympia Snowe and I had spent a lot of time since the 1990s trying, among other projects, to craft bipartisan, comprehensive health-care reform. Arlen Specter and I worked together and cosponsored a lot of legislation, including the first bill creating a new Department of Homeland Security in response to the terrorist attacks of 9/11.

I asked each of the three what they thought about Obama's stimulus proposal, and reiterated that their votes were critical. I also told them that Harry Reid had said that the president's proposal was "not fixed in stone." Each of them could have real influence on the final legislation. A day later, Susan Collins called and told me she had been asked to meet with Harry and Rahm. She requested that I come with her.

"Of course I will," I replied. "Do you want me to tell Harry I am coming?"

"I already told Harry I would ask you to join me, if your schedule allowed," she answered, "and he said that would be fine."

When Susan and I walked into Harry's office the next day, Rahm Emanuel, who is Jewish, said, "Hello, Senator Collins, I see you've brought your Jewish lawyer with you." After we all laughed—and without missing a beat—Susan said, "Senator Lieberman is my dear friend and trusted counselor." During that meeting and at least two others, we entered into a tough negotiation that changed Obama's proposal enough to get the support of the three Republican senators, but not so much as to lose the support of the more liberal senators and House Democrats whose votes were also critical to enacting an economic recovery plan.

Here's how it worked . . .

Harry and Rahm were professionals at the legislative process. Susan is, too, and she remains so in her current Senate role. She does her homework and is persistent but willing to compromise. My role, as I saw it, was to support her and try to mediate differences of opinion if I could. The original proposal President Obama sent to Congress was a $937 billion package, about two-thirds in new spending and one-third in tax cuts. That broke all previous records for a single piece of legislation, and that is what Susan Collins focused on. She ultimately negotiated the reduction of the cost to $787 billion, which was still the largest appropriation of its kind in American history.

I mediated one dispute about the president's proposal to add one billion dollars for research on responses to pandemic diseases. Susan argued that funding pandemic research was important and she would support it in a regular appropriation bill, but it didn't belong in an economic recovery plan whose purpose was to stimulate economic growth and new jobs. We were at an impasse, until I remembered that Susan was a strong supporter of federal support for Community Health Centers, which served low-income people. So, I suggested turning that one billion dollars into grants to the Community Health Centers for construction of new, job-creating facilities. Everyone liked the idea and agreed we would return to funding pandemic research in another bill.

The negotiations with Arlen Specter were the most memorable, and the most noble, political quid-pro-quo I ever witnessed in my political life. When Arlen sat down with Harry, Rahm, and others, including me, in Harry's office, he said he was happy with the changes that had been negotiated with Susan Collins. But he had a special, personal request to make. He would not support the bill without it.

Arlen was a truly heroic cancer survivor. He wanted more money in the bill for the National Institutes of Health (NIH), with most of it going to the National Cancer Institute to support the development of new cancer treatments. Harry Reid said he understood and respected that and asked Arlen how much more he wanted.

"Ten billion dollars more," Arlen calmly declared in his deep voice.

Rahm and Harry were stunned.

"Ten billion?!?" they both shouted.

"That is very admirable of you, Senator," Rahm said, "but $10 billion more is absolutely impossible."

Rahm offered to add one billion dollars.

Arlen did not budge, even as Rahm raised his offer a few billion dollars. My contribution to the negotiation was to say to Rahm and Harry, "We are already at about $800 billion on this bill. Can anyone possibly complain about spending $10 billion more to cure cancer?" Vice President Joe Biden made the same argument in support of Specter's bold demand.

In the end, Arlen got $10 billion for NIH cancer research and the Obama-Biden administration got the sixtieth vote they needed for the Senate to take up and pass legislation that would save our economy from going into a depression.

Afterward, Senator Reid received a lot of well-deserved credit for the passage of the economic recovery plan. "The bill was a team effort," he told a reporter from *Politico*, and added a metaphor from the casinos of his home state:

> I'm playing cards. They gave me three aces. Susan Collins pulls out a full house. No matter what I was dealt, she had a better hand . . . It's hard for the House [of Representatives] to accept that. But no matter what I did, Susan had the better deal . . . Nancy accepts but acknowledges a strong dislike for what I have to do over here.

There were times like that when I thought Harry Reid was channeling Damon Runyon.

I appreciated another sentence in that *Politico* article, one that I assumed Harry had inspired:

> Senator Joseph Lieberman, the Connecticut independent who infuriated Democrats by backing McCain in November, proved a much-needed conduit to Collins and the other moderates.

The next big project would have been Barack Obama's priority if the economy had not cratered in 2008: comprehensive health-care reform. In February 2009, the White House asked me to meet with the president in the Oval Office. It was just the two of us. He thanked me for my help on his economic recovery program, but wanted to talk about health-care reform which, as he said, the American people needed and he wanted to get done. "I am really going to need your help on health-care reform, Joe."

"I would be glad to help," I said. In fact, I had been working on health-care reform, usually with bipartisan groups of senators, since the early 1990s. I told President Obama what I guessed he already knew. The history of failed presidential attempts to enact health-care reform went back to Truman, Nixon, Carter, and Clinton—it was definitely not encouraging. The only exception and hopeful piece of history was the enactment of Medicaid and Medicare under President Johnson in 1965.

That was forty-five years ago. There were still millions of Americans, mostly lower middle income, who did not have health insurance. The insurance companies were still treating consumers unfairly in many ways. There was a real and present need for comprehensive health-care reform, but it would be very hard to achieve because of the increasing partisanship and the opposition of the business and professional groups involved.

"Mr. President, this is a fight worth taking on," I said. "I admire you for wanting to do it, and I will help in any way I can."

The specific advice I gave President Obama that day was based on the Clinton administration's failed attempt at health-care reform. "It is better to bring opponents inside your tent than to leave them outside where they will attack you," I said. I am sure I was not the only person to give the president that advice. He acted on it, and that was a major reason why he was able to do what his presidential predecessors couldn't.

My long history of working for comprehensive health-care reform was shaped by the Democratic Leadership Council and its think tank, the Progressive Policy Institute. In 1990, support for comprehensive health-care reform was greater than it had been in four decades. People were upset about the rising cost of health care. Many who did not receive health insurance from their employers could no longer afford it themselves. The debate in Congress in 1990 about how to fix the problem was between supporters of market-based reform on one side and advocates for a single-payer, government-controlled health-care system on the other.

During his 1992 presidential campaign, Bill Clinton chose the middle way and recommended reforms which he called "competition within a budget." That pleased us DLC New Democrats who were definitely against a single-payer system and were for market-based reforms that would not balloon the federal debt.

After the election, the president asked his wife Hillary to chair his Health Reform Task Force, which produced a complicated and government-heavy proposal. It was opposed by the DLC, which worked with Sam Nunn, Republican Senator David Durenberger from Minnesota, and me to write and introduce the Managed Competition Act of 1993. It would have provided comprehensive health-care reform, but relied less on bureaucracy and government regulation and more on market forces than the Clinton plan. Neither bill was ever considered by the Senate.

The Kaiser Foundation polled voters in the congressional elections of 1994 and found that a substantial majority believed that the Clinton's health-care reform proposals had too much government bureaucracy and threatened to reduce the quality of their personal care and increase its costs. That was one reason the Republicans swept the elections that year.

In the years between then and Barack Obama's presidency, I was involved in several bipartisan attempts at health-care reform: the Promoting Responsible Managed Care Act of 1999 with Republican John Chafee of Rhode Island; the American Center for Cures Act of 2005 with Senator Thad Cochran, Republican of Mississippi; and the Healthy Americans Act of 2007, spearheaded by Democrat Ron Wyden of Oregon and Republican Bob Bennett of Utah, which the Congressional Budget Office estimated would provide health insurance to 99 percent of the American people.

None of these proposals passed the Senate, but President Obama and his team had learned from all of them. He incorporated those lessons in his 2009 proposal. He began by reaching out to the groups that had opposed the Clinton health-care reforms, and his team negotiated agreements with them. The Health Insurance Association of America (HIAA) decided they would not spend the millions they had spent on television commercials against the Clinton proposal after they reached an understanding with the Obama White House. The Obama plan, after all, would give them between twenty and thirty million new customers.

In return, the health insurance industry would accept several reforms, including prohibitions against refusing to cover people with pre-existing illnesses and charging differential rates based on medical history or gender. Lifetime caps on benefits were also prohibited. The companies also accepted minimum standards for qualified health-care plans that required coverage for preventative tests like mammograms, and an option for young people to remain on their parents' health insurance until the age of twenty-six. The pharmaceutical companies were neutralized by the administration's promise not to push to allow re-importation of prescription drugs. Hospitals received increases in reimbursement schedules. In the end, all these critical and powerful industries, and the American Medical Association (AMA), either publicly supported Obamacare or remained neutral.

The Obama proposal was real reform. It required most employers to provide health-care benefits to their employees or pay a tax equal to a percentage of wages; expanded Medicaid to provide benefits to people earning up to 133 percent of the federal poverty level; and subsidized lower-middle income individuals and families so they could afford health insurance on the Obamacare exchanges that would also enable them to comparison shop for health insurance. People who could afford insurance were mandated to have insurance or pay a fine, a provision that had emerged from the conservative Heritage Foundation in 1989 and had been adopted by the moderate Republican Mitt Romney administration in Massachusetts in 2006. To pay for all this, various taxes were raised on higher-income taxpayers.

The three centrist Republicans who had supported the Obama economic recovery legislation were under persistent pressure from conservative Republicans, led by the Tea Party, because of their apostate bipartisanship.

Arlen Specter, who was up for re-election in 2010, responded to that harsh political antagonism by leaving the Republican Party and joining the Senate Democratic caucus in August 2009. That meant there were sixty Democrats in the Senate. Senators Collins and Snowe thought about Obama's proposal and talked to the president and his administration about it more than once, but they were reluctant to engage. I wondered whether—if the economy had not collapsed in 2008 and President Obama had not been forced to take up economic recovery legislation before his first choice, health-care reform—we would have had the support of Senators Snowe and Collins.

It was becoming clear to Senator Reid and the Obama administration that they would have to get all sixty Democrats to support the bill and vote to break a filibuster. It was rare for one party caucus in the Senate to have sixty members, but when it did, there would naturally be a great range of opinions among them. This would require movement to the center to hold all sixty votes. That is what happened in 2009 and 2010 to pass Obamacare. We moderates were empowered by the political reality the filibuster created, and we used that power in different ways. Some received greater benefits for their home states and others kept the overall proposal from going too far left, becoming too governmental, and costing so much money that it would put the federal government into even greater debt.

My main concern was with a proposal for a government-controlled, health-care system that had long been favored by many liberal Democrats. They were frustrated that President Obama did not clearly agree with them. I heard this frustration and anger in our weekly Senate Democrat caucuses that year, where some of my colleagues began to press for a foot-in-the-door compromise called a public option. It took various forms, the most common of which was to create a government-owned and financed insurance company that would compete with the private companies. It was clearly intended to be a first step toward federal government control of health care and health insurance. I made it clear from the beginning that I had been opposed to such proposals for the two decades I had been in the Senate. Several other Democratic senators felt the same way.

But the liberal Democrats understood that their votes were also necessary to get to sixty, so they persisted. Harry Reid and the administration tried to accommodate them. I never thought that the idea of a public option was that important to President Obama. In fact, he once described it during 2009 as only "a sliver of health-care reform." But Senator Chuck Schumer kept coming to me with new compromises. I kept saying no to him, to the Democratic caucus, to reporters' questions, and in op-eds, including one in the *Hartford Courant* on November 2, 2009, in which I wrote:

> A new public option will likely increase premiums for the 170 million Americans who already have private insurance, and let's not forget the warning of the Congressional Budget Office that the federal government will assume the financial risk that the premiums charged in a given year (for insurance from the public option company) may not cover all of the public plan's costs.

In an interview with Manu Raju in *Politico* on October 27, I said I would vote against the health-care reform if it contained a public option: "We're trying to do too much at once. To put this government-created insurance company on top of everything else is just asking for trouble for taxpayers, for the premium payers, and for the national debt . . . We have the opportunity to do some great health-care reforms now . . . Let's seize that opportunity."

The Democratic-controlled Senate Finance Committee had voted down two amendments to include a public health insurance option—one introduced by Senator Schumer, the other by Senator Jay Rockefeller—after which the Democratic chairman of the committee, Max Baucus, said, "If a public option is in this bill, it will hold back meaningful reform this year."

But the liberal Democrats refused to reject the "perfect" so we could all do "good." On the morning of Sunday, December 13, I went on *Face the Nation* on CBS and was asked about the public option. I explained why I was against it. Then the respected host, Bob Schieffer, asked me if that meant I would not vote to break a filibuster on a bill that contained a public option. I said that was correct, which I had said for months in public and private; but apparently, because of the forum, this was the first time many people heard it.

When I left the studio and got in my car, the phone rang. It was Harry Reid. He asked, "Did you just say on *Face the Nation* that you would not vote for cloture on our bill if it has a public option?"

I replied, "I did, Harry. That is what I have been saying for months."

Even though it was a Sunday, the Senate was coming into session that afternoon. Harry asked me to come to his office after the first roll call vote. When I arrived, I found Harry, Rahm Emanuel, Chuck Schumer, Dick Durbin, and some staff. After we discussed why I felt so strongly about the public option in any form, Rahm asked, "If we take out the public option, will you commit to support the bill?"

My answer was, "Yes, I will enthusiastically support the rest of the bill. It will be a major accomplishment for President Obama and this Congress and for our constituents. I will be proud to be part of it!"

"Ok," Rahm said. "The public option is out of the bill."

The Democrats who had been pushing the public option were outraged. Harry called a caucus for the next afternoon to try to quell an uprising. He asked that I attend, "even if you do not speak," he said. I went and did not speak. The caucus was held on Monday afternoon, December 14, and was a tour de force by Harry Reid:

> I know many of you are angry at our friend, Joe Lieberman, but he feels really strongly about the public option, though most of us disagree with him. With his support, we will have the great accomplishment of passing health-care reform, which will be so important to millions of our people and to President Obama. Without Joe's support we don't have the votes.

Then Harry went over five or six progressive bills favored by most of the Democrats that he said "would not have passed or even been taken up this year without Joe Liberman's support."

Many of my colleagues in the Democratic caucus were still unhappy, but they accepted Harry's appeal and rejected Howard

Dean's call for the Senate bill to be killed if it did not contain a government-sponsored option.

Nonetheless, a myth was born that I had stopped "real" health-care reform in order to accommodate the health insurance companies in Connecticut. In fact, I had a record of opposition in the Senate to government-controlled health insurance for more than two decades, which had begun in the work of the Democratic Leadership Council. The health insurance industry did not lobby me to fight against the public option; they had already made their own agreement with the administration not to oppose Obamacare. The myth also ignores the fact that the Affordable Care Act—for which I was the necessary sixtieth vote—was real and historic health-care reform.

The Affordable Care Act passed the Senate on Christmas Eve 2009 by a vote of 60–40. It then went to conference with the House, which ultimately agreed to the Senate bill on March 21, 2010. President Obama signed the law on March 23, and millions of Americans have benefitted since. It was not a bipartisan achievement, but was centrist enough to be enacted by all the Democrats in the Senate and most in the House.

My third leadership role among President Obama's first-term achievements was in the repeal of "Don't Ask, Don't Tell" (DADT). It was driven by the president and Democrats in Congress, but was more bipartisan in its passage than economic recovery and Obamacare. The reason was the extraordinary advocacy done across America by organizations for Lesbian, Gay, Bisexual, and Transgender (LGBT) rights, led by the Human Rights Campaign (HRC) and the Servicemembers Legal Defense Network (SLDN).

I had been a supporter of gay rights since I was in the Connecticut State Senate during the 1970s. Those were early days in the gay rights movement. Legislation proposed by one of my Democratic state senate colleagues would have prevented discrimination in housing based on sexual orientation. It was for me, as lawyers say, a question of "first instance."

I had not thought about it before. But as I did, it seemed to be an easy decision for reasons that were theological and constitutional.

LGBT people were as much children of God, our Creator, as every other human was. God's creation embraced diversity. America's legal system was built on that theological foundation. The Declaration of Independence and Constitution guaranteed every American "unalienable rights," including the overriding right to equal justice under law. I enthusiastically supported that first gay rights bill I had been asked to vote on. There was a tremendous legislative battle in Hartford over it, one that divided Democrats from Republicans and Democrats from Democrats. It did not pass the Connecticut legislature until years later.

When I arrived in the US Senate, the gay rights movement had made significant progress in law—but the United States was still a long way from providing equal justice to LGBT Americans. That was certainly true of those who wanted to serve in the US Armed Services. Prohibitions on homosexual activity in the military went back to the Revolutionary War. During the 1970s and 1980s, the gay rights movement began to raise the issue in response to dismissal of some heroic and honored service people who had suffered nonetheless because of their sexual orientation.

In 1990, a newly formed advocacy group called the Gay and Lesbian Military Freedom Project (MFP) started lobbying Congress to end the ban. During the 1992 presidential campaign, the cause of human rights for gay and lesbian Americans, including the right to serve in our military, received more public attention than ever before. All of the Democratic candidates—including the eventual nominee, Bill Clinton—said they would, if elected, try to repeal the prohibition on military service by gay and lesbian Americans.

After President Clinton took office, he decided to fulfill that campaign promise almost immediately. However, he ran into a lot of opposition from the Joint Chiefs of Staff and leading Democratic hawks like Georgia Senator Sam Nunn. His compromise was DADT. It was a contorted and unjust response to a real inequity. Homosexuality would remain illegal in the military. If a service man or woman were found to have engaged in homosexual acts or declared themselves to be gay or lesbian, they would be discharged.

But they would not be asked about their sexual orientation and were not required to reveal it.

I was one of five members of the Senate Armed Services Committee to vote against the compromise. I argued it was like a status crime under which people were punished for who they were, not what they did. In other words, the question the military should ask was how well people carried out their duties as soldiers, not what their sexual orientation was.

Since then, under the DADT policy, thousands of personnel who had been serving honorably were discharged from the American military only because of their sexual orientation. That was obviously unjust and usually disabling for them personally, and it also cost the US government millions of dollars to recruit and train replacements for them. During the 2008 presidential campaign, Barack Obama pledged to repeal DADT if elected. But here, too, he learned from Clinton. Once elected, he waited to take on this issue.

In an October 2009 speech to the Human Rights Campaign, he restated his commitment to end the ban, but didn't say when. Then, in his State of the Union address in January 2010, he declared: "This year, I will work with Congress and our military to finally repeal the law that denies gay Americans the right to serve the country they love because of who they are." A short while later, Secretary of Defense Bob Gates and Joint Chiefs of Staff chairman Admiral Michael Mullen announced that they supported the repeal of DADT. It was important, unprecedented support for the legislative efforts that followed. I know Gates and Mullen well enough to know that they were sincerely for the repeal of DADT, but it didn't hurt that the commander in chief had also made his position clear.

Throughout the campaign in Congress to repeal DADT, the gay rights movement was smart and strategic. I was honored when its leaders came to me early in 2010 to ask if I would be the lead sponsor of the repeal legislation in the Senate. I also appreciated their reasons for asking me. They said they knew that I had opposed DADT in 1993, and they added that they wanted a lead sponsor who had a record in support of the military and who was a hawk on national security. This pleased me because it summarized the centrist, independent Democrat I aspired to be—liberal on social issues, including human rights, and conservative on foreign policy and national security.

Early in March 2010, I introduced the repeal, titled "The Military Readiness Enhancement Act." The gay rights movement's leaders knew that if we were going to be successful, we needed sixty votes to break a filibuster. There were then fifty-nine Democrats in the Senate, and we couldn't assume we would get all of them. The advocates also understood that a change of this importance in military practice would best be achieved with support from both parties. They asked Susan Collins to be the lead Republican cosponsor. I was delighted that she was willing to take this cause on with me.

For the next few months, Susan Collins and I, in alliance with the gay rights organizations, worked senator by senator to describe our bill and ask them to cosponsor it. If they couldn't do that, we asked them to commit to vote for it when it came up on the Senate floor. We were impressed by how many of our colleagues told us that constituents in their states wanted them to support the bill. Feedback from constituents is incredibly effective in advancing legislation in Washington. People at home are much more persuasive than lobbyists in Washington. The gay and lesbian rights movement seemed to be organized better than they ever had been to make their case to Congress, regardless of party or ideology.

The first big test for our effort to repeal DADT came on May 27 in the Senate Armed Services Committee (SASC) during its annual "mark-up" of the National Defense Authorization Act (NDAA). Susan and I, both members of the SASC, decided to introduce our bill as an amendment to the NDAA, which had to pass every year for the US Armed Services to function.

The chairman of the SASC, Carl Levin of Michigan, was a strong supporter of DADT repeal. The passionate, lead opponent of the bill was my friend John McCain. He argued that we should not make such a disruptive change in military operations while at war. We argued that our amendment corrected an injustice that was depriving our military of capable people who wanted to serve when they were needed. This was the perfect time to make such a change.

Our amendment passed 16–12 with every Democrat but Jim Webb of Virginia voting for it, and every Republican but Susan Collins voting against it. On that same day, the House of Representatives took up the same bill, which had been introduced by Congressman Patrick Murphy of Pennsylvania. It passed 234–194.

In 2020, Winnie Stachelberg, who had been vice president of the Human Rights Campaign Foundation in 2010, and Rudy de Leon, who had been deputy secretary of defense, looked back and wrote: "The SASC vote on May 27, 2010, proved to be a key moment in the journey toward a fairer and more equitable America."

The NDAA bill was expected to come to the Senate floor sometime in the fall. In the meantime, Secretary Gates had appointed a task force to gauge opinion inside the military about repeal of DADT, and to consider its impact on military readiness. It was expected to be finished later in the year.

On September 21, Harry Reid and Carl Levin moved to bring up the NDAA with our DADT repeal in it. Much to our surprise, John McCain initiated a filibuster against this "must pass" legislation. The Republicans in the Senate were in an argument with Harry Reid about how many amendments they could introduce to the NDAA. The vote on closure was 56–43. We were four votes short of the sixty we needed to end the filibuster. Most observers felt that was the end of the effort to repeal DADT in 2010. But the gay rights movement—and Susan Collins and I—refused to accept defeat so quickly.

The fight for the repeal became more urgent on Election Day, November 2, 2010, when Republicans regained control of the House of Representatives in a landslide, 242–193, the largest loss by either political party in a House election since 1938. Republicans also picked up six seats in the Senate, which went from fifty-nine Democrats and forty-one Republicans to fifty-three Democrats and forty-seven Republicans. That would make it much harder for Democrats to stop Republican filibusters in the next session of

Congress. Thinking about the DADT repeal after that election, I remembered words from the Talmud:

"If not now, when?"

The Democratic leadership brought Congress back into session after the election because there were many bills they and President Obama wanted to pass before the next Congress, including the repeal of DADT and passage of the NDAA. On November 30, the Department of Defense task force issued its report, concluding that there was a "low risk of service disruption" if DADT was repealed. They also released polling of military personnel that showed good support for the change, more than most people expected.

SASC Chairman Carl Levin quickly convened two days of committee hearings on the Task Force Report on December 2 and 3. Secretary Gates and Admiral Mullen presented very effective testimony at those hearings. Gates noted that recently a federal court had found DADT unconstitutional, and that he would rather have Congress repeal DADT and give him time to implement the change—as our bill did—than have a higher federal court force him to do it overnight.

Admiral Mullen movingly spoke of military values: "Our people sacrifice a lot for their country, including their lives. None of them should have to sacrifice their integrity as well." The chiefs of all the military services testified that day. They were an impressive sight, sitting next to each other in uniform at the witness table. Half of them said they supported repeal and half had mixed feelings. The most clearly opposed was General James Amos, Commandant of the Marine Corps; but with the American military's characteristic sense of duty, he said: "If the law is changed . . . the Marine Corps will get in step and do it smartly."

A week later on December 9, Harry Reid and Carl Levin moved to take up the NDAA again in the Senate and, once again, McCain began a filibuster. This time, he added that it was unfair for Democrats to try to make this big change during a lame duck session. That was a familiar argument made by either party when they were about to take over one or both chambers in the next session. Harry decided there just wasn't time to repeat all the arguments on the repeal of DADT, because there was no new reason to believe we could get the sixty votes to break the filibuster. He reluctantly moved on to other legislation. The media now unanimously pronounced our effort to repeal DADT DOA—Dead on Arrival.

But we had come too far to give up. There was one option left. We had chosen to put the DADT repeal on the National Defense Authorization Act because we thought that bill had to pass. Now, maybe it was worth trying to raise our repealer as a stand-alone bill. We talked to Harry Reid, who agreed it was worth a try. He said he would use his power as majority leader to circumvent the normal committee process and bring our bill right onto the Senate calendar. Harry and the gay rights leaders also talked to Speaker Nancy Pelosi. I soon got a call from Steny Hoyer, the House Democratic majority leader, who said he thought a separate bill was a great idea. He had found a vehicle for moving it in the House and was prepared to go first; he knew it would pass in the House, and would have some momentum when it arrived in the Senate. I agreed.

We announced later on December 9 that we were introducing a stand-alone repealer bill, to great surprise. The *Washington Post* called it a "Hail Mary Pass." Susan and I went to work on all of our Republican colleagues who had not yet come out against repeal. And, more important, so too did the gay rights community and their allies throughout the country. In impressive numbers, they called and wrote senators, and visited them in their in-state offices. I asked one of my Republican colleagues who ultimately voted for the bill what made up his mind. His answer was revealing and encouraging:

> First, I had no idea there are that many gay people living in my state. Second, they made great arguments based on values I believe in.

The House took up the repeal bill on Wednesday, December 15, and passed it 250–175, with fifteen Republicans voting "aye" and fifteen Democrats voting "no." Debate began shortly thereafter in the Senate, with a cloture vote scheduled for later Saturday morning. It was the Sabbath for me, but it was my responsibility to be there. Harry said he would hold the vote so I would have time to go to the early service at our synagogue in Georgetown and walk in to participate in the end of the debate.

They asked me to give the closing remarks in favor of the bill and cloture. John McCain gave the closing statement against. There we were, two good friends, fighting passionately against each other. Susan Collins and I, and all the people with us for repeal, proved that we could be as combative and immovable as John—which wasn't easy.

The vote on cloture was sixty-three for and thirty-three against, with five other Republicans joining Susan Collins in support of repeal: Scott Brown of Massachusetts, Mark Kirk of Illinois, Lisa Murkowski of Alaska, Olympia Snowe of Maine, and George Voinovich of Ohio. We were ecstatic. Harry Reid, remembering the old political wisdom "When you have the votes, call the roll," scheduled the vote on final passage for 3 p.m. that afternoon. Two more Republicans—Richard Burr of North Carolina and John Ensign of Nevada—voted for the bill, and the final vote was a thrilling sixty-five for repeal and thirty-one against.

I can't remember a moment in my twenty-four years in the Senate when I felt more excited than I was when DADT was repealed. Part of the reason was that we had righted a wrong, and part of it was that both our opponents and the media thought more than once that we had lost. But we, and the people all across America who believed DADT was wrong, refused to give up.

On Wednesday, December 22, 2010, President Obama signed the bill into law in the jam-packed auditorium of the Department of the Interior in Washington. The feeling in that room was less like a bill signing and more like a college fieldhouse after the team had won a national championship. It was pulsating with chants of "Yes, we did!"

In talking with people there, I understood that what was being celebrated that morning was more than the repeal of DADT. It was also the coming of age of the gay rights movement as a political force in America. It was a turning point in the movement. As Winnie Stachelberg and Rudy de Leon wrote ten years later:

> The repeal was a landmark event for LGBTQ rights. Once the nation's largest employer changed policy based on the fact that it was wrong to discriminate against someone because of their sexual orientation; it helped lay the foundation for a decade of redressing further inequities. Chief among them was the glass-ceiling achievement in 2015 when the Supreme Court ruled in favor of same sex marriage.

And in 2020, Pete Buttigieg became the first openly gay candidate for a major party's nomination for president, and later the first openly gay member of a president's cabinet as secretary of transportation.

The law is the way we express our best values, our aspirations for ourselves and our country. And sometimes new laws change minds and behaviors. The repeal of DADT was one of those times. I was thrilled to be part of it. At that signing ceremony, President Obama was ebullient as he came to the stage to a roar from the crowd. He blurted out,

> I am just overwhelmed. This is a very good day . . . This law I am about to sign will strengthen our national security and uphold the values our military fights to defend.

Then he thanked "the Democrats and Republicans who put conviction ahead of politics to get this done together."

He was absolutely right. Without bipartisan support in the Senate, we never could have stopped the filibuster and passed the bill. And we never would have had that bipartisan support without the extraordinary work of the gay rights movement and its allies.

President Obama said a personal hello to each of the twenty or twenty-five people on the stage with him that day. When he got to me, we exchanged a big hug. I later joked with Hadassah that if I ran for re-election in 2012 and was challenged again by a Democrat in a primary, this time I could have commercials of me hugging a Democratic president. I guess that makes me a bipartisan hugger.

In fact, I had already decided that I would not run again. I had been privileged to have four terms, twenty-four years, in the Senate—which was, as I wrote earlier, my life's dream. It was time to move on to a new chapter. On January 19, 2011, I went home to Stamford, Connecticut, to announce that I would not seek re-election to the Senate in 2012.

> For the extraordinary opportunities to serve our state and country that I've had, I am personally grateful to the voters of Connecticut who I can never thank enough.
>
> I have not always fit comfortably into conventional political boxes. I have always thought that my first responsibility is not to serve a political party but to serve my constituents, my state, and my country.

And I promised, "I will keep doing everything in my power to build strong bridges across party lines."

My last two years in the Senate, 2011 and 2012, were the most partisan and least productive of my twenty-four years there. I worked hard, with *some* bipartisan support, to get something done on two big problems—climate change and cyber-security—but could not get to sixty votes on either one. Both were mischaracterized, mostly by Republicans, as being "against business" instead of "for national security and public health and safety." People asked me if I was leaving the Senate because it had become so partisan and dysfunctional.

"No," I answered, "but that makes it a lot easier to leave."

Because the president and Congress were in constant conflict in 2011 and 2012, very little of consequence was enacted. President

Obama turned, as often happens at such times, to foreign policy where his role as commander in chief gave him latitude to act. In March 2011, the US led an international military intervention in the Libyan Civil War. In May of that year, a team of US Navy SEALs, on a gutsy order from the president, killed Osama Bin Laden in a brilliant attack on his compound in Pakistan.

I also turned my attention to foreign policy, using the powers the Constitution gives members of Congress to legislate, advocate, and meet with friends and allies around the world. I did most of this in a bipartisan partnership with John McCain. Our friendship had fully survived the tensions of our disagreement over the repeal of DADT, which is the way it is supposed to be.

In February 2011, after the Arab Spring democratic revolutions broke out in the Middle East and toppled longtime rulers in Tunisia and Egypt, John and I were the first US officials to visit those two countries and to meet with the victorious revolutionaries. It was a thrilling trip during which we learned a lot and offered help to the new leaders. One memorable exchange happened at a dinner with leaders of the Tunisian uprising at the US ambassador's residence. During the discussion, one of them rose and said, "There is one American we would most like to invite to our country and we ask you senators to invite him for us."

McCain and I said, "Of course, we will try, who is it?"

The answer was thoroughly unexpected: "Mark Zuckerberg."

Why Zuckerberg? Because they had organized and carried out their revolution on Facebook. Zuckerberg had effectively supplied "weapons" to them in their successful, non-violent revolution. After John and I returned to Washington, we joined with John Kerry to introduce legislation to establish enterprise funds to support economic development and democratization in Tunisia and Egypt. The Obama administration embraced the proposal, and it was enacted.

After an uprising by the Libyan people in February, 2011 resulted in a brutal response by the Qaddafi regime, McCain and I urged President Obama to intervene militarily. When he did, we strongly supported him. In Syria, Bashar al-Assad turned his military on his own people when they also demanded change. Again, John and

I urged President Obama to call on Assad to step down, and we pushed the White House to impose tougher economic sanctions on Syria until Assad did so.

This time, the president was reluctant to get involved in any meaningful way to protect the human and political rights of the Syrian people. The violence in Syria developed into a nightmarish and long-lasting humanitarian catastrophe. John and I made three trips to Lebanon and Turkey to meet with leaders of the Syrian opposition to Assad to encourage them and try to help. We also met with Syrian refugees jammed in the camps set up in Turkey to tell them we were with them.

During 2011 and 2012, I continued my support of stronger economic sanctions and diplomatic pressure against the extremist, terrorist regime that held the people of Iran hostage. All of these initiatives began and ended successfully with a bipartisan group of cosponsors. In my last month as a senator, on December 6, 2012, I was grateful that the Sergei Magnitsky Rule of Law Accountability Act, which I had cosponsored with Senators Ben Cardin (Democrat of Maryland), Roger Wicker (Republican of Mississippi), and John McCain, was adopted by the Senate and enacted into law. Named to honor a lawyer who was arrested and murdered in Moscow by Russian authorities after uncovering massive tax fraud, the bill imposed sanctions against human rights violators in Russia, restrictions that would prevent them from gaining access to the US banking system or traveling to the US.

The 2012 session of the Senate ended in extended partisan conflict, which kept us in session through New Year's Eve to protect the country from going over a fiscal cliff that would have automatically raised taxes and cut spending at midnight on January 1, 2013. No one could remember when Congress had ever been in regular session on New Year's Eve. Two couples, Judge José Cabranes and Professor Kate Stith, and Dr. Alan and Deedee DeCherney, who were dear friends and had been spending New Year's Eve with us for twenty-five years spent this one at the US Capitol with us and the US Senate. We actually had a great time.

A compromise was finally reached to reduce the amount that taxes would be increased. It passed the House at 11 p.m. on December 31, 2012, and then the Senate around 2 a.m. on January 1, 2013. No agreement was reached on government spending, so it was kicked over to the next session (which would begin in three days) and helped create a serious debt limit crisis—but the new Congress and my successor, Senator Chris Murphy, would have to deal with that.

That chaotic ending to twenty-four years of productive service in the Senate convinced me of two things. First, it was the right time to leave; and second, I must look for a way from outside Congress to build more bipartisan, centrism inside. I found it in an organization called No Labels, which I will describe in the next and last chapter of this book.

LESSONS FOR CENTRISTS

1. After my support of John McCain in the 2008 election, President-elect Obama and Democratic Majority Leader Reid showed that they understood what Abe Ribicoff had long-ago taught me about John Bailey: "John never allows himself the luxury of revenge."

   When some of my Senate Democratic colleagues and the left-wing "netroots" began a campaign to deny me my Senate seniority and committee chairmanship because of my support of Republican McCain, Obama and Reid opposed such action. That made me grateful and eager to help them in the Senate. When the president and majority leader asked, I used my legislative experience and good relationships with moderate Democrats and moderate Republicans to help Obama enact three of his first-term priorities: economic recovery from the Great Recession of 2008; comprehensive health-care reform; and repeal of the discriminatory Don't Ask, Don't Tell policy of our military. The years 2009 and 2010 turned out to be two of the most constructive and satisfying of my twenty-four in the Senate because I knew I was making a difference for the better—and I was doing so in support of a Democratic president I admired.

2. In his first year in office, President Obama showed he had learned a major lesson from the first year of the Clinton presidency: stay away early on from controversial legislation that might not pass, like Don't Ask, Don't Tell.

He also learned that sometimes in government, a leader's personal priority has to yield to realities of the moment. In 2009, Obama wanted to tackle health-care reform first, but he wisely decided he could not because the American economy was still staggering from the collapse of 2008. He had to do an economic recovery and stimulus bill. That used up a lot of his political capital and made it harder to succeed when he got to health-care reform later in 2009. But he also accomplished that, this time by occupying the center-left of the Democratic Party. He had no choice—not a single Republican senator would vote for his proposals. I was glad to work with the small but very necessary group of moderate Senate Democrats who ultimately provided the votes to get to sixty to break the Republican filibuster of "Obamacare."

Then and after, I became the most visible—though not the only—Democratic opponent of the so-called public option. It was the Far Left's door-opener to government-controlled health care and an end to the employer-based insurance system that covered more than 150 million, mostly satisfied Americans. It would also have exploded the national debt.

I took a lot of criticism from some Democrats then and since for the Obama administration's removal of the public option, but it enabled us to get the votes to enact comprehensive health-care reform, a goal that had eluded presidents and Congress before Obama for decades, like the repeal of Don't Ask, Don't Tell.

3. The big lesson to be learned from repeal of "Don't Ask, Don't Tell" was that public support for a proposal can encourage members of Congress to work across party lines to enact

that proposal. For the economic recovery and health-care reform bills, there was clearly both public support and public opposition, and Congress heard from both sides.

When it came to a big social policy change like repeal of "Don't Ask, Don't Tell," many members of Congress assumed that most of their constituents were against it. Then the LGBT community organized as never before and convinced members of both parties that more of their constituents than they realized supported repeal of Don't Ask, Don't Tell, because it was the right thing to do.

There is a larger lesson to be learned from this experience. The president and Congress do not operate in an isolated bubble. In our democracy, they are moved by public opinion, and that can include being moved to the bipartisan center. It happened on "Don't Ask, Don't Tell" and can happen again whenever citizens organize, as the LGBT community did. The people have the power to encourage members of Congress to move to the bipartisan center to solve their problems and make ours a better country.

15

THE "NO LABELS" WAY FORWARD

Through the stories I have told in this book, I have tried to show that there is a treatment and cure for the diseases of extremism and partisanship that sicken America's government and politics. They are centrism and bipartisanship, and they are readily available to elected leaders who choose to use them. Centrism is not a new wonder drug. It is as old as the American Constitution—and the Greek classics and the Bible—and as young as the bipartisan accomplishments of Congress that I witnessed during my twenty-four years in the Senate. But success across party lines has come less frequently lately; and even after a significant national crisis, bipartisan unity does not always prevail.

When I left the Senate in January 2013, I wanted to find a way as a private citizen to help break the gridlock in Washington. I found it in No Labels, an organization I have co-chaired since 2014. There are other credible individual and organizational responses to the problems that have crippled America's government, including third-party movements and candidates; non-partisan primaries; public financing of campaigns; and the drawing of congressional district lines by non-partisan commissions rather than partisan politicians. These are all worth the effort, because there is not one response that will fix everything that ails Washington. We should try anything that makes sense.

I decided to focus my efforts on No Labels because its goal is to make our two-party system work again. It is also, of course, where I spent my years in elective office and what I know best. I ran as a third-party candidate in 2006 because I lost the Democratic primary. The two parties have changed their policies and priorities over America's history, but the need for them to work with each other for the good of the country never changes.

Michael Porter of the Harvard Business School has done some very insightful work with Katherine Gehl, a businesswoman and author, analyzing our political system through the lens of industrial competition. Their conclusions in an article for *Fortune* entitled "Why Politics is Failing America" strike me as unique and instructive:

> By nearly every measure the industry of politics itself is thriving. There's just one problem. The people whom the politics industry is supposed to serve have never been more dissatisfied . . .
>
> Competition in politics appears intense, which is usually good for customers. But today's competition is failing . . . The parties compete to divide votes/and serve special interests, rather than . . . find common ground to move the country forward.
>
> The politics industry is different from virtually all other industries . . . because the participants themselves control the rules of competition . . . Free from regulation and oversight . . . the duopoly does exactly what one would fear. The rivals distort the rules of competition in their favor.
>
> These biased rules have many competitive consequences, including a sharp decline in legislation passed and the near extinction of moderates in Congress.

No Labels was founded to restore healthy competition between the two parties, which will produce results for the American people by electing more centrist leaders to Congress and by changing the rules that work against bipartisanship. Change in our country almost always begins with one person who has a new idea and pursues it with courage, persistence, and resilience.

For No Labels, that person was Nancy Jacobson. She was raised in South Florida, educated at Syracuse University, and began her political life in Bill Clinton's 1992 presidential campaign. From there, she went on to be finance director of the Democratic National Committee and the Democratic Leadership Council where she met her husband, Mark Penn, the pollster, strategist, and business executive who polled for me in my 2004 presidential campaign. From 1995 to 2010, Nancy oversaw Senator Evan Bayh's political and fundraising operations.

Then, along with millions of other Americans, she got angry about the increasing partisanship and dysfunction in our politics— particularly as she watched Washington's rigidly partisan reaction to the Great Recession of 2008. That epic crisis should have motivated our leaders to put the national interest ahead of their party's interest, but it did not. Nancy saw how hard it was for the Senate to get sixty votes to end a filibuster so we could take up the economic recovery and stimulus program that President Obama had proposed in 2009.

Her disappointment with the status quo in our government and politics led Nancy to leave the work she had been doing for the Democratic Party and its candidates for more than two decades. She created a new non-partisan organization, No Labels, to bring bipartisanship back to Washington. She talked to me and many others at the time about her idea. I encouraged her because, from inside the Senate, I was feeling the same frustration about our politics. So too were most of the other elected officials Nancy consulted.

After a great deal of planning and advance work, No Labels was launched in New York City on December 13, 2010, with more than 1,000 people from across the country in attendance at the inaugural conference. A week before that, two first-rate political thinkers, Bill Galston—who had worked in the Clinton White House—and David Frum—who had been there during George W. Bush's administration—co-wrote a *Washington Post* column that was effectively a No Labels founding manifesto:

> In Congress, the center has collapsed and ideological overlap between the parties has vanished . . .
>
> At a time of national economic emergency . . . our government is routinely paralyzed by petty politics. The real American majority wishes to reassert control over a political system mired in brain dead partisanship.
>
> In an act as old as America, citizens are coming together [to create No Labels] out of frustration and patriotism to give their country a better future.

That is exactly what No Labels has done with increasing success since then. Not everything the organization has tried has worked. When something didn't pan out, No Labels tried something else. That is the way the rules of industrial competitiveness, as Porter and Gehl might say, should work in our political system. But the No Labels curve has trended upward. On balance, no group has done more to bring our government and politics back to the problem-solving center than No Labels.

First, Nancy and No Labels tried to get Republicans and Democrats in Congress just to sit down and talk together about the issues of the day, which was not happening at all anymore. Then, in 2011, No Labels ratcheted the discussions up a notch with a reform proposal called Make Congress Work—a response to the recurring and chaotic shutdowns and near shutdowns of the federal government due to the inability of both parties to compromise and reach agreement on something as fundamental as the annual federal budget. No Labels proposed a new law called "No Budget, No Pay," which would halt pay for elected officials if they didn't enact mandatory budget and spending bills on time. Another reform would require the Senate to vote on presidential nominees for executive and judicial positions no later than ninety days after submission, instead of holding them at will for months or even years.

These proposals were aimed directly at changing the rules that were strengthening the "duopoly" of the two parties but dividing and disappointing the country. I co-sponsored the No Budget, No Pay legislation, and on March 15, 2012, chaired a hearing of the Senate Homeland Security and Governmental Affairs Committee on the Make Congress Work package. Later in the year, a limited version of No Budget, No Pay—which would cover only the following year's budget deadline—was enacted.

In his State of the Union speech in 2012, President Obama endorsed the idea of the rules change to force a Senate vote within ninety days of presidential submission of a nomination. Prior to that State of the Union, 208 members of Congress supported an appeal from No Labels that there should be bipartisan seating at joint sessions of Congress such as the State of Union, instead of Democrats and Republicans sitting on separate sides of the chamber.

The Make Congress Work proposals and bipartisan seating didn't revolutionize Congress, but they made clear that No Labels was for real and clearly focused on changing the status quo—which, of course, pleased some and displeased others.

After I left the Senate in early 2013, Nancy Jacobson invited me to attend No Labels meetings. In 2014, Senator Joe Manchin, the Democrat from West Virginia—who had co-chaired No Labels with the former Republican governor of Utah, Jon Huntsman—decided to step down, and No Labels asked me to replace him as national co-chair. I was glad to. It was a real pleasure to work with Jon Huntsman until 2017, when President Trump asked him to be US ambassador to Russia.

In the 2014 elections, we decided to enter some of the Senate and House races to introduce bipartisanship and problem solving into the campaigns. No Labels certified some candidates as "Problem Solvers" based on their records and willingness to embrace a No Labels' brand of politics. Some of them used our "seal of approval" in their campaign advertising. We were trying to create incentives for members of Congress to put country over party.

In 2015, No Labels launched a new initiative called a National Strategic Agenda, which took on four major national problems, made recommendations for how to solve them, and set goals for when they could be accomplished. The four goals, which were crafted based on extensive polling of what the American people cared about, were: 1) Create 25 million net new jobs in a decade; 2) Reform Social Security and Medicare so that they would be secure for seventy-five years; 3) Balance the federal budget by 2030; and 4) Make America energy secure by 2024.

As constructive as these proposals were, No Labels soon recognized that the biggest problem in our politics was not lack of good policy or reform ideas, but a lack of political incentive to embrace them. We began to build a network of financial and grassroots supporters that would get behind members of Congress with the guts to break away from their party or special interest groups when they thought it was the right move for the country. We urged No Labels' financial supporters to contribute to the campaigns of these problem-solving members of Congress to liberate them from dependency on their parties or interest groups. All that our contributors asked was that members of Congress work across party lines to get things done.

In June 2015, Jon Huntsman and I visited the *Washington Post* editorial board to discuss No Labels and our National Strategic Agenda. Afterward, editorial page editor Fred Hiatt wrote a positive op-ed in which he noted that No Labels had signed up a half million members in the five years since it was founded and established branches on more than 100 college campuses. Congressman Tom Reed, Republican from New York and charter member of No Labels, told Hiatt that "No Labels taps into the silent majority and organizes them. This makes us members of Congress a little more comfortable sticking our necks out." No Labels could not have asked for a better explanation of our cause.

With no incumbent president seeking re-election in 2016, there were very competitive and very divisive campaigns for each party's nomination. No Labels decided to try to move the presidential process toward civility and problem solving. We convened a No

Labels Problem Solvers Presidential Convention in Manchester, New Hampshire, on October 15, 2015. Eight of the candidates appeared—Republicans Chris Christie, John Kasich, George Pataki, Donald Trump, and Lindsey Graham, and Democrats Martin O'Malley, Bernie Sanders, and Jim Webb. That positive response by the candidates was a sign of the growing credibility of No Labels.

Not surprisingly, Donald Trump drew the most attention. In fact, after No Labels announced he was attending, the number of reporters requesting credentials to cover our New Hampshire convention suddenly multiplied. The crowd and press reaction to Trump that day was mixed. Katie Glueck wrote in *Politico* that:

> The event organizers called for problem solving and civility, policy substance over sideshows. But Donald Trump just couldn't help himself . . .
>
> While other candidates and politicians noted their ability to collaborate, Trump trumpeted his ability to win a negotiation. Standing next to signs that read "stop fighting, start fixing," he jabbed at GOP rivals and bragged about poll numbers. And at a conference devoted to bipartisan bonhomie, he described himself as a "counterpuncher" . . .

In the *Keene (New Hampshire) Sentinel*, Steven Gilbert wrote:

> It was the kind of day political junkies yearn for . . . a glimpse of politics when solutions are encouraged and contempt discouraged. For one day at least, presidential candidates were cajoled into civility.

Of Trump, Gilbert wrote that he "seemed to try to tone down his bombast but couldn't really contain himself."

As the 2016 presidential campaigns went on, with Trump moving strongly toward nomination and Bernie Sanders giving Hillary Clinton a real battle, it began to feel like a No Labels partisan nightmare. We decided to become more deeply involved in congressional campaigns with the goal of building a stronger bipartisan center in Congress, regardless of who was elected president. That required a new strategy. We could not overcome the partisanship and extremism of politics with only bipartisan policy suggestions and pleas to candidates to be substantive and civil. We had to give them real political and financial support. So, we appealed to our contributors to give more to problem-solving Democrats and Republicans, many of whom won their elections thanks to support from the No Labels community.

We in No Labels were thrilled, and encouraged many of the Republicans and Democrats our supporters had helped elect to get organized into a formal House Problem Solvers Caucus. Their response was very positive. They wanted to get things done, and they knew the best way to do that was by working across party lines. In a Congress and country that were ever more deeply divided along party lines, it took courage for the twenty-four members—twelve from each party—to join this bipartisan House Problem Solvers Caucus. No Labels promised them we would not forget—and we haven't.

Early in 2017, the new caucus elected co-chairs, Democratic Congressman Josh Gottheimer of New Jersey and Republican Congressman Tom Reed of New York. They also wrote rules to make the group more cohesive. They said they would only accept new members in twos, with one from each party (the Noah's Ark rule). On proposals or legislation that they developed together, it would take the support of a majority of each party's members of the caucus, and 75 percent of all the members for the caucus to endorse the legislation and require all the members to support it. At the time of this writing in 2021, the caucus membership has grown to fifty-six, more than 12 percent of the House, which is more than enough to pull close votes to the center to secure passage.

During 2017, No Labels helped the Problem Solvers Caucus by hosting meetings with guest speakers like Microsoft founder Bill Gates, Treasury Secretary Steven Mnuchin, columnist David Brooks, and Professor Michael Porter from Harvard.

Later that year, the caucus began to meet once a week at 9 p.m. for tacos and beer without any media or much staff present. Real friendships developed among the caucus members from both parties. Several of them told me the caucus meetings were the best time of each week for them because there was open discussion across party lines that led to compromises and agreements.

The caucus ultimately produced six bipartisan proposals that year on problems that really mattered to their constituents—opioid addiction, health care, immigration reform, border security, infrastructure development, and gun safety. The proposal to respond to the opioid epidemic passed both houses and was signed into law. Another proposal on prison reform became part of a larger bill championed by Jared Kushner for the Trump White House and Van Jones, former adviser to President Obama, which was the most significant criminal justice reform in a decade. It passed the House with Problem Solvers Caucus support and was enacted in December 2018.

But Congressmen Reed and Gottheimer, the members of their caucus, and we at No Labels were frustrated that many of the Caucus's proposals on other big national problems never even got a vote on the House floor. To maintain their control over their members, the leaders of both parties did not want a bipartisan caucus to be too successful, so they used the restrictive House rules to block action on the Problem Solvers' proposals. Remember Michael Porter's observation that one of the ways the Democratic-Republican duopoly maintains its control over American politics is by writing the rules that regulate it. Some of the rules had to change for broad bipartisan problem solving to happen.

In the summer of 2018, No Labels created a reform proposal called The Speaker Project, in which we put forth several ideas to make it easier for bipartisan ideas to get a hearing on the House floor. We also identified how a group of members could use their votes as leverage to get these changes implemented, drawing on a notable example from 1923, in which frustrated House members withheld their vote for a new speaker until he agreed to embrace several rule reforms to give them a more prominent seat at the table. Soon thereafter, the Problem Solvers released their own rules reform package—which drew on many of the ideas in The Speaker

Project—called "Break the Gridlock." It proposed specific changes in the House rules which would strengthen House members and weaken the authority of the leadership to control which bills would be taken up and which amendments would be offered. One reform required that if 290 members (two-thirds of the House) signed a petition to take up a particular bill on the floor, it would have to be taken up; and if twenty members of each party co-sponsored an amendment, that too would get a vote. Then, the caucus members showed real courage. Prior to the 2018 election, many of them—from both parties—publicly pledged that they would not support any candidate for Speaker of the House after the 2018 elections who did not accept their proposed rules reforms, regardless of which party won a majority in the election.

In November 2018, the Democrats elected the majority in the House and Nancy Pelosi sought to become Speaker—but soon found she couldn't do it without some votes from the Democratic Problem Solvers led by Josh Gottheimer. They held their ground in the face of enormous partisan pressure and they compelled Speaker Pelosi to compromise and accept many of the "Break the Gridlock" reforms. When the Democratic majority put forth this rules package on the first day of the new Congress, three Republican members of the House Problem Solvers Caucus voted for it, the first time such a party crossover had happened in two decades.

The adoption of those reforms was the beginning of a new day for the House, the Problem Solvers Caucus, and hopefully for congressional bipartisanship. The new "290 rule" was used several times in the months after it was adopted to bring bills that were trapped in House committees to the House floor. One of those bills reduced backlogs for highly skilled immigrants seeking admission to the US; another prevented death benefits for spouses of servicemembers who died while on active duty from being taxed; and a third continued benefits to first responders who had health problems related to the 9/11 attacks when that law was set to expire. Most of the members of Congress who used the new petition path to get their bills to the floor for a vote were not members of the Problem Solvers Caucus. That was a surprise and good news.

With its newfound credibility and clout, the Problem Solvers Caucus helped break the gridlock on a range of important legislative measures. In spring 2019, a bill to provide humanitarian assistance for the large number of immigrants held on the southern border of the US passed the Senate with near unanimous bipartisan support. When it came to the House, the response of the core of both caucuses was reflexive and thoughtless. Liberal Democrats said the Senate bill did too little for the immigrants and to curb Trump administration immigration policies they did not like. Conservative Republicans said it did too much. There were not enough votes in the House for the Senate bill to pass. Then the bipartisan House Problem Solvers, remembering Voltaire's warning not to let the perfect be the enemy of the good, stood together in support of the Senate bill—and that made all the difference. It passed, and the immigrants received the humanitarian support they desperately needed.

In December 2019, the Problem Solvers also cast critical votes together in the House in support of the US Mexico Canada Agreement (USMCA) on trade, enabling it to pass. By early 2020, the Problem Solvers were increasingly viewed as the go to group to help advance must pass bipartisan legislation. So in March 2020, the day after Vice President Mike Pence was appointed chair of the White House Coronavirus Task Force, he invited fourteen members of the Problem Solvers Caucus to the Situation Room to discuss ideas for legislative relief. In April 2020, the Problem Solvers Caucus issued their "Reopening and Recovery Back to Work Checklist," making them the first group in the federal government to offer a bipartisan program for economic recovery from COVID-19. That began extensive work among the caucus's own members, and with the administration and leadership of both parties in the House, to formulate and pass a series of legislative responses to the pandemic which received impressively bipartisan support in a depressingly partisan age. There was a lot of partisan static in the air, but the catastrophic pandemic drew a mostly bipartisan legislative response in Congress.

It was time for No Labels, which had inspired and started the House Problem Solvers Caucus, to step back. The caucus was ready to run on its own, but knew it could turn to No Labels when and if it needed help. Supporters of No Labels committed to raise campaign money for members of the Problem Solvers Caucus who were running for re-election in 2020. Their bipartisanship had earned our continued support, and hopefully would encourage more members in the future to follow their example.

Then, No Labels turned to the Senate to organize a comparable bipartisan caucus there.

I knew it would not be easy.

Even in times of greatest partisan division, there was one thing both Senate party leaders could agree on: their opposition to bipartisan caucuses. On the rare occasion when a bipartisan, ad hoc working group was organized in the upper chamber, it was called a "Gang," as if it were somehow threatening and lawless. For example, I joined a "Gang" to protect the filibuster requirement for nominees to the higher federal courts, including the Supreme Court, and a "Gang" for immigration reform. The "Gangs" were for limited purposes, not to pursue the broad, bipartisan, centrist problem solving we had achieved in the House. But at the time, the "Gangs" were the best way to organize bipartisan groups of Senators to develop bipartisan solutions to big national problems.

In the Senate, we needed a different long-term strategy. Senators Susan Collins and Joe Manchin were naturals to help lead this new bipartisan Senate caucus and just as we had with the Problem Solvers, the No Labels community stepped up to provide political support for these centrist leaders.

I was frequently a part of conversations No Labels hosted with our top supporters—many of them notable business leaders—and I never heard them ask a self-interested question about their companies, taxes, or anything else. It has always been about how we together can restore bipartisanship and solve our country's biggest challenges.

In 2019, as No Labels started to bring more senators into our orbit, we also started working to build connections between House and Senate members by inviting them to join bicameral meetings. Those meetings worked beyond our expectations. Rarely do senators and representatives get together, and even more rarely across party lines. The conversations naturally turned to legislation that individual senators and the House Problem Solvers Caucus were working on, which led to bicameral, bipartisan legislative initiatives. The best, early example of that occurred in May 2020, when Senators Bill Cassidy, Republican from Louisiana, and Bob Menendez, Democrat from New Jersey—with support from the House Problem Solvers—introduced the SMART Act to provide desperately needed aid to state and local governments.

Later in 2020, No Labels announced that eight senators, almost 10 percent of the Senate, had formed a more formal bipartisan, centrist group. They included Democrats Joe Manchin, Jacky Rosen from Nevada, Kyrsten Sinema from Arizona, and Angus King, an independent from Maine who caucuses with Democrats. The Republican members were Susan Collins, Bill Cassidy, John Cornyn of Texas, and Todd Young of Indiana. Senators Rosen, Sinema, and Young were elected to the Senate in 2018 from the House, where they had been members of the Problem Solvers Caucus.

As No Labels built support in Washington, we continued to expand our work and base outside Washington, thanks to a robust digital education and engagement effort. In 2020 alone, No Labels:

- Hosted three "Congress Comes to You" events online, giving people opportunities to see members from both parties and both houses of Congress work together to solve the issues of day in real time.
- Reached people more than **fifteen million times** with educational content.
- Generated **seven million views** on educational videos.
- Engaged **more than 350,000 Americans** every month across digital platforms.
- Activated more than **60,000 people to take actions**, including calling or emailing their members of Congress.

And No Labels had a **20 percent engagement rate** on Facebook, higher than Justice Democrats, Club for Growth, the NRA, and similar organizations, proving that it is indeed possible to be a "militant centrist."

For an organization like No Labels, which was created to forge better relationships between leaders with different ideological points of view through personal discussions, the COVID-19 lockdown had the potential to take us off course. But our staff was smart enough to pivot and build an online community with opportunities for those most committed to our mission to find ways to get involved and stay engaged.

From the beginning of the pandemic, we attracted more than 100,000 people to calls with members of Congress and issue experts, including Governor Asa Hutchinson, former Governors John Kasich and Jeb Bush, current and former Treasury Secretaries Steve Mnuchin and Larry Summers, former US Trade Representative Charlene Barshefsky, Admiral Bill McRaven, and former White House Chief of Staff Mick Mulvaney.

After the pandemic started, we also began hosting weekly virtual meetings of the bipartisan, bicameral group we had hosted in-person pre-pandemic.

As of this writing in the first half of 2021, we believe this emerging bipartisan House-Senate coalition can and will coalesce into a formidable "swing faction" with the ability to set the agenda and shape the debate on key issues. Once this coalition can reach consensus on a solution, we want that measure to become the most likely solution that passes Congress.

Truth be told, the No Labels House-Senate bipartisan problem solvers coalition moved further faster than No Labels thought possible. After the 2020 election and before Joe Biden was inaugurated, President Trump focused on challenging the legitimacy of the election of Joe Biden, and the bipartisan leadership of Congress was unable or unwilling to work together to enact an extension of the COVID relief programs that millions of Americans desperately needed. Our bicameral bipartisan coalition (with a few additions from both parties) stepped forward and proposed a compromise $908 billion, four-month extension of many of the COVID relief programs. Trump, Biden, and the leaders of both parties in Congress said the bipartisan proposal was a good basis for an agreement. Before the end of 2020, it was enacted. At No Labels, it was a moment we had dreamed of, and it gave us hope that many more bipartisan successes could follow in the years ahead.

Democratic and Republican problem solvers will face real tests of their courage to continue such success. The Democrats in the Problem Solvers Caucus will be pressured by the left and Republicans will face similar pressures from the right. We in No Labels will do everything we can to encourage members of Congress to be bipartisan problem solvers, and we will work to re-elect them when they are challenged as a result of their independence.

No Labels has come a long way since its founding in 2010, but there is much more work to do to build a full-strength, permanent bipartisan problem-solving center in Washington.

On January 30, 1787, Thomas Jefferson, then-US minister to France, wrote to James Madison:

> I hold that a little rebellion now and then is a good thing and as necessary in the political world as storms are in the physical world. God forbid we should ever be 20 years without such a rebellion.

Today, No Labels is leading such a rebellion against the status quo in Washington to fix our political system, end divisive partisanship, and restore trust to the relationship between the elected leaders who govern and the citizenry that is governed. In the end, in this great republic that Jefferson, Madison, and their contemporaries created for us, we, the American people, will decide by our action or inaction whether our future will be as good as we want it to be.

And, I am confident, No Labels will continue to show us the way.

ACKNOWLEDGMENTS

This is a book I have been thinking about writing for years. The truth is that the stay-at-home social distancing of the COVID-19 pandemic of 2020 gave me the extra time and motivation to do it.

I want to thank my constant companion for the last year of the virus and wonderful wife for thirty-eight years—Hadassah Freilich Lieberman. She encouraged me to write this book about the importance of bipartisan centrism, tolerated the time I spent writing it, and thoughtfully informed what I have written.

I also thank Nancy Jacobson, the founder and chief executive officer of No Labels, for her encouragement and support of this book, and for all she has done to return bipartisan, centrist, problem-solving government to Washington.

Whatever I accomplished in my career in government and politics would not have happened without extraordinary help from the gifted and good people who have been my political supporters in campaigns and my co-workers in office. As representatives of all those wonderful people, I want to thank two who have been at the heart of my career for a long time:

Clarine Nardi Riddle, who joined me in 1978 as deputy counsel when I was state senate majority leader, later served as my deputy attorney general, and then succeeded me as attorney general. Later, she was my chief of staff for ten of the years I was a US senator.

Sherry Brown, who impressed me so much as a volunteer in my unsuccessful campaign for Congress in 1980 that I asked her to manage my campaign for attorney general in 1982, which was successful. And she managed every other winning campaign I ever ran, ending in my independent re-election run for the Senate in 2006.

ACKNOWLEDGMENTS

Sherry and Clarine have been indispensable to my service and success and are like members of our family.

I also want to thank Marc Kasowitz, Dan Benson, and Hector Torres, the founding partners of Kasowitz, Benson & Torres, the law firm I have practiced with since I left the US Senate in 2013, for supporting my work as a lawyer and also for being supportive of my other activities, including the writing of this book. I am personally grateful for the help of my executive assistant at the law firm, Vernell Glover, and Tara Leach who sat in for Vernell while she was out on pregnancy leave.

It has been a real pleasure to work with the professional and talented team at Diversion Books, beginning with its publisher, Scott Waxman. Diversion's executive editor and editor in chief, Keith Wallman, really improved what I gave him. Thanks to Scott and Keith.

I am deeply grateful to everyone who helped me live the stories I tell in this book and helped me write them. But of course, I take full responsibility for everything I did and have written.

Joe Lieberman
March 2021

INDEX

INDEX

INDEX

INDEX

ABOUT THE AUTHOR

J oe Lieberman served in public office in Connecticut for forty years—ten as a state senator, six as state attorney general, and twenty-four as a United States senator. In 2000, he was the Democratic Party candidate for vice president of the United States. Senator Lieberman became known as a national leader who works across party lines to get things done and speaks up for what he believes is right, regardless of the political consequences. He now serves as national chair of No Labels, a political organization that works to build centrist, bipartisan coalitions in Washington, and as chair of United Against Nuclear Iran, a bipartisan advocacy group whose name describes its purpose.

Since 2013, he has been senior counsel at the law firm Kasowitz Benson Torres LLP in New York, taught political science courses at Yeshiva University, served on the board of two companies—Victory Park Capital and Park Hotels—and on the board of several nonprofit organizations, including the McCain Institute, American Federation for Children, Institute for the Study of War, Center for a New American Security, and Cohen Veterans Network.

Senator Lieberman is the author of eight previous books on history, government, law, and religion. He is married to Hadassah Freilich Lieberman. They have four children and twelve grandchildren.